THE BELLY DANCE BOOK

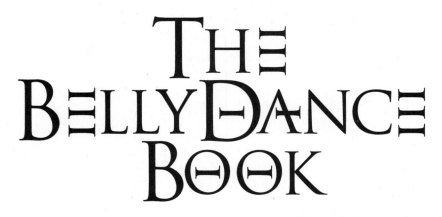

Rediscovering the Oldest Dance

EDITED BY TAZZ RICHARDS

BACKBEAT
PRESS

The Belly Dance Book
Rediscovering the Oldest Dance
©2000 Tazz Richards

Editor-in-Chief	Tazz Richards
Senior Editor	Jenni Morrison
Art Director	Kate Reed
Book Design	Morris Design, Carmel, California

Editors	Lauren Nelson
	Farah Jahan Siddiqui Bullara
	Janet Morrison
	Stephen Richards
	David Himmelreich
	Toni L Whyte
	Morocco
	Kris Ashley
	Josh Berkus

Cover model	Nymue
Cover photographer	Michael J Monson
Cover shoot director	Caroline Slack
Back cover model	Carolena Nericcio
Back cover photographer	Jay Richardson

Illustrators	Kate Reed
	Dina
	Karol Henderson Harding
	Alan McCorkle

Library of Congress Card Number: 00-191474

ISBN 0-9700247-03

Published by
Backbeat Press
PMB 253
1647 Willow Pass Road
Concord, CA 94520

WWW.BACKBEATPRESS.COM

Caduceus, page 72, Coliseum, page 173, and lamp icon ©1999-2000 www.arttoday.com.

Text is printed on recycled paper with 85% recycled content, 10% post-consumer.

1 2 3 4 5 6 7 8 9 10

ABOUT THE BELLY DANCE BOOK

While rehearsing in my dance partner's garage for the 1999 Rakkasah Middle Eastern Dance Festival, an authenticity question came up. I don't remember what it was, but I do remember thinking that the information should be in a book somewhere. This thought spurred the idea of a complete information source for belly dancers. Dancers needed one place to get all the answers. I wanted to create the gospel, the bible of belly dance. I wanted this to be the be-all end-all of belly dance. I wanted a book that told everything—history, costume, music, dance, sources. And snakes—there had to be something about snakes.

I knew I wasn't knowledgeable enough to write the book, but with my publishing background, I could definitely produce it. I put out the call to the belly dance community, asking for articles, photos, recommendations, information. Dancers and dance enthusiasts from around the world sent materials and their support.

This book was made by the community, for the community. It is the textbook, the starting point, the welcome mat for the world of belly dance. It is not the Belly Dance Bible. There is more information about belly dance, and all of its predecessors and spin-offs than would fit into one book. At least, not one the average reader could lift. There is, however, enough information wrapped up in this tome to give anyone inside the community a place to learn more about their passion, and anyone outside the community a good idea of what the whole thing is about.

One of the challenges of belly dance research is that much of the information is ambiguous or incomplete. Anyone studying the history follows a maze of historical presumptions, assumptions and inaccuracies. No one can really know how the dancers moved in Ancient Egypt or Constantinople or the 1893 Chicago Exposition. There is no hidden videotape waiting to be discovered in the temples of Isis. Well, probably not anyway. As information is passed down from generation to generation, it distorts, changes with the times. The information here is the current gospel of belly dance.

Much controversy surrounds the world's oldest dance, including what to call the dance, and what it encompasses. I've decided to let the authors explore those deeper areas. Some of the information will conflict. Opinions will clash. There are as many different reasons to embrace the dance as there are definitions of it. To agree on everything will limit the potential experiences the dance has to offer. I think you will find as I have, that everyone has their own dance, and we are still part of the same circle.

ACKNOWLEDGMENTS

To David, for saying yes, and still remaining my friend. To Jenni, for becoming the guardian angel of the book when I was ready to give up. To Kate, for always being there, putting up with me, and becoming whatever I needed you to be while remaining yourself. To my parents, Mom, Dad & Margie, and all of my family, for your love and support. To Lauren, for getting me behind closed doors, and doing what you do best: showing people how to make their dreams real. To Siobhan, my dance instructor, for giving so much of yourself to me and the world of dance. To my fellow dance students, for your ideas, support and pictures. To the crew of the Kali Ma: If you have to ask, you have to drink! To Irene, for making me make the book better. To Morocco, for being the matriarch of the dance. To the Reed family, for all you've done. To Diane Pedersen, Todd Hensley and the cast and crew of C&T Publishing, for teaching me the game, perhaps better than you thought! To all of my editors, authors, photographers and illustrators for putting up with last minute demands, late night phone calls, and learning the process with me. To Autumn, for being Autumn. To Stephanie, Caroline, Meleah, Mike, Nymue, Thalia, and Farah for the photo shoot. To Shira, for all your expertise, and wonderful online glossary. To the Society for Creative Anachronism for giving a lost spirit a place to run. To two great teachers, Ann B. Justus and Jayne Kyl, for teaching a distracted teen the most important thing: how to learn. To everyone not listed, everyone I've forgotten and everyone who hasn't forgotten me. And for planting the indelible words in my mind: "A writer writes!" to April, wherever you are.

Thank you. May your days be spent in pursuit of your dreams, and your nights be filled with dancing!

Tazz

IN MEMORY: KEITH DROSIN

Keith Drosin left this world at 2:00 a.m. Saturday, August 19, 2000. He succumbed to liver cancer. He will be remembered for his outstanding photographic depictions of Middle Eastern and other dance forms. According to several of his subjects, at various times he "recorded the beauty of the dance and the beauty of the woman dancing", with "a gift for timing" that "expressed his appreciation of the art and also the love for what dancers do as artists." He captured us with his heart and soul on film, in our lives and beyond. Now he is dancing with the devadasis.

—*Djahari, Anaheed, Fahtiem, Marguerite*

PAPER CASTLES

Building paper castles at the
  kitchen table
Your kingdom colored, seamless
Mine a tower paper white,
  tape showing
You say
When
I say
When I'm ready
You wait You laugh when I
drop paste on my shirt When I
can't cut a straight line You help.

The white tower gains a courtyard
  a banquet hall
a moat wrapping your kingdom
around my kingdom around
  your kingdom
I say
When
You say
When you're ready
I ask Will you help me build one more
  building
We build a tower I've wanted to
  build all my life
With a bridge to your castle
With a place to sit under
  your window
a place to watch you
All day long.
You know that I am finished,
  but you ask
When
And I say
Now.

to Katie
love, Tazz

Dedication

Introduction

Yesterday & Today

Spirit

Snakes

Props

Make-Up

Costumes

Business

Music

Table of Contents

BELLY DANCE IN BRIEF

By Kajira Djoumahna

KAJIRA DJOUMAHNA
IN AMERICAN TRIBAL
COSTUME
Photo by Chuck Lehnhard

Introduction

9

Belly Dance—In Brief

By Kajira Djoumahna

TODAY THE DANCE IN MANY VARIATIONS IS ALIVE AND WELL ALL OVER THE WORLD, AND IN A GREAT MANY INTERPRETATIONS.

One of the first things to know is that the term "belly dance" is only used in the United States, Britain, Australia, and a few other English-speaking regions. In countries of the dance's origin, it is known by different names. There are many reasons why people believe the term "belly dance" came into popularity in the U.S. There are some who love the term and embrace it because the belly is the source of power and creation. Others feel it is a misnomer and an insult that came out of the Victorian era when dancers appeared at the Chicago Exposition. Still others feel that the term came from the Middle Eastern word *"beledi"* which means "my country" or "country".

Belly dance is considered a derivative of the world's oldest known documented dance forms. Artifacts from Ancient Egypt and Sumer portray dancers. Many statues from Greece also show dancers, some with veils. These depicted meneads; maidens who performed Baccanalian rituals. It is believed that early civilizations used dance to worship deities as well as in religious ceremonies. Dance was, and is, used to pantomime the sowing and harvesting of crops, to bless and heal, to prepare for childbirth and the wedding bed, and for secular entertainment. Dancers also mimicked daily activities, such as the application of make-up. An excellent example of this in use today can be seen in Persian dance. Some believe there were temple dancers as well, similar to the dancers of ancient India known as the *devadasi.*

Somewhere around the 11th century, groups of wanderers left northern India *en masse.* The proper name for these groups and their descendants is "Romany" or "Roma". In Hungary, they are Czingany. In Russia, they are Tsingane. In India they are Banjara and in Spain they are Gitano. In Egypt they are called Nawar and Ghawazee. There are dozens of proper names for this race of people, none of which are "Gypsy".

Europeans mislabeled them as "Gypsies" because they were believed to have come from Egypt. The Roma traveled into Pakistan and Afghanistan, into the Persian Gulf and Arabian Gulf. Some traveled into Egypt and Africa, and others into Turkey, the Caucasus Mountains, and then Eastern Europe, Russia, Western Europe and finally down into Spain.

10

Through all of the countries in which the Roma passed, they left some of their music and dance. Along the way, these new dances mingled with the indigenous dances already in those countries. Results can be seen in folk dance and belly dance. There are common aspects in the Romany dances of many countries including India, Egypt, Morocco, Turkey and Spain, such as stomping and rhythmic hand clapping. During the 700 year Moorish occupation of Spain, flamenco was born. It was originally known as *Zambra Mora,* or "Moorish dance". This dance form includes more torso and hip isolation than traditional flamenco does today. It is performed barefoot, and often incorporates the use of finger cymbals— called *chinechines*—instead of castanets.

Today in the Middle East and North Africa, the majority of Oriental dance occurs in women-only groups. The sexes are still segregated in those countries. The men have separate parties from the women. In the women's parties, they all dance and play music for each other, but a "good Moslem woman" would never dream of dancing for a mixed gender audience unless they had no other means of financial support. Men's parties usually hire a troupe of entertainers that may include dancers along with the musicians and singers.

Generally speaking, a dancer who dances for men in the Middle East is disparaged. There are exceptions. For example, in Egypt, it is always the custom to have dancers at one's wedding, who perform for guests, and lead the wedding processional, called a *zeffa*. When leading a zeffa, the dancer wears a *shamadan*, or candelabra, with lit candles several tiers high on her head. This originated before streetlights as a means of lighting the way of the bridal party. Some say it has more symbolism as well, including the fact that fire stands for cleansing and new beginnings in many parts of the world.

In Morocco, *Schikhatt* dancers are hired to help acquaint the new bride-to-be with what is expected of her in the wedding bed. They do this through dance pantomime, some of which is tasteful, and some of which is not. This is done with a sense of humor, and only by married women, since they are the only ones that have carnal knowledge. Schikhatt comes from the word *"Sheika"*, or *"Sheik"* which means "one who possesses knowledge." Also in Morocco and other parts of the Middle East, women practice abdominal movements akin to belly dancing in preparation for childbirth. Some of the movements are similar to the Lamaze Method of childbirth technique.

Men also dance, both in the U.S. and the Middle East. Styles in the U.S. are usually more relaxed for men and may include not only traditional folkloric pieces, but interpretations and adaptations of women's solo styles as well. In the Middle East, they usually do a more masculine version, wearing long cloaks or *djellabiyas* over their clothes. This was not always the case. There are long periods of time in the histories of Egypt and Turkey where boys dressed as women and danced publicly because women were banned from doing so. In Turkey, these rather famous and popular dancing boys were, and still are, called *kochek*.

11

Both women and men traditionally sing and play instruments. These activities are not, and never have been, considered dishonorable. Some of the most revered people in the Middle East have been singers and composers. Some of these people include Farid el-Atrash, Umm Kulthum, Warda and others. Some dancers have achieved a high level of stardom in recent years, especially in Egypt and Lebanon. These dancers include Dina, Lucy, Nagua Fouad and Amani today, and Sohair Zeki, Samya Gamal, Tahiya Karioka and Naima Akef of yesterday. Today there is relatively little public dancing in Egypt, as the religious climate is increasingly terrorist and dangerous. They have forced nightclubs out of business that featured dancing. Recent tourists in Egypt have reported a revival of dance in some areas, though not to the extent it was enjoyed in the past.

Today the dance in many variations is alive and well all over the world, and in a great many interpretations. Some examples of these include the people who work diligently at the preservation of traditional forms. These dancers usually study in the countries of origin at some point during their research, and with teachers from the countries they are studying. As examples, Morocco, Eva Cernik, Elizabeth Artemis Mourat, Laurel Victoria Gray, Kay Hardy Campbell, Aisha Ali and Robyn Friend come to mind. In some cases, these researchers may be some of the last to be performing older dances as they were done around the turn of the last century and throughout the 20th century. This is because in many places all over the globe, people are changing and re-interpreting their dances, as all living art has always done. That is how the dance evolved originally. The difference today is in mass communication. Now things everywhere change much faster. In one generation of today's dancers, a whole style can be lost. This has already happened to Romani dance gestures, the Guedra blessing ritual and many more forms too numerous to mention.

As for the forms already lost, we can only guess as we look into past depictions of these dances in drawings, paintings, lithographs and written descriptions by historians and travelers. There are people who re-create some of the lost dances of antiquity. These people do so by studying historical books, archaeology, history of daily life, textiles, metal working, period instruments, agricultural and hunter-gatherer societies. There are more factors to consider while reconstructing ancient dances, such as religion and politics of the time. Even historical records can be biased, depending on who has written them and why.

Many dancers enjoy the solo forms that have arisen from the Middle East and elsewhere. These are the most popular styles in restaurants and nightclubs. These styles have evolved into high art only within the last century in the Middle East, and within the past fifty years in North America. Before that, groups of traveling musicians, singers and dancers were the norm in the Orient. Solo dance is most commonly characterized by the flashy two-piece *bedlah* (bra, belt and accessories set) with skirt and sometimes, a veil. It is designed to accentuate the female form. This costume is less modest than that found in folkloric dance.

Some examples of various solo forms include the popular modern Egyptian form, which is contained, fluid, elegant and controlled. American dancers Shareen el Safy and Sahra Kent are excellent examples of pure Egyptian solo dance. Both women have lived, danced and studied in Egypt for years, and have gained the respect of the Egyptian people for their dedication to this art form. Turkish Oryantal is flashier, typically with more floor space covered (not as contained within the body's own shape as with Egyptian styling) and is generally more playful and robust. Many Turkish dancers appear less modest than their Egyptian counterparts. American dancers Eva Cernik and Artemis have the Turkish style down, after spending many years in Turkey researching and perfecting it. Dancers who enjoy Lebanese style may use more leg kicks than their sisters in neighboring countries. Catch a show by Americans Jawahare, Tasha Banat (first generation American) or the Lebanese Amani to see an example of this form. American dancers have evolved veil work into a high art not seen anywhere else! Check out Delilah's veil work to see what I mean. Aneena is famous for her double veil, which is also an American contribution to our art form.

Other famous dancers who are American and have an American style of dance include Suhaila Salimpour, Ansuya Rathor, Mesmera, Atlantis and Suzanna del Vecchio. These women have created something uniquely theirs by blending movements from many Mideastern countries, and in some cases with their own classical Occidental dance backgrounds. These are not even counting each individual dancer's own interpretations, no matter which style they are doing. Remember that Oriental dance has always depended upon the expression of the individual.

Some of the modern American dancers can also be considered innovators due to their fusionary approach to traditional Oriental dance styles. John Compton and Rebaba of Hahbi'Ru have created a wonderful form combining different ethnic styles. Dalia Carella's Dunyavi Rom (Gypsy) fuses traditional Romany movements from India, Turkey, and Spain. Another popular example of fusion is the phenomenon of American Tribal Style belly dance as interpreted by Carolena Nericcio of FatChanceBellyDance. This style was created for groups, and is unusual due to its group improvisational format, colorful and original costuming, and on-stage camaraderie between members. Movements for this style are drawn from solo and folkloric dances from countries along the Romany Trail.

Which approach is closest to your heart matters not. What does matter is the fact that dancers in the United States and elsewhere have kept alive the world's Oldest Dance, which is in danger of extinction in its native countries due to religious, political and social mores. Knowing these facts makes any form of belly dance all the more precious.

■ *For contact information see: Kajira's Black Sheep Bellydance, Books, Bodywork & Bazaar, page 195.*

13

TERMINOLOGY

By Tazz & Shira

What is the proper term for Belly Dance? Throughout this book, many terms are used. We've chosen to allow each writer to call the dance what they feel is the appropriate title. The following is a list of common terms and what they generally specify:

Belly Dance

A popular, but debatable term. The term possibly originated from the French *Danse du ventre,* "dance of the stomach." Another theory is that it originates from the Arabic, beledi meaning "country." While some dancers feel the term is offensive and sexist, others relate the belly with maternal, goddess, and world beliefs. Many dancers embrace the term simply because it is the common term of today, and started "belly dancing" before knowing what else to call it. In this book, belly dance is viewed as a culmination of traditional styles from the East, along with modern influences.

Oriental Dance

This refers to dance of the Orient, or East. This term seems to imply any Oriental dance, including dances of China and Japan. In common usage, the term is limited Middle Eastern, Near Eastern, Indian, Egyptian and some Eastern European styles, and Americanized versions.

Middle Eastern Dance

Dances specific to the Arabic countries including Iran, Iraq, Sudan, Jordan, Morocco, Lebanon, Saudi Arabia, and Americanized versions.

Near Eastern Dance

Dances specific to the Middle East, and surrounding countries including Greece, Spain, India, Egypt, Northern Africa, and Eastern Europe.

Raks Sharki (also Raqs Sharki)

Arabic for "dance of the East". While referring to cabaret-style dances of Arabic countries, this term has become an American synonym for any Middle Eastern dance.

Cabaret

An American term for the Egyptian nightclub style of dance.

American Tribal Style

A style created in California, using dance and costume styles from a multitude of Eastern countries.

14

TAHIYA KARIOKA
WITH FEIRUZ
Photo courtesy B. Lüscher/RMI

Yesterday & Today

15

Dancers of the Long Night

By Virpi Virtanen

THE DEVELOPMENT OF ORIENTAL DANCE IN FINLAND HAS
FOLLOWED A DIFFERENT PATH THAN IN MOST
OTHER COUNTRIES.

In the northeast corner of Europe lies a country whose roots and heritage originate from the cold mists of Central Asia. Although this country is now one of the most modern and industrialized countries in the world, there are still mysterious echoes of the East. This country is Finland— a land of a thousand lakes and forests, a land of the short exploding summer and the long dark winter. During the last ten years, it has also started to become a land of Oriental dance.

The first breezes of Oriental dance touched Finland about the same time as they reached the rest of Western Europe. The influence of the romantic and mysterious image of the Orient has spiced Finnish Arts since the end of the 19th century, but except for a few short glimpses of dancers in some 1940s wartime movies, there was not much opportunity to see many foreign dances. In the 1970s, media and travel brought the outside world closer to the common people. Finnish dancers were first tempted by Flamenco and African dances, but when they finally discovered Oriental dance it soon became the most popular dance form among women.

The credit for the bringing Oriental dance to Finland belongs to two women: Eva Hemming and Shoshana Sfaradi. Eva Hemming, a famous actress and dancer, discovered this fascinating dance in New York, where she was studying tap-dancing. By chance she saw a group of women in Oriental outfits dancing at Serena Wilson's dance studio. She was so thrilled about this dance that she joined the group. Soon after returning to Finland, she started her own classes with the title *Joyful Exercise for Women*.

Shoshana Sfaradi, an Israeli-Persian dancer, brought her own dance traditions to Finland after marrying a Finnish man. Her opulent, joyful dance style soon attracted Finnish audiences ranging from restaurant performances to more sophisticated dancing for politicians and VIPs. Shoshana still continues her colorful dance career.

Eva's students, especially Irene Jelin, have had an enormous influence on improving the reputation of Oriental dance. Today they are accompanied by dozens of teachers, performers and thousands of dance enthusiasts. Some statistics have counted as many as 20,000 hobbyists in Finland, a country of population 5 million.

Many well-known foreign teachers are annual visitors to Finland, and have influenced the dance scene with their talent. They have had an essential role in the Finnish dance scene as it is today. Finnish Oriental dance is almost purely Egyptian. Folk dances and group dances are a specialty, due largely to the teachings of Mahmud Reda, Raqia Hassan and Yousry Sharif.

The development of Oriental dance in Finland has followed a different path than in most other countries. There have never been significant Arab or Muslim minorities. The Oriental restaurant and nightclub scene does not exist. Most of the dance performances are seen in theaters and dance festivals. Unlike other countries, Oriental dance was never considered controversial in Finland. It is considered an art form—a beautiful example of the colorful dances of the world.

BIBLIOGRAPHY
Sirke, S. Itämainen tanssi (Oriental dance book). Tammi, 1993.
Tanssi-lehti (dance magazine). No. 2 and 3, 1996.

■ *For contact information see: Afsana Magazine (Virpi Virtanen) and Afifa Studio, page 203.*

The Golden Age of Egyptian Oriental Dance

By Dr. Barbara Lüscher/Aischa (Switzerland)

SHE WAS AT THE SAME TIME A LADY AND FEMME FATALE,
A QUEEN AND PEASANT GIRL.

In the 1940s and 1950s, Cairo was the cultural center of Middle Eastern entertainment, trying to adapt to the musical comedies from Hollywood through their own newly founded film industry. It was the time of famous names like Tahiya Karioka, Samya Gamal and Naima Akef, who all debuted in Cairo's first professional dance theater, run by the Lebanese dancer and entertainer Badiaa Masabni. Their appearances in many black and white movies have heavily influenced today's dancers, not only in Egypt, but also all over the world.

BADIAA MASABNI

Where it all began...

Today we would probably call this Lebanese dancer, singer and actress a real "entertainer". Her casino-theater was the place to go in her time. In the 30s and 40s in Cairo it was the meeting place for all kinds of artists. It was on her stage that stars were born! Dancers like Tahiya Karioka, Samya Gamal, Naima Akef, Beba Aizzeddin, Huriya Muhammad and Hagar Hamdi made their first appearances here as well as actors, musicians or singers like Farid el-Atrash, Muhammad Fawzi and many others.

Badiaa Masabni was born probably in 1892 in Beirut (other sources mention 1894 in Damascus) as daughter of a Syrian mother and a Lebanese father. When her father's soap factory was completely destroyed by fire, the family fell apart. Badiaa and her mother left their home-country together. They had to struggle to make their living, and young Badiaa even stayed in a Lebanese brothel for a short time.

She escaped to Egypt where she worked in different clubs, casinos and small theater troupes. Her big chance came when the famous actor Naguib er-Rihâni discovered her and made her the star of his troupe. They married in 1925 but separated after a short time. Badiaa started her own business, soon changing the location of her casino to be beside the river Nile where the old Cairo Sheraton stands today. This place gained such notoriety that the people of Cairo named the bridge beside it Kubri Badiaa. Badiaa invited and supported not only artists from Egypt but also from outside the country. She hired dancers from Sudan as well as circus-artists and magicians from Europe. Her choreographers came from abroad and her stage shows and dance theater had heavy foreign, and especially western influence.

18

It was in this cultural melting pot that today's *Raks Sharki* style of oriental dance, with glittering costumes and glamorous stage-show, began.

Badiaa Masabni appeared on screen, in a film called *The Queen of Theatres* (1935 by Mario Volpi).

Her star began to fade after the 2nd World War. During the revolution in 1952, many casinos, clubs, cinemas and places of western entertainment in Cairo were destroyed. Badiaa Masabni finally left Egypt during the 50s and returned to Lebanon, where she died in 1976.

TAHIYA KARIOKA

The Queen of Oriental Dance

Tahiya Karioka was one of the last legends of the famous Golden Age of Oriental Dance in Egypt. Although she stopped her dancing career at the young age of 32, she continued to perform as an actress in theaters and film throughout her life.

She was born on February 22, 1919 (other sources give 1915, 1921 and 1923) in the district of Ismailiya in the Egyptian delta. Her real name was Badawiya Muhammad Ali el-Nidâni. Her father made a living for his family with a few sailboats, shipping from Ismailiya to Port Said and the Red Sea. Badawiya was the daughter of his seventh wife, who took Badawiya back to her own family after the death of Badawiya's father.

TAHIYA KARIOKA
Photo courtesy of
B. Lüscher/RMI

She had a miserable life, living with her mother's family in Egypt. Her elder brothers kept her in the house like a prisoner and prevented her from going to school. Finally, at the age of about 15, she escaped to Cairo and went to Alexandria where she spent some time at the house of a woman named Mahâsen, a friend of her family. Mahâsen used to perform at weddings and theaters as a singer and dancer. Through her, Badawiya met the famous dancer/entertainer and casino-owner Badiaa Masabni.

Badawiya started as a background dancer in Badiaa's troupe in Cairo. Work was strenuous, with several performances a day plus many hours of rehearsals, but Badawiya, who had now named herself Tahiya, was ambitious. She worked hard on her technique, and took some ballet classes. She finally advanced to the status of solo performer in the troupe. Her special performance to a Brazilian dance called "Karioka" gave her the stage name of Tahiya Karioka.

Like other dance stars of the time she started a big film career, which took her to America and to Twentieth Century Fox. She worked with all the big names of Egyptian cinema and theater, impressing kings as well as common people with her stage and screen-presence, her soulful interpretations of the music and her genuine, heartfelt way with typical Egyptian dance. She was at the same time a lady and femme fatale, a queen and peasant girl.

She even went to prison for a short time for her political statements and activities. Therefore she worked a lot outside of Egypt, especially in Lebanon. Although her many love affairs, marriages and divorces filled the gazettes of the time, she always stressed that her art was the only real love and passion in her life.

Tahiya Karioka passed away on September 20, 1999.

SAMYA GAMAL

A Touch of Hollywood

Like others before her, Samya Gamal started her glamorous career as a background girl in Badiaa Masabni's famous casino-troupe in Cairo. Samya was born in a small village in the Egyptian district of Beni Suef, as Zeinab Khalil Ibrahim Mahfûz. Her Moroccan mother was her father's second wife, with whom he had three children. They soon moved to Cairo where they lived in a poor district near el-Ghûri, not far from the well-known quarters of el-Azhar and el-Hussein. Her father was a strictly religious man who would not allow his daughters to attend school. No mirrors were permitted in the house, no pictures taken. At the age of nine she lost her mother. After that, her life deteriorated. She was beaten by her father and abused as a cheap maidservant by her stepmother. Later, she was sent to work in a factory to support the family. At about age 14 she left home and stayed for a time with one of her elder sisters.

She always loved to go to the movies and watch the old films, especially those with dance scenes. She would practice at home, dreaming of becoming a famous dancer one day. Her chance came when a friend introduced her to the famous Lebanese dancer/entertainer Badiaa Masabni. Badiaa gave Samya a job as a background dancer in her troupe. Samya had her own special style, being much more a solo dancer than a group dancer, because she had problems following the strict choreography. She worked hard, took ballet lessons and practiced with the troupe choreographer, Isaac Dickson, until she was allowed to present a solo dance.

Although her first performance flopped, she did not give up. She started to let herself flow with the music and improvise rather than stick to a fixed choreography. The audience loved her! She advanced to the star of the troupe, now as Samya Gamal, and it was not long until she debuted in films. Her film career was largely connected to her love affair with the famous Lebanese composer, singer and oud player Farid el-Atrash. He wrote many wonderful love songs and dance pieces for her. Together they starred in numerous films and traveled all over the Middle East, from one success to another.

Oud
an Arabian lute

She also was the absolute favorite dancer of King Faruq. Samya and Farid were considered to be a beautiful and admired couple on screen. Unfortunately they were not as they appeared. Samya Gamal was desperate to get married, but Farid el-Atrash constantly refused, saying that as son of a Lebanese Druze prince he could not marry a dancer. Finally they separated in private life and career and Samya worked for some time outside of Egypt.

21

In France she appeared in a film called *Ali Baba and the Forty Thieves* (1954), with famous comedian Fernandel. In Hollywood, she worked with Robert Taylor in *Valley of the Kings,* (1955). She married an American who converted to Islam for her, but their marriage did not last long. Returning to Cairo, she worked again for some time with Farid el-Atrash, then married the famous Egyptian actor Rushdi Abaza with whom she had a daughter. After her second divorce she retired completely from the field of cinema and stage. Her last film was in 1972, and after a short comeback as a dancer in 1984 she disappeared from public life and hardly left her home. She refused all offers to teach or perform and led an extremely quiet life until her death in Cairo on December 1, 1994.

Her dance style has influenced generations of students, and continues to do so today. Her vivid and fluent veil work, her gracious arm movements and her elegant attitude combined with a real Hollywood smile made her one of the most glamorous dancers of the so-called Golden Age of Egyptian dance history.

NAIMA AKEF

The "Isadora Duncan of the East"

Together with Samya Gamal and Tahiya Karioka, Naima Akef was one of those famous stars that helped write the Egyptian dance history of the 20th century. Sadly, her early death that prevented her from having the fame and reputation she deserved outside of Egypt.

Naima Akef was born in Tanta, Egypt on October 7, 1929 (other sources give 1932 or 1922), to a poor circus family. As one of four girls, she never had the chance to go to school, though she could read and write.

Her grandfather, a former school teacher of gymnastics in Giza, got so fascinated by the performance of an Italian circus in Cairo that he decided to quit his job and found his own little circus, the Akef-Circus. By the age of three Naima was already a performing artist and acrobat, and by ten she was a tightrope walker.

After Naima's parents divorced, her mother founded her own acrobat troupe with her girls, Awlâd Akef. They performed with great success in different clubs and casinos in Cairo. It was in the Casino Badiaa that Naima's career as a dancer started. Although Naima Akef was never an official member of Badiaa's troupe she occasionally substituted when someone was absent or ill. Her big chance came at her sixteenth birthday when Badiaa allowed her to dance a solo part in her show. Her talent was obvious! The audience adored her, but at the same time it brought her the envy and jealousy of the other troupe members. She left the Casino Badiaa and went to its rival, the Kitkat-Club, run by a former student of Badiaa Masabni whose name was Beba Aizzeddin.

The next step in her career was from the stage of the casinos and clubs into the film studios. It was by chance that she met the famous film-director Hussein Fawzy who remembered her as that talented dancer he once saw in the Kitkat Club. Although he was already over fifty and Naima still under twenty, they had a love affair that ended in marriage.

Her successful film career as an actress, dancer and singer began. She also continued performing in clubs and theaters. The first official Musical and Opera Theatre was run by the government under the director and founder of the modern Egyptian theater Zaki Toleimat. Naima Akef and the later famous dancer and choreographer Mahmoud Reda were playing the main parts in the operetta *Ya Leil Ya Ain*. In 1957, when the theater was invited to perform in Moscow, Naima Akef participated in a dance-festival and unexpectedly won the first prize in the legendary Bolshoi Theatre. Her picture was in all newspapers, and they titled her the "Isadora Duncan of the East".

Besides performing on stage, Naima Akef continued her successful film career. After about ten years she divorced Hussein Fawzy. Her second marriage, to Samy Abdel-Halim, produced a son named Muhammad.

In the midst of her successful career she died on April 21, 1966 in Cairo from cancer. Through old black and white film clips we can still admire her soulful and expressive dance style as well as her beautiful voice. She was one of the rare all-around talents in Egypt, and she will continue to inspire many dancers throughout the world.

■ *For contact information see: Aischa, page 203.*

It's Not Just for Women—
Men in Oriental Dance

by Tarik abd el Malik
Illustrations by Alan McCorkle

THE MALE DANCERS OF TUNISIA PERFORM A DANCE
BALANCING A STACK OF WATER JUGS ON THEIR HEADS.

WESTERN CULTURAL PERCEPTION OF ORIENTAL DANCE

In its native settings, *Raks Sharki* is done primarily at family and community celebrations, by men and women of all ages. At the turn of the century, the role of professional male dancers was eclipsed by female performers. This was due in large part to the demands of male European tourists and Westernization.

The general Western public's only exposure to this dance is through professional entertainers in nightclubs and films, who are now almost exclusively female, thus they assume it is a women's dance. Lack of cultural and historical information results in many erroneous speculations about the origins and nature of Raks Sharki. The resulting vacuum has been filled with a misleading mystique of exoticism and eroticism. Speculations that it was originally a fertility ritual, the dance of temple prostitutes, seductive dance of Salome, or practiced by harem concubines to sexually arouse the Sultan further confuse the issue. These are all theories reflecting the popular stereotype of the dance as explicit feminine sexual display.

Western culture historically has made women feel ashamed of their sexuality, as well as the natural fullness and curves of their bodies. In the late 1960s and 1970s, women began to challenge these negative messages. As a result, many women saw the assertive and graceful movements of the hips and torso in Oriental dance as a celebratory affirmation of womanhood and female sexuality which created an explosion of interest in the dance. The belly dance fad swept the nation—for the first time it could be learned in formal classes accessible to the public.

The intention of this article is to examine the dance from the perspective of cultural and historical reality. I hope to show that in its countries of origin the dance is also traditionally done by men, and thus challenge those stereotypes held by the general public of this dance as an invention of concubines and harem girls, done by women to entice men. Oriental dance is simply one of the movement expression of North African, Near and Middle Eastern peoples, no different in nature than the Salsa is to the Puerto Rican or Cuban, the Samba to the Brazilian, or Hip-Hop is to the average American youth. By illustrating this fact, I hope that more people will be inspired to pay it the scholarly and artistic attention which it has been denied for far too long.

24

It's Not Just for Women — Men in Oriental Dance

ORIGINS OF RAKS SHARKI

In her article, "Dances of the Muslim Peoples", Lois Ibsen Al Faruqi categorizes Raks Sharki as a solo improvisational dance. Performed by an individual or groups of individuals, there are no set patterns or sequences of movements. Each dancer uses the movement vocabulary to express the music as he or she pleases. The vocabulary of the dance consists primarily of movements of the torso, which include twirling, twisting, circling, shaking, lifting and dropping of the hips, undulating and waving motions of the trunk and abdominal region, shaking and waving of the shoulders. The hands and arms wave and spiral to create abstract patterns which frame the body, while the head and neck can be slid back and forth on a horizontal axis.

VALENTINO

Photo by Walter Rasmussen

Yesterday and Today

There are ancient Roman documents which report dances with some of these movement qualities being done in the Mediterranean regions, but we cannot give a specific age or place of origin of the dance with any certainty. We can however, by dissecting the movement vocabulary, tell that it has roots in the various cultures that border the Near and Middle East. If we look at the articulated hip movements, we can see similarities with the dances of Sub-Saharan Africa, as well as the dances of African origin in the Americas, such as the Brazilian Samba, Dominican Merengue and the various Vodoun dances in Haiti. On the other hand, graceful, fluid movements of the hands and arms are central features of Asian dances, especially those of Central Asia.

This should come as no surprise, because the Middle East and North Africa are at the crossroads of these regions, as well as the Mediterranean and Southern Europe, and has attracted waves of migration from them for millennia. These peoples came to settle in the regions as traders, slaves, mercenaries, pilgrims, conquerors or refugees, intermingling with the indigenous populations and creating new vibrant cultures in the process.

This is the true origin of the dance: Not segregated secret societies hidden from the eyes of the uninitiated or in secluded temples or harems, but evolving over the centuries in community celebrations and the hearth and home of the family. Even in the Middle East today, this is the milieu in which the majority of dance takes place and it is the only dance "school" where one learns Raks Sharki.

RAKS SHARKI TODAY IN ITS COUNTRIES OF ORIGIN

In this natural arena of community and family, male and female children, are taught to dance by imitating the movements of their parents and older siblings. In its native setting, dance is used to mark the special occasions of life: the birth of a child, a circumcision, a wedding, a good harvest, a religious holiday, a family gathering or an informal congregation of close friends. It is a dance of joy and celebration. Most of these people would be shocked and perplexed to learn that in the West, many people view it as something women do to seduce men.

Although there are exceptions, men and women, even among the westernized upper classes, rarely dance with each other unless they are related. In conservative areas, even this is frowned upon. Therefore, men and women generally dance with and for members of their own sex. Often, virtuosity may be lacking among urban men of the upper classes. Some may feel that dancing is undignified, while others may be more acculturated to Western music and dances, creating the mistaken impression that Arab, or Middle Eastern men are not good dancers.

MEN PERFORMING RAKS SHARKI IN THE MIDDLE EAST

The first time I witnessed male dancers who were true technicians was 1988 in Luxor, while part of the dancer Morocco's "Secret Egypt" tour group. As part of the real cultural entertainment, Morocco hired Mohamed Murad's band, "Musicians of the Nile", with dance performance provided by Osman Balata, a local merchant in the nearby bazaar. Although not a professional, he is a skilled dancer, who readily seizes any opportunity to show his ability.

Kocheck and buffoon dancers performing at circumcision ceremony.

It's Not Just for Women—Men in Oriental Dance

Rabbaba
a one or two stringed bowed instrument of Upper Egypt.

—

Mizmar
a doubled reeded woodwind instrument similar to a zurna.

Kockeck wearing turban and robe.

As the *rabbabas* and *mizmars* stirred the air, Osman took command of his dance space with a dignified air. The musicians played the Jihanni rhythm, (named for the famous dancing horses) and he began to do the Upper Egyptian men's stick dance, Raks al Assa. His feet marked the heavy, syncopated rhythm, as he imitated the steps and hops of the dancing horses, while using his *assa*, (large cane reed walking stick carried by many Saidi men) to frame his movements. This first part is the same type of Saidi men's stick-dance commonly presented by the various Soviet influenced Egyptian folk and theater groups. What is not commonly presented however is the rest of Osman's dance.

After a few minutes of manipulating his assa, the rhythm changed. He balanced the assa on his head, while removing the long wool muffler worn around his neck and tying it around his hips. He then proceeded to execute a series of hip articulations with amazing precision for a man his size. The stick was now used to highlight his hips and torso, as he twisted, shook and undulated, all in time to the music. His movements were very earthy and interspersed with heavy footwork, which I had never seen done by women. At times he balanced the assa on his head and at others, he used it to underline his hips.

The following evening the group was entertained by the Banat Mazin Ghawazee. The Ghawazee are sedentary Sinti Gypsies who, until recently, earned their living by singing and dancing. Their dance is characterized by a rapid double side-to-side movement of the hips. With the exception of occasional shaking of the shoulders and neck slides, the upper body remains still. The arms are generally motionless being held out from the body at chest level, while they continually accompany themselves with finger cymbals.

After an hour the Ghawazee took a break and the musicians entertained with a musical interlude. At this point, one of the musicians, a young man in his late teens, got up and began to dance. He did the very same rapid staccato hip movements that the Banat Mazin sisters had just done.

It is not at all uncommon in Egypt to see a young man spontaneously begin to roll his shoulders or rotate his hips if he hears a strain of music he likes from a passing car or coming out of a storefront speaker.

Once, back in Cairo, I had another opportunity to see dancing in a disco on Pyramid Street. The clientele were mostly male college students on semester break. At first the DJ was playing American dance music, but as soon as he began playing Arabic pop music the crowd really came to life. Their movements were less earthy and the vocabulary more complex than I had seen in Luxor. The dance skills of many of them could easily rival that of some of the best professional female dance stars appearing in the five star hotels of Cairo.

It is obvious to the cultural observer that movements considered "feminine" in the West are, in their own cultural contexts simply part of the native movement vocabulary. Men perform these dances with and for their friends at weddings, discos, or other informal gatherings. The only context where they are not currently seen doing these same dances is professionally on stage, but this was not always the case.

Because of the plethora of images in movies, paintings and nightclub stages around the world of female Oriental dancers in exotic costumes, it is hard to believe that only a little over a hundred years ago it was also possible to see this ancient dance being performed throughout the Middle East by young men and boys.

The best documentation currently available of the existence of male dancers comes from Turkey, most of it by way of European travel accounts from the late 16th to early 19th century. In addition to these, we also have pictorial evidence. Among Turkey's many notable artistic accomplishments is a rich centuries old collection of miniature paintings. The dancing boys known as *Kocheks,* were a favorite subject, mostly depicted playing wooden clappers and dressed in colorful, multi-layered outfits.

The upper part of the costume was a close fitting tunic with a short collars, which fell to mid thigh, often made of velvet, buttoned down the front and from the forearm to the wrist, held in place by a belt with a heavy clasp, or a sash. Over the tunic, (just below the belt), was a skirt made of silk or some other rich fabric. They often wore a double skirt, the first being shorter and a different color than the second. Underneath they wore fitted trousers ankle high boots or slippers. On their heads, they wore skullcaps or a fur cap called a culpack.

This complex costume came into vogue in the 16th century. Earlier depictions show them wearing a much simpler costume, consisting of an intricately embroidered robe (the same as men of the upper classes), tied with a sash and either a turban or a culpack on the head. Turkish people of all classes took great pleasure in the performances of these entertainers, who were so popular that in the 1700s they were required to repeat their shows in several sections of Istanbul during festival days.

Chengi dancer.

Another type of male performer was called a *Tavshan* (rabbit). One of the dances they did, called a *Tavshan Raksi,* (Rabbit Dance) consisted of making facial contortions, hops and skips, imitating the mannerisms of rabbits (1). The main difference between these dancers and the Kochecks was costume. They wore a high collared shirt, over which was an embroidered fitted vest, over which was worn either a jacket or a looser vest, also intricately embroidered, a pair of baggy trousers around which was wound a long sash, and a pointed cap on the head. They are often depicted playing finger cymbals, or snapping their fingers in time to the music.

Although there were female dancers in Turkey, (known as *Chengis*), they did not perform in public. According to tradition, men and women did not socialize together. Public space was male space. Therefore, when women appeared in public, they were required to veil themselves. The home was considered female space and in many circles a "good" woman was one who left the house only on the day she married and the day she died. Since women did not have the freedom to socialize in public, female dancers were hired to perform in the private residences of those who could afford them, for the amusement of the women in the household. The public bath, or *hamam,* was another place female dancers performed. The hamam had certain days or hours that were reserved for women. This allowed women of different households a socially acceptable opportunity to see each other.

It's Not Just for Women—Men in Oriental Dance

Chengi dancer wearing double skirt costume.

For this reason a visit to the hamam was as much a social outing as an opportunity to bathe. It was not uncommon for the bath to hire Chengis to add to the social atmosphere of the occasion.

The Kochecks on the other hand, performed in public. Prior to European influence, there were no special buildings with raised stages for performances. Performers were a part of the community and exhibited wherever they could: public squares, yards, coffee houses and private residences. Sometimes, temporary pavilions of two or more stories were erected on festival days, so that important dignitaries could have a better vantage point of the activities. (2)

The Kochecks performed a variety of Anatolian, Greek and Balkan dances, some of them acrobatic in nature. Among these dances was a form of Oriental dance. Witnesses described it as consisting of quick steps, "wriggling", undulating, twisting of the body and pulling the stomach muscles in and out.

The Kochecks were not strictly dancers. They were members of theatrical companies, or guilds called *kols,* similar to the Chinese Opera. A complete performance blended music, dance, athletic feats, drama and comedy. No one element took precedence over the other. Therefore, as performers, the Kochecks had to be multi-faceted. (3)

Some kol were owned by independent entities, others were attached to the various trade guilds in the city. In the early 17th century, the two most popular kols in Istanbul were the Jeweler's Guild troupe in Edirne and the Gardeners Troupe. The Sultans also had troupes of Kocheks and Chengis attached to the palace.

One 17th century French observer reported that dancing boys performed in the palace from 3:00 p.m. till evening to the accompaniment of the court musicians. It's interesting to note that when they played for the Chengis, they were required to be blindfolded. In addition to this, many taverns throughout Turkey had small groups of performers.

According to 17th century Turkish traveler Eviliya Chelebi, in 1638 there were twelve kols in Turkey with over three thousand performers. These troupes frequently were hired to entertain the crowds at public festivals by the dignitaries of state who organized them and could also be seen at processions and parades. When the Sultan's armies left for battle or returned, musicians, clowns, jugglers and dancers preceded them. The parades of the trade guilds were also carnival-like atmospheres and each guild would parade past the Sultan on large elaborate floats, which depicted the activities of their trade. Many of these guilds owned kols, which were parts of their processions. On Friday afternoons, the eminent members of Turkish society patronized many of the best taverns, where these male performers entertained them with dances, songs and pantomimes.

Sometimes the crowds became over enthusiastic in their admiration and on many occasions quarrels broke out among the spectators, especially if spirits were involved, not unlike overzealous sports fans today or teenagers after a rock concert. Unfortunately, performances often devolved into fights and riots. These were so common that in order to put an end to the quarrels among his *Janissaries* (soldiers) Sultan Mahmoud first forbade and then passed a law prohibiting the performances of Kocheks in 1857. (4) Many of them fled to Egypt, where they were employed by Mohamed Ali Pasha.

3 0

Ironically, twenty-three years earlier in 1834, Mohamed Ali banished the female dancers (Ghawazee) from Cairo in an attempt to keep them from the view of European men.

Unfortunately, there is not as much detailed information about the male dancers of Egypt. As with Turkey, our primary source for information comes from the reports of European travelers. For the most part, accounts we have for Egypt were written in the 19th century, a period which saw the overlapping of several social and cultural movements: the Victorian era, the Romantic age and the Orientalist movement. Each of these influenced the opinions and tastes of the travelers and how they perceived what they saw.

In the arts and philosophy, Romanticism was the most influential of these movements. It was a departure from the values and ideals of Classicism, which embraced the artistic conventions in art and architecture of the Greco-Roman world. In Classical art, the male form was seen as ideal of beauty and harmony, exemplified in the sculptures and paintings of Michaelangelo. Romanticism celebrated women and the female form as the epitome of beauty, grace, and artistic inspiration. Women were placed on a pedestal.

This sentiment was expressed in ballet in several ways: the female heroine, not the male hero, became the leading figure in the dance. The ballerina went on point, focusing on her physical virtuosity. As a result, segments of ballet, previously created to show off male athletic prowess, were eliminated. Ballerinas were the stars and the number of men in ballet began to decline sharply. Had the upper body strength of the *ballerino,* (male dancer), not been needed to lift the ballerina in simulated flight, the presence of the male dancer would have been erased entirely. Where male dancers were once revered for their athleticism, they were now ridiculed and lampooned as effeminate and deviant.

Male Tavshan dancer.

WESTERN EXOTICISM OF THE MIDDLE EAST

This was the socio/cultural context in which the Orientalist movement was born. Technically, Orientalism was the study of Eastern arts and subjects, but for many Westerners, Orientalism was the adventure and sex fantasy of its day. The East was the Other, the Unknown, the Mysterious: far away lands of fantasy and magic. In the minds of Europeans, it was seen as a feminine entity; but whereas the European woman became the pinnacle of virtue, chastity and spirituality, her Oriental counterpart became the exact opposite: sexual, tempting, voluptuous, decadently luxurious and sensual. Many travelers of the nineteenth century (particularly males) came to the East to escape the restrictions of puritanical Victorian society. Reports of exotic dancing girls fired their imaginations, justifying their desire to indulge in behaviors and activities that would have caused social ostracism back home.

The reality they encountered was often disappointing. They frequently complained that the dancing girls were not the dark-haired sylph-like sirens with creamy complexions they imagined, but kinky-haired, dark-skinned, plump, earthy and graceless creatures with screeching voices. If the dancing girls failed to live up to their sensual image, the discovery of dancing boys did little to make up for it, especially given the aversion to male dancers in their own culture.

It's Not Just for Women—Men in Oriental Dance

If mentioned at all, they were dealt with in dismissive tones, or stereotyped as cross-dressing degenerates.

The most well known accounts of male dancers in Egypt are in Gustave Flaubert's *Travels in Egypt,* and W.E. Lane's *Manners and Customs of the Modern Egyptians.* These accounts, however, give scant information and have contributed to a general misunderstanding about the nature of these performers.

In the chapter on public dancers, Lane devotes only two paragraphs out of six pages to the male dancers. He reports that in addition to the female Ghawazee, young men and boys, called Khawals, who danced in the same manner as the Ghawazee, were hired to perform at weddings and festive occasions. Although few in number, many people preferred them to the Ghawazee. This was probably because public space was considered male territory. No doubt, many people considered unveiled women, calling attention to themselves in public, a bad example for their family women.

He also mentions the existence of another group of dancing boys and young men, known as *Ginks,* who were not Egyptians, but Jews, Greeks, Armenians and Turks. Unfortunately, this is all the information we are given about them.

Flaubert mentions seeing Khawals on two separate occasions. The first, a dancer named Hassan Belbesi, in a wedding procession, the second in his hotel by Hassan and another dancer.

Kocheck dancing as a woman.

Neither Lane nor Flaubert did any research on the subject of dancers in general, or male dancers in particular, other than casual observation. After all, anthropology is a relatively young discipline and dance ethnology younger still. People simply did not think in terms of cultural investigation at all, and even less so for dance. They seldom bothered to look beyond momentary observations, or think to question casual information given concerning dancers. These were taken at face value without consideration of the context of the performance, or whether or not their informants were relating fact or what they thought the traveler wanted to hear, or that individual's particular prejudices. For instance, in respect to the Ghawazee, closer inspection finds that reports of their supposed prostitution tend to be greatly exaggerated. This is also the case when it comes to male dancers. The variety of costume, how they came to be in the profession, whether they worked freelance or were attached to a guild, what they did after retirement, whether or not femininity was a required part of the profession and why are but a few of the questions an unbiased researcher would ask today.

MALE DANCERS ARE NOT ALWAYS DRAG QUEENS

In the face of incomplete information, these two works have led to the incorrect assumption that all male performers were female impersonators and male prostitutes. This is a gross overgeneralization due to several factors: 1) the European prejudice that considered movements of the hips and torso as well as fluid arm and hand movements feminine, 2) seeing male dancers who performed in drag, wearing long braided hair in the female fashion, 3) their own bias against male dancers and notions of cultural and racial superiority, and 4) confusing the dancing outfit for female dress.

32

On the first point, as I have shown, Raks Sharki is not exclusively a woman's dance, but a folk dance performed by both sexes. It is interesting to note that although Lane lived in Egypt for several years, he gives the impression that the only dance in Egypt was by professionals. Had he seen family celebrations of ordinary people, perhaps he would have realized it was indeed a unisex folk dance. One can only speculate that as a foreigner, a Christian and a male, he could never make the kind of connections that would allow him access to these activities where men and family women were present.

As to the second point, transvestism, or dancing in drag, did occur in several contexts. In Turkey, dancers were members of entertainment troupes in which several arts were blended. Pantomimes, mimetic dances and farce were all parts of an evening's entertainment. Since these troupes were all male, they would have had to perform female roles as well, if it were called for. It should be noted that female dancers also played male roles for the same reasons. According to Turkish dance historian Metin And, there are still mimetic folk dances in Turkey in which it is common for men and women to play the roles of the opposite sex. "O Olmasin bu Olsun," (Let It Not Be That One, But This One), from Erzurum, done by two men, in which one plays the fiancee of the other and Sudan Gecirme, done by two women in similar manner as the first, are but two of many such dances to be found in Turkey. (5) No doubt this also was the case in dramatic or comedic skits.

Although we do not have as much detailed information on Egypt, there is no reason to suppose that they did not have as rich a performance tradition as well. Female impersonation is a tradition that can be found all over the world and in all periods of time. Remember that in Shakespeare's time, all roles were played by men. In our own time, Milton Berle, Flip Wilson, Dame Edna and The Kids in the Hall are but a few modern day examples of male performers, who are famous for playing female roles. How ridiculous it would seem if someone suggested that stand-up comedy was a woman's art just because they saw one of these performers!

Druze warrior
performing dagger dance
in pleated skirt.

There is another possible context in which cross-dressing occurred: some male performers actually lived as women. Recently, the term Gender Dysphoria was coined to describe people who feel that they are trapped in the bodies of the opposite sex. In today's society, many of these people opt to have a gender reassignment operation to become the opposite sex, or they may simply choose to dress and live as the sex they believe themselves to truly be.

This may have been the case with some of the Khawals that Lane and Flaubert saw. The word "Khawal" means effeminate. Flaubert described Hassan Belbessi as having his hair braided and wearing makeup. Lane also describes seeing dancers in like manner and mentions that some of them even veiled themselves as women did, when not dancing. This was indicative of a female identity that was independent of the stage, part of the individual's everyday life. (6)

WHY MEN DANCED

In a society where a man was expected to marry and sire a family, embracing an alternative lifestyle would have caused him to be marginalized. The only professions open to him would have been those that were considered equally marginal, such as becoming a public entertainer. During the Golden Age of Baghdad, there was a group of effeminate singers and musicians, who performed in drag. They were known as *Mukanaths,* a word that also means effeminate.

Music, dancing, singing and acting were all considered low professions. People who engaged in them were generally poor and uneducated (or considered such), orphans, slaves and women who had to support themselves, etc. In cases of extreme financial difficulty, performers might have also engaged in prostitution in order to survive. If the cases of people who were marginalized and also lacked social protection, such as orphans, slaves, young people and abandoned women, they might have been exploited by disreputable individuals and forced to prostitute themselves. Flaubert mentioned that Hassan Belbessi was accompanied by his pimp when he performed. (7) Might he have been an orphan or slave who was raised to be a dancer and male prostitute for this pimp's profit? We may never know, but can be sure he led a hard life.

COSTUMES IN MALE DANCE

Albanian soldier doing Sword Dance. Notice pleated skirt.

Many Europeans, such as Lane, who saw male dancers, described their costume as being half male, half female: the upper half being a shirt of some kind or a vest and the lower half what they called a petticoat. (8) To them the sight of a brightly colored skirt suggested femininity. This, again, was a cultural misunderstanding. Ordinary men and male performers can be seen wearing outfits of this description throughout the Mediterranean and Asia. For example, Greek soldiers, called *Evzones,* wore an elaborate pleated skirt and still do for special occasions. The male dancers of Tunisia perform a dance balancing a stack of water jugs on their heads. Their costume is the same as mentioned by Lane, a shirt with a vest and a "petticoat" which is ankle length, with a sash tied around the waist. Sometimes the skirt reaches the shinbone. As late as 1926, there was a dagger dance performed by the Druze warriors of Syria in which they wore a large pleated skirt, used only during this dance. Even as far away as Tibet and India, male dancers can be seen wearing a costume with a wide multicolored skirt.

Several travelers to Turkey mentioned that the female Chengis were jealous of the notoriety of the male Kocheks and imitated their dress and dances. In miniatures of Turkish female dancers, they are shown in a dress similar to what the Egyptian Ghawazee wore. A typical costume would be a long overcoat with flowing sleeves and baggy pants. European drawings also show them in the single or double skirt of the Kocheks. Eyewitnesses also mentioned that the hems of Kocheks' skirts were weighted so that when they spun or pivoted, they flared out like a fan. Given this evidence, it is my belief that it was worn both by male and female performers. It was not everyday dress, but costume designed for dramatic effect. The fact that male dancers also wore ordinary robes as well as trousers shows that a variety of costumes were worn. With the exception of performing female roles in a skit or mimetic dances, the claim of the men wearing "female dress" shows itself to be an oversimplification of their roles as performers, to say the least.

In addition to cultural misunderstanding, Europeans were also influenced by the colonialist/imperialistic attitudes of the day—the belief that they were racially, morally and spiritually superior to the different races and cultures they encountered. This conviction was one of those used to justify their rush to colonize these peoples. Portraying the male and female dancers they saw as prostitutes and sodomites reinforced their notions of moral superiority. Lane himself described the women of Egypt as being the most licentious in the world (9). Because they preferred to believe this sentiment to be true, they saw no need to investigate further or challenge these statements.

Those who choose to ascribe to the views of Lane and Flaubert on male dancers would do well to remember that at the period those letters were penned, young boys were being castrated in Italy in order to maintain their soprano voices. These eunuchs, known as *Castrati,* sang in the opera houses and cathedrals throughout Europe. Many of them even played the female leads in operas. Despite this past and the prominent position women hold in Opera today, I doubt anyone would agree that it is a female art and that men who sing it are sexual deviants who imitate women.

THE DECLINE OF MEN IN MIDDLE EASTERN DANCE

Despite the fact that male dancers were plentiful and much enjoyed throughout the Near and Middle East, the 19th century saw their decline and disappearance from the performance scene. In Turkey, an edict of 1857 made their performances illegal. There is evidence that there were Kochecks in the Imperial palace at the turn of the century, indicating that the edict was eventually lifted, but their numbers never again rivaled that before the ban. By the late 19th century, Turkey had already embarked on a course of rapid modernization and social reforms in order to maintain its position as a world power. Many of the old customs and traditions quickly died. By the beginning of the 20th century, even the institution of the Chengis had vanished. The political and cultural reforms of Kemal Attaturk in the 1920s saw the deliberate abolition of traditional dress, speech and education as Turkey sought to severe its ties with the East and reinvented itself as a modern European nation.

Egypt also began to experience a decline in its traditional culture. From the beginning of the 19th century, European travelers had begun to monopolize female dancers. The dancers, most of whom lived from hand to mouth and experienced periods of unemployment, now found steady work performing for the droves of tourists who descended on Egypt. Unfortunately, because of their prejudice, male dancers did not share this opportunity. During the course of the century, the British began to exercise more and more influence over the culture. Lane himself commented on the rapid erosion of the very traditions he was documenting. By the end of the century Egypt was a British colony. The elite classes embraced British fashions, education and tastes in an attempt to align themselves with their ruling class.

Male Tunisian folk dancer balancing water jugs.

There is no record of exactly when the tradition of male dancers ended. By the end of the century there was no mention of them. Although there was a Syrian male dancer named Mohammed at the Chicago Exposition in 1893, there were no male dancers in the Egyptian theater. (10) Pictures of the Fair show only Ghawazee dancers. Similarly to the Chengis of Turkey, the Ghawazee also declined in number, surviving only in the remote regions of Sumbat in the Delta and around Luxor in southern Egypt. It is possible that as more and more Egyptians adopted a European worldview, they also adopted a prejudice against professional male dancers. Whereas in the past, the upper classes once hired them to enliven their family celebrations, they now regarded them as old fashioned, backward and an embarrassment. Because of the lack of patronage and the erosion of traditional social structures, young men and boys, who once would have become dancers, pursued other professions.

At the turn of the century, dance halls (patterned after English dance halls) began to appear in the Ezbekiyah district of Cairo, which catered to the British colonial administrators, tourists and the Egyptian upper classes. The dancers who performed in them were not the Ghawazee, who had once dominated the dancing scene, but newcomers. A new era in the history of the dance began, culminating in the 1920s and 30s, with the introduction of European-style nightclubs and an age of glamour and conspicuous wealth. Dancers reflecting the spirit of the times, adopted the two-piece costume, which was originally a Western fantasy of female Oriental costume, based on the *cholis* and flared skirts of Indian women. The elements of specially orchestrated dance music, as well as a more liberal use of space, were also introduced at this time.

A leading innovator in the field was a Lebanese woman named Badiaa Masabni, whose Casino Opera nightclub in Cairo launched the careers of legendary stars such as Tahiya Karioka, Samya Gamal and Naima Akef. The motion picture industry in Egypt turned these dancers into superstars and the Golden Age of Oriental Dance was born. This new image of the dancer was exported through North Africa, the Near and Middle East, Central Asia and around the globe. In the 1930s there were still people who remembered the old days, but that world was long gone and forgotten. Younger generations have no idea that this dance that they see performed by women at weddings, in movies and nightclubs, and which they do themselves in social settings, was also once performed professionally by men.

Tunisian drummer.

3 6

CONCLUSION

In summary, we have seen that Oriental dancing is in fact, not gender specific, but a folk dance practiced by both sexes. As professional entertainment, it was performed by both men and women. In certain countries, like Turkey, male dancers were numerous and performed in public, as well as in private residences. Female dancers performed primarily indoors, with and for other women. In Egypt, although there were public female performers, there were also public male performers as well.

Many European travelers described male dancers as female impersonators. This however, was an oversimplification of their roles as performers. Dancers were all-around entertainers versed in acting, comedy, singing and music. Since performing troupes were sex segregated, male and female troupe members were required to play the roles of the opposite sex when needed. This tradition can still be seen in some Turkish folk dances today. Some male dancers may in fact have had a condition known today as Gender Dysphoria, meaning they believe they are women trapped in male bodies. This may explain why some of them continued to dress as women in their private lives.

The 19th century was marked by political and cultural tensions in the countries of the East, which altered the traditional roles of both male and female dancers. Although very popular at one time, the tradition of male performers died, due to the combined effects of colonization, Westernization and the demands of a European tourists to see female, rather than male dancers. However, the folk tradition of male amateur dancers survives and many men continued to play a role in the professional arena as choreographers for the dance stars of Egypt.

At present, in the United States, Europe and in Turkey, a handful of men have began performing as professional Oriental Dancers, reviving an age old tradition.

This work has only scratched the surface of a rich and fascinating history and culture. I hope that it will inspire others to do further study and research free of ethnocentrism, fantasy and speculation. By doing so, the dance known as Raks Sharki will eventually gain the respect and recognition as one of the world's classic dance forms which it deserves.

Male dancer, based on 17th century engraving.

ENDNOTES

1. And, Metin (1976) A Pictorial history of Turkish Dancing. Dost Yayinlari, Ankara, p 139.
2. Ibid 135.
3. Ibid 133.
4. Ibid 141.
5. Ibid 164-165.
6. Lane, E. W. [1836] (1978) Manners and Customs of the Modern Egyptians. East West publications, p 377.
7. Flaubert, G (1979) Flaubert in Egypt. Ed. F. Steegmuller. Chicago: Academy Chicago Limited.
8. Lane, p 377.
9. Ibid 297.
10. Carlton, D (1994) Looking for Little Egypt. IDD Books. Bloomington Indiana. p 94.

■ *For contact information see: Tarik abd el Malik, page 200, and Walter Rasumssen Photography Studio, page 197.*

It's Not Just for Women—Men in Oriental Dance

American Tribal Style Belly Dance

By Zenuba

IN ATS, DANCERS PERFORM TOGETHER WITH THEIR "TRIBE."

In the world of *Raks Sharki,* a dance style has emerged which is uniquely American, artistically distinctive, and has become extremely popular: the American Tribal Style (ATS). This unique American creation emerged approximately twenty years ago. Although it was born in the Western United States, its appeal is spreading across the country and throughout the world, as many dancers are interested in learning more about ATS, and in creating a "tribal look" of their own.

What elements make Tribal style dance distinctive? The most instantly recognizable aspect of ATS is the elaborate costume, with an ornately wrapped headpiece and multiple layers of fabric and antique jewelry. But it is more than the costume that defines this dance style as Tribal—there is a unique on-stage characteristic that defines a performance as Tribal.

COSTUME

The ATS costume can be contrasted with the popular and glamorous look of the Egyptian-style costume, a style that swept the country during the 1980s and remains popular today. This popular costume style often features, for example, beaded fringe, sequins and sequin appliqués and costume pieces made from iridescent or diaphanous fabrics. In contrast, the ATS costume incorporates natural fabrics, fringed scarves, and antique jewelry. Diverse costume elements are drawn from many sources, including Berber culture, or from the Afghani or Moroccan peoples and culture, and elements from India and Pakistan, such as fabric embroidered with shisha mirrors. A costume often incorporates voluminous skirts, pantaloons, and a *choli* top, and may include tassel belts, coins, long rayon fringe, and Turkish or Russian scarves.

The elaborate headpiece, which is most often a turban style, gives the tribal dancer a regal demeanor. The specific style of the head wrap varies among the different ATS dance companies. Other important costume elements include facial *bindis* and theatrical make-up. Many dancers have tattoos and body art. The combined elements of the Tribal costume evoke a sense of strength, power and tradition. They are colorful and complex. However, it is more than the costume that makes ATS a unique dance form: group performance and the element of group improvisation make ATS special.

Choli

An Indian fitted blouse with a bare midriff.

—

Bindi

An indian facial decoration placed over the "Third Eye."

38

PERFORMANCE

The group performance and presentation of ATS contrasts the American Classical style of Raks Sharki. In general, Raks Sharki consists of solo performances, which have intricate, subtle musical interpretation, and often a more flirtatious style. ATS is typically a group presentation. In ATS, dancers perform together within their "tribe." An ATS performance may incorporate duets, trios, circles, and solos, within the group context. While the featured dancer performs, the other dancers provide a continuous backdrop or "chorus line". The steps and movements used by the chorus line compliment the featured dance. However, the dancers in the chorus line do not merely perform a choreographed dance—their movements and steps are improvised on stage during the performance. It is this unified whole which is presented to an audience.

The key element of ATS is "group improvisation." In traditional Raks Sharki, the dancer as soloist often performs in an improvisational style, but when dancing in a troupe the dances are choreographed. However, in Tribal style dancing, the troupe performs as a cohesive unit, with all of the dances, transitions from one dance to another, "chorus line" movements to accent the featured dancer(s) performed as group improvisation. For group improvisation to be successful, the ATS dance company, or tribe, learns a common dance vocabulary, which enables all dancers to follow cues initiated by the designated leader, and make seamless transitions to new movements.

As can be imagined, it is very important for the tribal dance company to work together so that the improvisation of several distinct individuals merges to create a unified look. In addition, each tribe has its own performing style, which includes unique methods for cueing changes in movements. This may take the form of various arm placements, which may signal specific hip articulations. These cues signify transitions, and allow a Tribal performance to flow seamlessly. As an ATS dance company evolves, it creates an artistic union of dance movements, group dynamics, and a unique costume style that singularly defines their tribe.

When considering Tribal style dance, some of the most common questions are: What are the origins of Tribal style? From what country or countries did it originate? Why is it so popular? Tribal style seems to have evolved from the dancing, performance style, and teaching of several influential teachers on the West Coast, specifically Jamila Salimpour and Carolena Nericcio. Jamila Salimpour is credited as being an important progenitor of Tribal style, and many artists acknowledge her influential teaching, technique, and the stage performances of her troupe "Bal Anat" as a creative inspiration from which ATS evolved. The most well known tribal dance artist, Carolena Nericcio, developed Tribal style, and founded the first Tribal dance company, FatChanceBellyDance. Her approach has become the primary interpretation of ATS, as it is known today. Two important teachers who have furthered the development and popularity of Tribal style are Kajira Djoumahna and Paulette Rees-Denis. These dancers teach Tribal style dance and technique at seminars, as well as offer instructional material for those interested in learning more about ATS.

In ATS there is a fusion of ethnic elements, so that the costume and dance steps are drawn from the many different cultures that have contributed to Raks Sharki, but it does not represent an authentic ethnic style of costume or dance from any one specific culture or people.

Why has Tribal style become so popular? That question may be the hardest to answer, as the popularity of any dance style is highly subjective. It may fill several needs in the Raks Sharki dance community, including the desire for something new, the chance to try a different performance approach, and a new costuming look. For the dancers involved in Tribal dancing, the element of "group improvisation" requires teamwork and a spirit of cooperation that can be very rewarding. Many dancers enjoy the element of body art and tattooing that is common to many Tribal performers, and the costume itself often draws a lot of attention. Finally, although Tribal style has become very popular, there is no requirement that a dancer "go tribal" if that's not what she/he is looking for in Raks Sharki. Most importantly, Tribal style has emerged from what may originally have been a West Coast phenomenon, to take its place in the world dance community.

BIBLIOGRAPHY

Djoumahna, Kajira. *The Tribal Bible, or What the Heck IS American Tribal Style Bellydance, Anyway?,* Santa Rosa, CA 1999.

Nericcio, Carolena. *Telephone interview. 29 September 1999.*

Rees-Denis, Paulette. *Telephone interview. 24 September 1999.*

■ *For contact information see: Beledi Magic Dance Company (Zenuba), page 200, FatChanceBellyDance, page 194, Kajira's Black Sheep Bellydance, Books, Bodywork & Bazaar, page 195, Gypsy Caravan/Sister Caravan, page 200.*

4 1

American Tribal Style Belly Dance

Dances of Ancient Egypt
(revised and abridged)

By Elizabeth Artemis Mourat

THE DANCERS BECAME THE DIVINE AND THE DIVINITY BECAME THE DANCERS.

The grandeur of ancient Egypt was reflected in the splendor of its art. People from every social class were exposed to music and dancing. Priests and priestesses used dance as a mystical too. The great Pharaohs performed ritual dances, and as early as 3000 B.C.E., King Semti danced as a form of prayer in motion.

Tomb painting and engravings provide a wealth of information about the significance of these ancient dances. Foreign influences left indelible traces on all of the arts. Evidence of the ancient dances was buried for thousands of years. Only in the last few centuries have archeologists, historians and dancers uncovered them.

A BRIEF HISTORY OF ANCIENT EGYPT

The early history can be divided into three periods.

Period	Centuries B.C.E.	Dynasties
Old Kingdom	27-21	I-XI
Middle Kingdom	21-16	XI-XVII
New Kingdom	16-10	XVII-XXI

The ancient dances that will be focused on in this section are primarily from these time periods.

The area known as Egypt was at one time geographically divided into two kingdoms: Upper and Lower Egypt. In 3100 B.C.E., King Menes conquered Lower Egypt and united the two into one nation. His was the First Dynasty. The Old Kingdom was known as the "Age of the Pyramids. "This was a time of great artistic growth; however, internal political struggles were prevalent.

42

The Middle Kingdom saw some relief from political turmoil. Trade was expanded into Phoenicia, south into Nubia and the lower Sudan, and east into Palestine and Syria. In 1730 B.C.E., the Hyksôs conquered Egypt. The origin of these people is unknown, but the Egyptians called their leaders the "Princes of the Shepherds." (Holum) The Hyksôs are variously believed to have been Asiatic, Arabic or Canaanite. The Egyptians learned military skills from their captors and expelled the Hyksôs in 1576 B.C.E.

Egypt regained its magnificence and its Nubian allies. The New Kingdom was born. This era is sometimes referred to as the "Empire Period." Expanded trading expeditions went further into Africa. Military campaigns continued and Egypt grew. In 1370 B.C.E., King Amenhotep IV drastically changed the already existing religious structure. He insisted on monotheism and proclaimed Aten, the sun, as the god of all Egypt. He then declared himself as the son of Aten, and took the name Akhenaten.

He was the first pharaoh. His wife was the lovely and famous Nefertiti. Akhenaten's obsession with this new religion resulted in self-imposed isolation. Egypt was left defenseless against the Hittites. Shortly after Akhenaten's death, Tutahkhamon was made Pharaoh. The old religions were reinstated. Egypt's "Golden Age" came not long after in the XIX Dynasty. Egypt once again recovered its status and strength.

Women had always passed on the royal lineage in Egypt. A woman became a queen by birth, but a man could only become king by marriage. The Pharaohs often married their daughters. Eventually, a succession of ineffective Pharaohs weakened the internal structure of the country.

General Horemheb seized the throne in the XVIII Dynasty and rebuilt the army. Other fine leaders built temples and rebuilt monuments. They also conquered the Libyans, but Ramses III was the last of the great pharaohs. His successors were becoming weak and ineffective due to their domination by the priests.

Egypt fell prey to many invaders in the centuries that followed. Libyans ruled it for 250 years commencing with the invasion of 950 B.C.E. The Sudanese briefly established their rule. The Assyrians took over in 671 B.C.E. The Persians conquered and ruled Egypt for over 200 years.

In 332 B.C.E., Alexander the Great drove out the Persians. Egypt came under Grecian rule and influence for 300 years. Once again, it regained its grandeur. The Greek rulers were called Ptolemies. Cleopatra was the last of the Ptolemies. Egypt's new capitol, Alexandria, had a magnificent library and museum. This was not a museum in the modern sense of the word. It was a center where great thinkers of that era would gather to worship and do research.

These philosophers would pay homage to the muses through creative thought on the arts, philosophy, astronomy, history and science. The Ptolemies supported this and Egypt became an intellectual, artistic and religious center of the world. It also became an irresistible target for Rome. In 30 C.E., Egypt was conquered by the Roman Empire. In 395 C.E., it fell under Byzantine Rule. This was followed by the Arabian conquest of 641 C.E. (Holum)

CLASSIFICATION OF DANCES

Everyone danced, whether they were a slave or a king. The occasions were plentiful. The dances can be divided into six types: religious, nonreligious festival, banquet, harem, combat, and street.

The most prevalent dances were for religious purposes. Some were for private rituals, but many were for public festivals. Women within the harem used dance to amuse others and charm their husbands or masters. Mock combat dances were carried out for entertainment or to symbolize mythological or historic events. The common people performed dances in the street. Traveling troupes of artists entertained the viewers in public squares and peoples' homes.

Religious Dances

Dozens of ritual dances were performed for sacred purposes. Athotus is sometimes credited for having been the first "inventor" of dance, but cave paintings depict ritualistic dancing seven thousand years earlier. Athotus, however, was an early choreographer. He noticed that during religious sacrifices, people would naturally move in accompaniment to the music, so he used these natural movements in his choreographies. (Kirstein, p. 12)

Several of the gods danced. Bes used dance to protect Ra, the sun god. Ra's offspring, Osiris also danced. It was believed that Hathor and Isis gave dance to the people. There were entire dance troupes attached to the temples to honor the deities. Some of the dancers were royal priestesses who entered this profession at an early age.

Each town employed special dancers for rituals. (Lexová, p. 68) In later Egyptian history, temples and royal houses employed independent dance troupes. (Kraus and Chapman, p. 34)

In religious ceremonies, dancers represented the divinities. (Kinney and Kinney, p. 4) In ritual dance, the priest or first-dancer not only impersonated the god, but also symbolically and magically became the god. The dancers became the divine and the divinity became the dancers.

The Dance of Stars—The Astronomic Dance

The ancient Egyptian clergy possessed great power and wealth. Their mystique was enhanced because many rituals were conducted in private. One such secret ritual was the Dance of the Stars, also known as the Astral Dance or the Astronomic Dance. It commemorated both astronomy and astrology.

The priests wore "scintillating" clothes. (Kirstein, p. 13) They surrounded the altar as the planets surround the sun. They then made signs...

> for the Zodiac with their hands, while turning rhythmically from east to west, following the course of the planets. After each circle, the dancers froze into immobility to represent the constancy of the earth. (Kirstein, p. 14)

The priests' movements imitated the heavenly bodies as they moved in their course. (Clarke and Crisp, p. 25) It has been speculated that this dance was the predecessor of all circle dances. (Sorell, p. 22)

44

Dancing for the Deities

The Pharaohs were considered to be the sons of Hathor; they are often depicted as jingling a sistrum before her while the priests played clappers and danced. (Kirstein, p. 12) Annual festivals were held at Bubastis for Artemis or Bastet, both of whom represented an aspect of the great universal mother goddess. In the New Kingdom, a celebration in honor of the god Amon was depicted in wall paintings at Luxor. There were strong African influences in the religious festivals, particularly in the ecstatic dances that included frenzied dancing, excessive drinking and moments of bliss. (Olivová, p. 60)

Harvest Dances

Harvest dances were offered every year. The king or his representatives would perform a dance of thanksgiving at harvest time in honor of the fertility god Min. (Olivová, p. 54) Farmers would also bring their sacrifices to the god, and then dance. One account from the Old Kingdom describes men as "performing quick movements and holding canes in their hands, clapping them together." (Lexová, p. 9) Dance was also used in celebrations honoring Sokar, Amon, Bastet and Artemis.

Fertility Circle Dance

At Giza there is a relief on a tomb showing a circle dance done for the purpose of fertility that dates back to 2700 B.C.E. Fertility rituals were at one time quite common in earlier Egyptian history but eventually the aristocracy frowned upon this practice. (Clarke and Crisp, p. 25)

Osiris and Isis Festival Dances

The most famous religious celebrations pertained to the worship of Osiris and Isis during the New Kingdom. These spectacular festivities were directly related to the irrigation of the great river Nile.

Funeral Dances

The Egyptians saw the rebirth of their beloved god Osiris as a symbol of their own ability to continue in a life after death. The funeral itself became a Feast of Eternity. There were several different dances performed. The most important dance was of prehistoric origins, and may have disappeared during the New Kingdom. This ritualistic dance was

> ...always performed by several men and women dancers who are accompanied by mates, slapping their hands rhythmically. The women or men move erect with a free dancing step keeping their hands raised about the head. (Lexová, p. 36)

In this posture, the palms were turned upwards towards the sky with fingertips facing the dancer's head. They were placed just above the head and the inner elbows were facing the ears.

There were certain expressions of grief that could be considered as dance gestures and postures. Perhaps these gestures grew out of natural movements and eventually became a part of the Egyptian dance vocabulary. They may have served some ritualistic function.

The festivals for the goddess Hathor were full of dancing and rejoicing. In her Dendera temple, it is written:

We beat the drum to
   her spirit.
We dance to her Grace,
We raise her image up to
   the heavenly skies;
She is the lady of sistrum,
Mistress of jingling
   necklaces...

She is the lady of cheers,
   mistress of dance,
The lady of sistrum,
   the mistress of song,
The lady of dance, the
   mistress of wreathmaking,
The lady of beauty,
   the mistress of skipping

When both her eyes open
   —the sun and the moon—
Our hearts rejoice,
   seeing the light.
She is the lady of
   dance wreaths,
The lady of intoxication,
We dance to none, we cheer
to none, but her spirit.

(Lexová, p. 40)

45

Nonreligious Festival Dances

The great Pharaohs decreed the need for frequent, massive festivals. There were public festivals, jubilees and processions to celebrate anniversaries, birthdays and marriages of the royal families as well as historic events. At one time there were 162 festival days in one year. The people danced on each of these public occasions.

Banquet Dances

The Pharaohs and other members of the aristocracy hosted elaborate banquets and dinner parties. There was even a hierarchy for performers. The wealthy took great pride in owning or employing entire dance troupes, singers and musicians. Little is known about dance training for men, but women began training at an early age.

Slower Dances

Some of the banquet dances were stately. In one dance, the women's movements were ". ..quiet and restrained. The dancers followed one after another, hardly lifting their feet from the ground and moving their hands; sometimes other women beat time clapping their hands."(Lexová, p. 9) These dancers usually performed in groups of two or more and their movements were slow. They often played instruments including the lute, lyre, harp, and flute while dancing.

Acrobatic Dances

The acrobatic dances were incredible spectacles of agility. They performed splits, backbends, tumbling, and walked on their hands. They also performed sleight of hand, juggling and balancing tricks. The dance position known as the bridge was used, and may have had some ritualistic significance. Women would perform the bridge as part of a religious dance in the temple of Queen Hatshepsut at Karnak circa 1480 B.C.E. (Olivová, p. 53)

Many of the acrobatic dances were performed in short wrap-around skirts, a kind of loincloth, a hip scarf, or in the nude. This allowed for the necessary freedom of movement, while accommodating for the heat of North Africa. It also permitted the audience to admire the beauty of the dancers' well-proportioned bodies. The dancers sometimes wore dresses, which gathered under the bodice, exposing both breasts. Some of the dresses had a ribbon over one shoulder or crossed in front. The dancers sometimes wore wrist cuffs, bracelets, ankle bracelets, earrings and collars. The hair was styled in several different ways, including braids, full curls or a cap with tassels. It is also possible that their hair was cut short, thus giving the impression of a tight cap.

Pair Dances

There are numerous references to dances involving two people. Themes illustrated in pair dances included longing, emancipation, secret abduction and depression. Either two women or two men who executed symmetrical movements in mirror image of each other performed these dances. (Lexová, p. 26) Thus, the dancers were not performing the same movement identically, but in reverse.

There is a beautiful illustration from the VI Dynasty of a paired dance involving two women dancing with canes decorated at the tops with small gazelle heads, which may have been rattles. In pair dances, the partners were usually wearing belts or skirts trimmed with several pieces of long wide fringe. They occasionally danced nude.

Harem Dances

The women of the harem were known as the "adorned ones", and they were there to please and delight their master. Harem women and ladies of high society were instructed by choirmasters and mistresses of dance as part of their education. (Wenig, p. 38) There are a few extraordinary engravings from Amenhotep IV in the XVIII Dynasty, which depict palace harem scenes. They show the king's harem dancers practicing their dance while women musicians played harps, lyres and lutes.

Dances for Banquets, Dinner Parties and within the Harems

These dances were dissimilar from the religious or acrobatic dances. In these dances, performers created solos, pas de deux, pas de trois, and group dances.

Male dancers were quite spirited. They often jumped in the air exuberantly and usually danced with great enthusiasm. They wore short apron-like skirts or belts, which suspended a panel or fringe. The boys or young men of the Old Kingdom sometimes danced nude. Hair was generally worn short or tucked under tight-fitting caps. (Lexová, p. 62)

In ancient Egyptian dance, the feet were always bare. Traveling steps were based on the most natural of movements. The dancers used simple or vigorous walking, stamping, running, short hops and leaping. They rotated completely and also made 180° turns. A bas-relief dating back 3500 years shows a *pirouette* (where a dancer turns on one foot with the other foot raised). An *entrechat* (where a dancer jumps up and tightly crosses her feet in the air) has also been identified.

The hand was usually "soft", relaxed and open. Sometimes, however, the palms were flat, rigid and geometrical. There were some dances that were done with the fist clenched and occasionally thumb and/or first two fingers were extended from the fist. The arms were often, but not always symmetrical and point in the same or opposite directions. Many right angles were employed. A gesture indicating the act of addressing someone is performed with one arm bent slightly at the elbow and extended outward and upward in front of the body. The palm faced out and was usually level or above the head. The other hand was down with the palm facing the hips or the back of the thighs. The hieroglyphic for this gesture means "to speak" or "to call." (Lexová, p. 53)

The Egyptians were comfortable with nudity or semi-nudity. In the Old and Middle Kingdoms, women frequently wore short skirts and danced bare breasted. They sometimes wore dresses that came to the knees or mid-calves and had a wrap-around effect, which allowed the legs to move freely. Some of theses dressed hung from the left arm with the right breast uncovered. In the New Kingdom, the women ordinarily wore a long transparent dress with either narrow or broad sleeves. Dancers adopted this style, sometimes wearing hip belts underneath their dresses. They occasionally danced nude, except for hip belts and sometimes jewelry.

Egyptian women sometimes cut their hair short or wore wigs. In the Middle and New Kingdoms, some dancers pulled their hair back and arranged several braids each ending with a tassel. The dancers from the Old and New Kingdoms wore ribbons and garlands.

Due to foreign influences during the New Kingdom, women were more inclined to follow changing fashions. There was more variety in the dancers' coiffures.

Egyptian women adorned themselves with ornaments. They wore wreaths of flowers and particularly adored lotus blossoms in their hair. Jewelry was extremely popular, as it not only beautified the wearer but added mystical properties. Women wore pearls and semi-precious stones, as well as jewelry made from copper, bronze, silver and gold. The artwork frequently reveals women who were wearing bracelets on the wrists, upper arms, and ankles. They also wore necklaces or decorative collars made of malachite, lapis lazuli, carnelian and glazed earthenware. Earrings appeared during the New Kingdom.

The Egyptians cherished cosmetics. They were valued for their beautifying effects and their medicinal and magical properties. The eyes were heavily painted with kohl. Henna was used to stain hands and nails. (Murray, p. 89) Lipstick was worn (although perhaps only by prostitutes). There are many recipes for cosmetics which could heal the eyes, blacken the hair or make "...an old one young." (Wenig, p. 43)

Combat Dances

The combat dances were a way of perfecting military skills. At the same time, they celebrated great victories and portrayed mythological events. Soldiers also performed dances for their own amusement. Some dances were choreographed, while others were improvised based on a theme.

Dances of the Street

Little is known about the dances of everyday citizens since their history was not meticulously preserved. It is known, however, that the common people had a passionate love for dancing and they performed their own dances, which were burlesque in style. There were wandering dance troupes that performed in the streets and in private homes. They did acrobatic and mimic dances. Members of the group played instruments and sang. They may have also been skilled in midwifery. (Maspero, p. 39-41)

INSTRUMENTATION

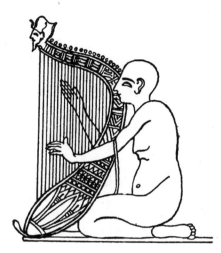

No description of ancient Egyptian dance would be complete without a discussion of the musical instruments of that time.

During the Old Kingdom, percussion was provided by hand clapping, finger snapping, rhythmic shouting and foot stomping. The percussion instruments were clappers made of wood, bone or ivory. Two clappers were held in each hand and played much like castanets.

Eventually, finger cymbals were introduced which may have been played with only one in each hand and later with two in each hand. It is unclear when the drum was first introduced, but a conga-type drum was used in a military dance during the New Kingdom. The god Bes danced with a tambourine. This is one of the instruments used in secular as well as sacred dances. The tambourine seems to have been introduced during the Middle Kingdom.

The *sistrum* was an important instrument primarily used in Isis cult rituals. This sacred instrument was believed to have the ability to drive away stagnation by the use of agitation as it jingled. The *menit* (or *menyt*) was another mystical instrument that was worn between the shoulders. It dangled down to the middle of the back and made a sound when the dancer moved. This instrument was primarily a mystical charm, which by the power of the goddess Hathor protected its wearer against physical or magical attacks from behind. (Murray, p. 138)

Flutes and pipes were also popular in ancient music. The flute was sometimes short but there was also a large flute that rested on the ground so that the performer had to play while sitting. This instrument appeared in the early IV Dynasty. There were double flutes as well, which first appeared in the XII Dynasty. These were two flutes, attached near the mouth and played simultaneously. Trumpets appeared around the XVIII Dynasty and were most likely to have been of foreign origin. (Murray, p. 143) Ancient Egyptians also played clay and bone whistle as well as buzzers.

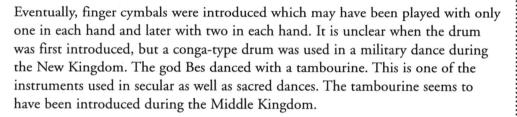

The harp was the first stringed instrument of Egypt. In the Old Kingdom it was usually played by women. Other stringed instruments played in ancient Egypt but of foreign origin were the lyre and lute. The lyre originally had three strings, which were stretched over a tortoise shell and up onto a crossbar made of wood. Protruding from the shell and attached to the crossbar were two arms that formed a horseshoe shape. The arms were made of horn or wood. The lyre first appeared in the artwork at Beni Hassan during the XII Dynasty in the Middle Kingdom. This wall relief shows a lyre being played by a desert nomad who is identified as a Bedouin. (Murray, p. 143) Dancing girls more often played the lute. This instrument closely resembled a small-bodied *oud*. It was pear-shaped and made of wood, sometimes with a long neck.

EVOLUTION OF EGYPTIAN DANCES

The dances of ancient Egypt evolved with each phase of Egyptian history. There were foreign influences from Phoenicia, Syria, Palestine, Nubia, the Sudan, Ethiopia, and the Bedouins. Dancers were "imported" from other countries and foreign customs and tremendous wealth poured into Egypt. Around 1500 B.C.E. the Egyptians brought the *Bayadeers,* magnificent and elegant temple dancers of India. An ancient text described

> ...the lines flow softly and pleasantly; nowhere do they bend sharply or break; and even where the mood is impetuous and impassioned, the movement remains close. (Süheyla, p. 84)

The dances were becoming more fluid and graceful.

After the New Kingdom there was a turbulent time with many invasions. The Libyans, the Sudanese, the Assyrians, and the Persians brought their influence into Egypt. In the 3rd century B.C.E., Alexander the Great brought Grecian rule for over 300 years. During this time, the arts flourished and Greek dancing masters were brought to Egypt. In 30 B.C.E., Egypt became a Roman province, and the Romans brought their decadence with them.

In 395 C.E., the Roman Empire divided and Egypt fell under Byzantine rule. Christianity became popular with some Egyptians and the Christian Church eventually discouraged dance. In 641 C.E., the Arabs conquered Egypt and it became a Moslem nation. This began another exciting chapter of Egyptian dance history.

Egyptian Oud player, 1860

50

BIBLIOGRAPHY

Bland, Alexander. *A History of Ballet and Dance in the Western World.* New York: Praeger Book Co., 1976.

Clarke, Mary and Crisp, Clement. *The History of Dance."*London: Orbis Publishing, 1980.

Ellis, Havelock. "The Dance of Life." Cambridge, Massachusetts: The Riverside Press,
    Houghton Mifflin Co., 1923.

The World Book Encyclopedia. "Ancient Egypt." United States: Field Enterprises Education Corp., 1963, 5.

Graves, Robert. *The White Goddess.* New York: Creative Age Press, 1948.

Grove, Lilly. *Dancing.* London: Longmans, Green and Co., 1895.

Holum, Ph.D., Kenneth. *Lectures.* University of Maryland: College Park, Maryland.
    October 13 and November 16, 1987.

Kinney, Troy and Kinney, Margaret West. *The Dance.* New York: Tudor Publishing Co., 1914-1936.

Kirstein, Lincoln. *Dance—A Short History of Classic Theatrical Dancing.* New York: Dance Horizon
Publication, 1935, 1977.

Kraus, Richard and Chapman, Sarah Alberti, *History of the Dance in Arts and Education.*
    New Jersey: Prentice Hall, Inc., 1981.

Lexov·, Irena. *Ancient Egyptian Dances.* Prague, Czechoslovakia: Oriental Institute. 1935.

Maspero, Sir Gaston. *Popular Stories of Ancient Egypt.* London: H. Grevel and Co., 1915.

Murray, Margaret A. *The Splendor that was Egypt.* New York: Prager Publishers, 1964.

Olivov·, Vera. *Sports and Games in the Ancient World.* London: Orbis Publishing 1984.
    Republished in New York: St. Martin's Press, 1985.

Shawn, Ted. *Dance We Must.* London: Dennis Dobson, Ltd. 1964.

Sorrell, Walter. *The Dances Through the Ages.* London: Thames and Hudson, 1967.

Süheyla. *The Ancient and Enduring Art(Dance Oriental.* Ann Arbor, Michigan: Edward Brothers, Inc. 1977.

Wenig, Steffen. *The Women of Ancient Egyptian Art.* New York: McGraw-Hill Book Co., 1969.

Wolinski, Arlene. "Egyptian Masks: The Priest and His Role." Archaeology, 1987,
    40 (1) January/February.

■ *For contact information see: Elizabeth Artemis Mourat, page 198.*

Dance As Community Identity in Selected Berber Nations of Morocco:

From the Ethereal & Sublime to the Erotic & Sexual

by Carolina Varga Dinicu, p.k.a. Morocco

ALL BLUE PEOPLE ARE TUAREG,
BUT NOT ALL TUAREGS ARE BLUE.

This article was first presented by request at the combined annual conference of the Congress on Research in Dance, Society of Dance History Scholars, American Dance Guild & Dance Critics Association at the Library for the Performing Arts in Lincoln Center, New York City, June 1993. It was published in their proceedings, then in segmented form in Habibi in 1994 & 1995. It was delivered again as part of the Keynote Session at the Annual Conference of the International Council on Physical Education, Recreation, Sport & Dance (a UNESCO international organization) in Cairo, Egypt, in July 1999 .

GUEDRA

Spreading Soul's Love & Peace to the Beat of the Heart

In classical Arabic, the word *guedra* means cauldron/cooking pot. That pot was covered with an animal skin to make a drum, also called guedra, to play the heart-beat rhythm (life's basic rhythm)—also called guedra, for the female performer—also called a guedra, of the ritual, which is also called Guedra only as long as it is being done on the knees: when the guedra stands up (or starts the ritual standing up), it is called *T'bal*. In the 37 years I've been researching, doing and teaching Guedra, nobody has been able to explain the reason for the difference—not even my teacher, B'shara. I have come to my own conclusions, based on language, which I won't go into here.

Guedra belongs to the Blue People of the Tuareg Berbers, from the Sahara Desert, which ranges from Mauritania into Morocco and Algeria, all the way to Egypt. When, due to current long- term drought or economic conditions, Blue People choose to live in a town in Morocco, it is usually Goulmime or TanTan.

Why are they called Blue People? Because they love to use indigo "stones" to color pieces of fabric by pounding the "stones" into powder and the powder into the fabric—as versus dying by hot-water dip. The bluer and shinier the resulting fabric, the more beautiful the item of clothing and the higher the status of the wearer, since more was spent to get the richer color.

52

In the course of wearing fabric so treated, some of the blue powder gets on the skin of the wearer. In a desert, one can't take daily showers, so the wearer's skin actually takes on a bluish tinge, which is considered beautiful and desirable. The good news is that this powder also protects the skin from drying out from the terrible desert sun and heat by locking in natural moisture and acting as an extremely effective sunscreen. All Blue People are Tuareg, but not all Tuaregs are Blue.

The Blue People have a matriarchal society: unusual enough in terms of Western cultures, more so in context of what is assumed to be Islamic. Women keep all the household keys, show off their strength by impromptu wrestling matches, go unveiled—while the men modestly cover their noses and mouths with the end of their tagelmousses (several meters of gauze, wrapped around the head in a turban), and have equal—if not greater rights to choose/take as many lovers as they wish before marriage: it only increases their value, skill and desirability. (1,2,3)

Why do Blue men, feared to this day for their ferocity and skill as warriors and respected as businessmen, "veil"? Because of their belief that the world has a great number of evil "spirits" eager to invade the body via any opening—especially the mouth and nostrils, so they must cover and/or protect the entranceways, but since women know the secret of life: only they can conceive and give birth, they have natural protection against these evil spirits and don't have to "veil".

For the Blue People, Guedra isn't merely a dance, it is a ritual in which anybody and everybody can participate, although the central figures are the female guedras (sometimes two women do it together, or a man and woman or woman and child of either sex). Unlike the *Zar* (Sudan/Libya/Egypt), Stambali (Tunisia) or Hadra (Morocco), the Guedra's aim is NOT to exorcise a person or place of evil spirits, but to envelop all present with "good energy", peace and spiritual—not carnal—love, transmitted from the depths of the guedra's soul via her fingers and hands.

The entire accompaniment consists of the drum (guedra), which can be played by anyone, of any sex or age, with the skill and desire to do so, and rhythmical clapping and chanting by any and all others present. Nowadays, a slapped and shaken gourd instrument is sometimes added.

Chants are in Tamahaq (their own language) or Maghrebi (Moroccan Arabic) and can be about anything from Islamic exhortations calling on the name of Allah: El hamdu l'Illa, Allah, Allah (all praise to Allah, oh Allah, oh Allah); Wahad, Wahad, Wahad (God is one); to praise King Hassan II or expressions of thanks for good fortune or a wish granted. Most often, they call upon God and goodness, to be shared with all humanity.

Clothing often has a tremendous effect on the movements and styles of dances and rituals, especially in ethnic forms, where tradition leaves very little leeway for individual choice or expression. Those garments, their styles and reasons for being that way, usually pre-dated the dances and rituals done while wearing them. Not so theater dance, where costumes are (hopefully) designed to facilitate and accentuate the choreography.

Usually over a *caftan* (long, loose robe), sometimes not, Blue women wear a length of fabric, five to six meters long by about two meters wide. Wound around the body, folded over a bit in the front, both front and back portions are caught at the collar bones after each turn by two elaborate *fibulae*: the world's first "safety pins". Long chains are suspended from the fibulae to hold them in place and as ornamentation. A rope or belt is tied around the waist and fabric pulled up for a blouson effect and so the skirt just reaches the top of the foot. The last two meters are left unwound, to be pulled up and draped over the wearer's headdress, should circumstances or the desert heat require it. This train-cum-veil plays a very important part in desert survival—and the Guedra.

The Blue woman's unique headdress is also a result of adaptation to desert conditions —and germane to the overall effect of the Guedra. Anywhere from two to six inches high (or more), the front is made of leather, canvas, felt or woven horsehair decorated with cowry shells, silver coins, turquoise, coral and the occasional mother-of-pearl button or Coca-Cola bottle top: whatever appeals or is valuable to the wearer.

From this front, a circlet of twigs, thin bones or wire sits on the crown of the head and the wearer's hair, interwoven with horsehair and braided over and down, fastening it firmly to the head. Cowry shells, silver, turquoise and coral beads are also woven into the multiple braids. From the back of the circlet, a "handle" rises to the same height as the front piece, up and over the center of the head, approaching but not touching the front "crown". Horsehair or wool is woven around it.

Such a time-consuming and elaborate hairdo is usually redone every one to one and a half months. The headdress supports the aforementioned two-meter fabric end, keeping it off the wearer's head and leaving an air space that maintains her normal body temperature of 98.6°F, thereby keeping her cooler in the heat of the day and warmer in the cold desert night.

Guedra is a nighttime ritual, around a fire under the light of the moon or inside one of the larger tents. When done for real, as versus for an audience, it's most often in a circle. The drum throbs with the heartbeat rhythm: da da dum da da, da da dum da da and the clapping starts. Shrill guedra (ululations) ring out, the chanting swells.

Inspiration calls, a woman from the circle answers: for now, she is the guedra. Pulling the tail of her robe over her headdress, so it covers her head, face and chest, she puts on the "magic" necklace. It's up to her as to whether she starts standing up or on her knees.

The "veil" covering the guedra's head, shoulders and chest signifies darkness, the unknown, lack of knowledge. Her hands and fingers are moving under the covering, flicking at it, trying to escape into the light. When she feels the time is right, the guedra's hands emerge from the veil's sides.

With hand-to-head gestures, she salutes the four corners: North, South, East and West, followed by obeisances to the four elements: Fire (the sun), Earth, Wind and Water. She touches her abdomen, heart and head, and then quickly flicks her fingers towards all others present, in life or spirit, sending blessings to them from the depths of her soul's energy.

Why does she touch her abdomen? In the East, the heart is known to be fickle and unreliable. When somebody wishes to convey true depth of affections or emotions, the way of expressing it is to say: "You are in my liver" not "You are in my heart" as we do in the West. By indicating any approximate spot on her abdomen—not necessarily the anatomically correct location—the guedra underscores the depth and sincerity of her blessing.

In the West, we used to believe the third (ring) finger of the left hand lead to the heart, ergo the custom of wearing engagement and/or wedding rings there. Blue people believe their second fingers to be direct lines to the soul, with power to transmit blessings or curses, so the guedra directs most of her mini-bolts of energy through them, gently holding them a bit lower or higher than the others. This energy can be specifically focused on an individual, present or not, to a group or the entire world.

Once again, when the guedra feels the time is "right", she takes off the magic necklace, uncovers her face, drapes the fabric on top of her headdress or out-of-the-way, replaces the necklace and focuses her gaze and blessings more strongly and specifically. The drumming, clapping and chanting increase in tempo and intensity at each phase, as does the guedra's breathing.

If her hands flick to the front, the guedra sends blessings for the future, to the side—the present, in back—the past. Overhead—to the Sun, down—to the Earth, from side to side—to the waters and winds. Time is a circle. In the Guedra, the vast majority of movement flows from the fingers and hands, with some arm movement from the elbows down.

The ribcage is lifted and lowered/relaxed, as in some African dances, when extra emphasis is called for. The head can be gently turned from side-to-side, causing the braids to sway. As the Guedra comes to a crescendo, accent in the chest movements transfers from lift to lowering and the head swings more strongly from side-to-side with chin lifts, causing her braids to "fly".

When done "for real", the Guedra goes on for quite awhile, gradually increasing in tempo and intensity, but still keeping the heartbeat rhythm. Likewise, the guedra's breathing also increases in depth and intensity, until she collapses in a trance.

Dance as Community Identity

When a man joins in, it is as an accompaniment, to induce a woman of his choice to accept the magic necklace from him and bless him—and the others with her soul's energy via the Guedra. After she accepts and takes the necklace, he unfolds the shoulder drapings of his *dra (ghandoura)*, holding it out in his fingers to its full width, dipping and swaying from side to side, until she is ready to focus her energy and go on with the ritual alone. In the group, the men concentrate on driving and maintaining the clapping and chanting that encourage the guedra and deepen her trance.

Blue people consider Guedra their direct contact with the elements, spirits and universe, the deepest expression of their souls and protection against a hostile environment and evil spirits.

So seriously is it taken by Moroccans in general, that his majesty, King Hassan II, had his own personal guedra, B'shara of Guelmim, who I was fortunate enough to have known as a friend and teacher from 1963 to her death from cancer in 1992.

BETROTHAL DANCE OF TISSINT

Pursuit, Persistence and Victory

Tissint is located in the south of the Anti Atlas, about 40km from the Algerian border.

The women's festival clothing is marvelous: a long, flowing black overrobe with multicolored zigzag embroidery at the shoulders and across the chest, tied at the waist with a multi-colored woven wool belt ending in tassels that hang almost to the feet. The black head veil is held in place by embroidered bands hung with silver coins and almost unbelievably elaborate large silver jewelry, chains and ornaments. Very large silver hoop "earrings" hang from both sides of this headwear. Many necklaces of graduated size, made of silver coins, some interspersed with large amber, turquoise and coral beads, adorn the chest. Large silver bracelets circle each wrist.

The men wear flowing blue ghandouras over white caftans, with black cloth wound into turbans on their heads: similar to, but not as big or elaborate as the dras and tagelmousses of the Blue Men. Each has a dagger at his left hip, its sheath attached to a braided cord hung over the right shoulder and across the chest. Some ghandouras have elaborate, thin-cord embroidered ornamentation on the chest and pocket.

The *bendir* players, clappers and chanters are from the community and not professionals. They sit in a circle, in the center of the dance space, not only musicians and accompanists for the festivities, but chaperones making sure the limits of propriety are adhered to by all participants.

After the group of mostly young men and women dance a while to a relatively lively tempo, one of the young women detaches herself from the group. One of the young men stands, holding overhead the corded belt from which his silver dagger dangles: he offers his protection. It is an official, public proposal of marriage. (Usually known about and agreed to in advance, but not always: surprises do occur.)

He dances after her, whirling and swooping, the dagger, held high, swaying on its cord. She constantly flutters her shoulders like a frightened bird, hands palms up, elbows gracefully bent, while she flees from him for awhile, then approaches, coyly whirling and escaping at the last moment.

When done "for real", this "mating dance" goes on for quite awhile, to show that she is "hard to get" and he is undaunted in the face of resistance, because he truly wants her for his wife.

Once she lingers in front of him long enough for him to slip the corded belt over her head, they are officially betrothed. He kneels before her beauty and acceptance of his proposal. She, shoulders still fluttering, makes a last circuit of the group, showing off his dagger around her neck: she is under his protection.

This danced ceremony, involving the whole community, predates Islam. It continues in spite of efforts by conservative religious elements and bureaucrats to convince the people of Tissint to abandon it as heretical and against the Hadith, and use only religious contracts, ceremonies and bureaucratic paperwork to legalize their unions. Fortunately, its continued inclusion in the Marrakesh Folk Festival by the Ministry of Culture kept the anti-dance wolves in Tissint at bay for a while. I don't know if the unfortunate ending of that wonderful festival has had any effect as yet.

AHOUACHE OF IMIN TANOUT

Dancing the Night Away

The musicians sit in a circle around the fire, heating their bendirs and getting ready for a long haul. The night air is still, then the bendirs and small drums start to thrum and reverberate.

The *rais*, or leader, prepares to direct the group's formations and sequences, somewhat like a square dance caller, but in a more general, laissez-faire manner: closer to a traffic cop on a crowded urban street. He is there mostly to make sure the proprieties and distances are kept, for this is a dance in which only the unmarried can take part: it is their socially acceptable way to "check each other out"—all night.

Dance as Community Identity

Everyone wears his or her best: the men in long, loose, hooded white dras over close-fitting white *thobes,* white head wraps and with the requisite daggers on thick cord belts draped over their right shoulders, resting at their left hips, yellow *babouches* on their feet; the girls, some very young, in individual, multicolored kaftans and *d'finas,* over which all have tied white "skirts" made from lengths of wide fabric, folded over cords to form two tiers and gathered (no sewing needed, just fold to store away!) under their belts, fringed, patterned headscarves (red a predominant color) held in place by two-rowed bands of silver coins attached with chains and hooks, the babouches on their feet and, most important for this dance, around their necks, each young girl has a many-tiered, large chest piece of silver coins and semi-precious stones.

Standing in a line shoulder-to-shoulder, the (mostly) young men sing their paeans to the young women's beauty. They clap rhythmically, as the young women, in a separate line of their own, sing out their answer. This call-and-response alternates for a bit.

At a signal from the rais, keeping their line, the young girls run forward, stop, and, holding hands, both feet flat on the ground, bob up and down to make their heavy chest pieces jingle loudly. Arms pumping with the beat, the sound of the coins becomes part of the music.

They divide into two lines, with the rais at the center, and run towards each other, form a circle, drop to one knee, join hands and, swinging their arms back and forth to the beat, vibrate their chest pieces again. Jumping up, they form two lines again and drop to one knee, facing the young men, to repeat the arm swinging and coin vibrating. This continues for a while, since their main purpose is to show off for their possible future husbands: not only their beauty, but even more important in the harsh realities of the Berber world, their physical strength and endurance.

When it is the men's turn, they sing, clap rhythmically, lean from side-to-side in unison, then run forward, stop and stamp their feet furiously to the beat. Which group does what and when is up to the rais, who usually alternates the men and women every fifteen minutes or so. The dancing is over at dawn.

These *Ahouaches* are held at every appropriate holiday or public event, since this is the only way young people can get to know who is eligible outside of their immediate families: teen hangouts, school dances and Western-style dating are totally unknown and unacceptable within this mainly traditional, agrarian culture.

Imin Tanout is located halfway between Marrakesh and Agadir. Ahouache is danced all over southern Morocco, in the High Atlas, Dades Valley, Ouarzazate and Kelaa M'Gouna as well as Imin Tanout. Often, the distinctive dress of the women of each Berber tribe is the only way to determine which is dancing.

Yesterday and Today

Unbelievable Precision Amid the Scent of Roses

El Kelaa M'Gouna (sometimes called Kelaa des M'Gouna) is on the Casbah Road, in the Dades Valley, 90 kms north of Ouarzazate and south of Tinghir. A place blessed with abundant water and fertile soil, it has a rich agricultural tradition. World famous for its vast, fragrant rose gardens, it holds an annual Rose Festival in May. It is believed that these rose fields are of Yemenite origin, but the houses of the Ait Atta, strangely resembling those of Nepal, and their high cheekbones and slanted eyes point to more Far Eastern Oriental origins.

Their dance is a type of *Ahidous,* very similar to the Ahouache, but a bit more "dignified", with the rais in total control of the movement shapes and sequences. As with the Ahouache of Imin Tanout, only unmarried women can participate in the dance and it is the village's socially acceptable venue for its young people to get close enough to look each other over and make (hopefully) lifetime matches.

The men wear the same sort of white thobes and hooded dras as those of Imin Tanout, with one significant exception: in place of the daggers hanging on thick cords at the left hip, they have leather bags.

Over their caftans and d'finas, the women's dress is something else entirely: a floor-length piece of black cloth passes under the right arm, over the chest and back, caught at the left shoulder by a fibula, while a second piece of white cloth passes under the left arm, over the chest and back, caught at the right shoulder by the second fibula, a chain hanging from the bottom of both fibulae. Several red cords are tied around the waist; the ends left to dangle in bunches at the front. They wear decorated leather shoes with front and back pieces that come up over the ankle. Necklaces of large amber beads, interspersed with silver, adorn each neck, as do second necklaces of elaborately twisted strands of colored beads.

They all have the same hairdo (sometimes a wig): very short, fluffy bangs and one big braid, doubled over, at each ear. Their high headpieces, held in place with tiny gold chains circling their foreheads under the bangs, are covered in strands of colored wool with metal sequins dangling down all over. Hanging from the back of the headpiece is a black kerchief, fringed with short strands of the same colored wool.

All the men play bendirs while they dance, including the rais, who's there to direct the movements and make sure the men and women don't get too close.

The women cross their arms in front and take a hand of the dancer on each side. The men, shoulder-to-shoulder, play their bendirs. They rush towards each other, almost meet, then return, moving backwards. Forward again, only to separate at the last moment into four sides of a square.

The two male sides rush towards each other, swivel by one another in the middle and change sides. The women do likewise. Both figures are repeated several times, then both sides circle one another, going in opposite directions: men on the inside, women always on the outside—it wouldn't be right for them to be surrounded by men.

Forming a cross, they move with strides of varying length in order to keep its shape as they circle counter-clockwise. The precision of their patterns and movements, especially their rushing feet, is mind-boggling.

HOUARA

Mother of Flamenco

South of Agadir, less than ten km inland from the Atlantic coast of Morocco, lies Inezgane, home of the Houara tribe, branches of which are also found in Ouled Teima, approximately 30 km to the east and slightly north, midway between Inezgane and Taroudant. Although in the heart of the Berber Souss, the Ait Houara speak and sing in Arabic.

The men are all in white thobes and hooded *djellabas,* with babouches on their feet. Sometimes the djellabas have black vertical stripes. The women are in belted kaftans and d'finas. Fringed scarves, tied in the back, hide most of their hair.

The main instrument for the Houara, aside from coordinated staccato clapping (as in Flamenco), is a metal tire center, played with two long metal nails or sticks: da-da dum da-da, da-da dum da-da.

The group is almost entirely composed of men, with one or two women: the best dancers and most daring souls of their sex from within the Houara.

This dance isn't a religious communion with the spirits and sharing of the soul—like Guedra, nor a group courtship "look each other over" dance—like the Ahouache of Imin Tanout or the Kelaa of the Ait M'Gouna (or all Ahidous), nor an actual ancient wedding rite—like the betrothal dance of Tissint. This is a show-off demonstration of superior skill for one's friends and peers, pure and simple.

They start by singing in loud voices, short bursts of song followed by crescendos of rapid footwork as a group. Two or three rounds in this manner, then the next bursts of song end with one or two of the men running forward, beating feet like crazy for a few seconds, then rushing back to the line. As it goes on, the men end their solos with high leaps or sharp flamenco-like barrel turns *(vuelta quebrada)*, sometimes both.

After several rounds of these macho outbursts/challenges, when the rhythm and excitement reach their peak, one of the women rushes forward. Her footwork is even more skilled and complex than the men's, her solo longer. Flinging the front halves of her d'fina, she makes several vueltas quebradas and jumps into the air, bending her knees, tucking her calves to her thighs. Sometimes, her hips move with the footwork, sometimes she uses them to manipulate a dagger under her d'fina, moving as if she's on horseback, her feet the horse's hooves.

After a while, one of the men, unable to resist, rushes forward and, facing each other, they begin to dance together. He blends his footwork with hers, they spin and leap in unison, his arms, elbows bent, in front and behind him as he spins, she, flinging her d'fina furiously as she spins. They resemble the courtship fight of a rooster and hen—or Kate and Petrucchio in *Taming of the Shrew.* Occasionally, two women from the circle challenge each other.

60

*Do you like Flamenco?
Meet its mother.*

The Moors—that is, the Moroccans—ruled Andalucia for 800 years. Approximately five percent of the Spanish language has Arabic roots, e.g.: *el algodon, el alfombra, el almoada, el aceituna, el Alhambra, el Albaicin, el Cid, ojala, Olé* (just try shouting "Allah" under Ferdinand and Isabella, who threw the Moors and Jews out of Spain, and see how fast you'd be turned into a crispy critter by the Inquisition...). The very word "Flamenco" comes from Arabic, though some try to translate it as "flamingo" or, worse yet, "Flemish". The root is the Arabic word *"fellah"*: peasant, farmer, poor person.

SCHIKHATT

*From Sex Education to
Social Recreation*

In Classical Arabic, the word *sheikha* is the feminine of *sheikh:* a person with knowledge, experience, wisdom. In Maghrebi (Moroccan Arabic), sheikha limits its meaning to specify a woman with carnal knowledge extensive enough to teach others.

Under prevailing interpretations of Islam and Sharia, both the bride and groom, but certainly and especially the bride, are expected to be virgins before their wedding. In many areas, to avoid any possibility of dishonoring a family via an illegitimate pregnancy, girls are sometimes married even before puberty.

Before the marriage ceremony, at which, as custom demands, the young bride is conspicuous by her absence (she is represented by a male relative), there are many sex-segregated festivities and ceremonies. For at least three days, sometimes a week or more with wealthy city families, preceding the signing of the marriage contract and ritual carrying of the bride to the house of the groom's family, day-long women's parties are hosted in the home of the bride's family to display her dowry, clothing and beauty.

She sits motionless on a "throne" set apart, eating nothing all day, leaving only to change her elaborate clothes at least three times a day, while the massed female relatives loudly discuss her flaws and attributes in front of her. Several times a day, she will be lifted in her chair by two or three women and carried around the room, to better show off the details of her finery.

Fortunately, the family has hired a sheikha and her all-female group of *schikhatt* musicians and dancers to liven things up.

The sheikha, who usually knows all the local gossip and, therefore, everything about everybody at the party, begins by singing impromptu raucous verses poking fun at the foibles and defects of family and guests alike. Between the verses, her troupe vigorously dances the Schikhatt, exaggeratedly moving hips, stomach and breasts, for this is very definitely an erotic dance and the movements have to be visible in spite of the large, loose caftans and d'finas they wear.

The Schikhatt has nothing to do with Raks Sharki, despite the fact both consist mainly of control and articulation of torso muscles versus limbs, as in Western dance. Lately, however, due to recent exposure to Lebanese and Egyptian movies and videotapes, Raks Sharki movements are showing up in the Schikhatt of sophisticated city-dwellers, in an effort to make it more varied and artistic.

Musical accompaniment can be as simple as bendirs, clapping and voices singing the refrain to the sheikha's ribald improvised verses, or with a *guimbry* (stringed instrument, held horizontally, plucked and played like a banjo) or *kemanjeh* (violin, held vertically on the knee and bowed) added.

More skilled Schikhatt dancers play *sagat* (finger cymbals), but only three—not four: two on the right hand, one on the left; some hold a small *taarija* (drum) in one hand, hitting the other hand with it as they dance; some play bendirs while executing the movements.

When she feels the time is proper and her "stage" has been set, the sheikha, herself, dances in front of the bride to be, singing verses about the pleasures of marital relations that await the bride after the ordeal of the wedding night, and the loss of her virginity. With the Schikhatt movements, she demonstrates how the bride will be expected to move in the marriage bed.

Both before and more so after the sheikha's dance for the bride, all the women get up at one time or another to dance with the troupe and each other, until they are tired and ready to go home for the day.

Depending on her finances and personal scruples, the sheikha will either go home or to the men's party, to entertain them with much bawdier songs and behavior.

62

It's not socially acceptable for a "good" woman to be a professional Schikhatt dancer, but everyone dances the Schikhatt—at home and at parties. It's OK for a man to take a Schikhatt dancer as his second, or better yet, third wife, but she is forbidden to perform in public as long as the marriage lasts.

Men do Schikhatt at family parties too, but if they are professionals—and there are many—they dress in drag or, at the very least, wear a woman's caftan and d'fina, to acknowledge that it's a woman's dance.

Family men come home from work for their main meal at midday, nap, and then return to work until evening. The household women's whole morning is taken in its preparation. Leftovers, bread and cheese suffice for dinner, so after the men go back to work, the afternoon is for a bit of diversion with one's fellow females. Typical, respectable Moroccan city women have no access to exercise centers, spas, dance classes, movie matinees. They must make their own amusements at home, within the family enclosure or visiting the other women in their homes. They don't "lunch".

What they do do is dance the Schikhatt with and for each other, making up verses or repeating those they've heard and liked. They egg each other on and do their own steps and variations solo or duo. They add movements seen on television and at other women's parties. City Schikhatts are far more "laid back" and varied than the *schleuh* (village) variety, which tend to be more direct and energetic.

CONCLUSION

There are about two hundred different Berber tribes in Morocco, each with its distinctive dress—especially the women's, language, dance and social customs. For each and every one of them, dance is an integral and constant affirmation of who and what they are: a form of self and group expression and pleasure: they dance throughout their entire lives.

Some tribes pray and send blessings by dance; others celebrate plantings, harvests, holidays, seasonal changes and births with dance; so many meet and court during dance; challenge one another, show off and communicate in dance; several seal marriages with a dance; most city and many country women get their sex education via dance; most tribes have their macho, warrior dances for the men.

All these dances are assimilated—as versus studied—in the normal course of family and tribal life and not in special schools or courses. It's not for a theater show or to play a part. It is their pride, a statement of their specific ethnicity: for each village, tribe, age, sex, class has its own special dance with which it identifies and declares itself.

It's interesting to note that, in a culture where a woman's public role is so circumscribed and her behavior so restricted vis-a-vis men, references to and discussion of matters sexual and physical are so much more frank, open and specific by women with and among other women and within the circle of the family.

Dance as Community Identity

ENDNOTES

This study (& all my others) is based on over 39 years of frequent in person observation & conversation and:

1. National Geographic:
Ref.- household keys: Aug., 1973 - pp. 222-3.
Blue Men's veils: ibid-pp. 220, 228; Apr., 1974 - pp. 552-4 & May, 1958 - pp. 689 & 691.
Matriarchy: May, 1958 - p. 689 .

2. Natural History Magazine, Volume 101 Number 11, November, 1992
"Where All the Women Are Strong" pp. 54-63.

3. Gersi, Douchan. Faces In the Smoke. Jeremy P. Tarcher, Inc., Los Angeles, 1991:
Why are Blue Men blue: p. 69.
Sexual freedom: p. 76.
Men's veiling: p. 36.

■ *For contact information see: Morocco, page 199, and Yasmin, page 202.*

Spirit

In Touch

By Yemaya

IN THE END, THERE IS ONLY THE PERCEIVED DIFFERENCE
BETWEEN THE AUDIENCE AND PERFORMER.

One who is in touch flies effortlessly through the dance, letting the music and the other dancers be her guide. One who isn't in touch tries to control the situation and focuses outside the music/lead and more often than not ends up missing cues (visually from the other dancers and musically) and therefore alienates herself from the other dancers and the audience. This then, just results in more and more distance from the security of the troupe.

—Carolena Nericcio, director of FatChanceBellyDance

Perhaps the most elusive and the most prominent part of a belly dancer's performance is the dancer's relationship with her self, and the communication of what that relationship is to the self. Fewer barriers allow more direct contact with the audience. The magic begins with the ability of the dancer to be open and honest in her expression. This honesty gives rise to a larger and subtler range of expression, during which the audience begins to see themselves in the dancer, and the dance. Thus the separation between the audience and the performer begins to blur. The experience becomes one of merging; each individual adding to the experience of the other. Any dancer who sees themselves as separate from their audience is sorely mistaken. The audience's reaction and energy create a dynamic that colors the entire performance.

Movement itself is an abstract, emotional, spiritual communication. Body language is louder than words, and has the ability to transport the dancer into realms beyond the physical. Dance carries within it the ability to heal and inspire. Like any other art form, there is the artist's unique energy behind the creation. This energy has a rippling effect on the participants. This wave of creative energy can be directed, and experienced on a variety of levels, depending on the awareness of audience and performer.

What one focuses on expands, whether it is ego, love, joy, or power. With this knowledge comes the incredible power of transformation as well as the incredible responsibility of awareness. If the performer chooses to be aware of their power to transform the audience, and themselves, through dance, it requires strict personal honesty, and courage to allow the transformation to take place.

This ability to change comes from the oldest part of ourselves, and can be traced back to ancient ceremonies, and civilizations, where dance was used as a vehicle for spirit. As seen on the cave drawings in Catal Hayuk, the soul was believed to be released into the spirit world during dance. The function of dance was a bridge between the human experience and the spiritual experience.

Belly dance, when performed with integrity, honesty, and courage can be a vehicle for the spirit of dancer to engage the spirit of the music and to communicate this experience with the audience. This eliminates the difference between the performer and the observer. In the end, there is only the perceived difference between audience and performer. When magic really occurs, all the separation dissolves into one pulsating, vibrating, expression of life of which we are all a part.

■ *For contact information see: Yemaya, page 197, and FatChanceBellyDance, page 194.*

In Tribal Style, the dancers are surrendering to their fellow dancers. They are all in a set-long trust fall. Everyone has to cooperate, or the show falls apart.

—Carolena Nericcio

YEMAYA

Photo by Modia Cook

The Spiritual Connection

by Shira

THE PALM OF THE RIGHT HAND FACES TOWARD THE SKY
TO RECEIVE THE BLESSINGS OF HEAVEN.

From ancient shamans to energetic gospel choirs, movement has long been integrated into spiritual practices. The Middle East has several traditions of movement meditation, and many modern-day dancers have incorporated the dance into their own personal spiritual lives. People often refer to these as "trance dances", but "movement meditations" or "rituals" would be a more accurate description.

MOVEMENT MEDITATION TRADITIONS

Traditional spiritual movement has taken many forms throughout the Middle East and northern Africa. People in these regions continue to practice these rituals today.

In Morocco, the *Guedra* is performed as a ritual of blessing. According to oral tradition, it is many thousands of years old, part of the traditions of a sub-grouping of the nomadic Tuareg. The Tuareg known as the "Blue People" because of the indigo dye they use for clothing and protecting their skin from the elements. Guedra is also the word for the cooking pot used by the tribe. When a skin is stretched over the pot, it serves as a drum, also called a guedra. Finally, the term guedra also refers to the woman who performs the ritual.

The physical movements of the guedra are simple hand flicks. Members of the tribe accompany her with drum, clapping, and chanting. The repetitive background sounds and movements lead the guedra, and often the participants, into a trance.

Like many esoteric traditions, the guedra begins by acknowledging the four points of the compass. She also makes hand flicks to bless heaven, earth, wind, water, the past, and the future. Then she moves on to hand flicks that are not so specifically directed. As the ritual progresses, she may repeat these acknowledgments if she chooses. As the guedra enters a state of trance, she may eventually sink to her knees and perform the remainder of it from there. At times, one guedra may move out of the center of the circle to sit on the sidelines while another takes her place. Once started, a Guedra may go on for many hours.

68

The Zar

The *Zar* is a ritual used to perform a cathartic type of healing on behalf of someone, usually a woman, who has been possessed. Although technically forbidden by Islam, it continues to be an essential part of some cultures. It appears mostly in Egypt, Sudan, Somalia, and Ethiopia.

The instrumental accompaniment to the Zar is a drum rhythm, which strongly resembles a heartbeat. Sometimes the Zar leader sacrifices a chicken, pigeon, sheep, or other animal as part of the ritual. The ritual often ends with all participants eating together.

Hadra

Hadra, which is part of a ceremony by a Sufi brotherhood called the Aissawa, is another exorcism ritual. It opens with improvisational vocals, and moves on to accompaniment on *bendir* (frame drums with bells), and the *taarija,* a very small drum. A *ghaita* (similar to an oboe) plays a melody line. The participating men move slowly at first, then as the accompaniment picks up speed their movements become wilder and faster. Eventually they move into a trance.

Sufi

The image of the whirling dervish has captured the imagination of people worldwide. The Sufi sect of Islam uses whirling as a devotional tool as part of a spiritual group event known as a sema. It moves the practitioner into an enhanced state of awareness, a kind of ecstasy.

While whirling, the individual holds both arms outstretched to each side at shoulder height. The palm of the right hand faces toward the sky to receive the blessings of heaven. The left palm faces toward the floor to channel the blessings to earth. The eyes slip out of focus, which protects against dizziness or motion sickness.

NEW SPIRITUAL CONNECTIONS

The Lutheran and Episcopalian denominations of Christianity have both been progressive in introducing liturgical dance to the altar at their church services. Although their liturgical dance workshops focus on ballet and modern dance movement vocabularies, some Middle Eastern dance artists have successfully introduced our art form to their congregations as liturgical dance. Of course, these artists don't wear the midriff-baring nightclub costume. The mood they portray is one of worship.

On the Web

The Internet has offered a meeting place for dancers who seek a spiritual connection through the dance to gather and discuss their common ground. A list server named Sacred Movements *available on* www.onelist.com *offers opportunities for dancers to exchange e-mail with others making a similar journey.*

MARGUERITE
IN A SPIN
Photo by Keith Drosin

69

Thank You

I am deeply indebted to Morocco for freely sharing the knowledge she acquired of Middle Eastern dance and ritual traditions through her on-location field research. Much of the information here comes from what I have learned from her. I also want to thank the many dancers who have shared their spiritual journeys in dance with me, especially my Inanna sisters.

The Unitarian Church has long supported the use of the performing arts at the altar. Folk dances from Eastern Europe are sometimes performed as part of a church service. Many Unitarian congregations have welcomed performances by Middle Eastern dance artists as well.

Even more conservative Christian denominations have accepted Middle Eastern dance as part of special events: parish talent shows, shepherdess portrayals in Christmas pageants, and celebratory dances in Palm Sunday services, to name a few. Biblical costumes and moods appropriate to the role being portrayed (such as joy for Palm Sunday) are often the key to earning the trust and respect of the congregation.

Many modern-day Pagans who also happen to be part of the Middle Eastern dance community have brought their dance talents into their religious practices. Some have studied the Middle Eastern rituals and brought modified versions of them into their own lives. However, the majority draws from their own creative energies to find spiritual fulfillment.

In one moving California show, Bonney Meyer performed a dance she called "Blessing of the Moon Goddess" at a benefit for a woman who had recently fallen on difficult times. The sense of warmth and blessing for everyone in the room was palpable.

Delilah from Seattle has sponsored retreats focused on the myth of Inanna's descent to the underworld, with a ritual applied to Inanna's passage through each of the seven gates. The group Goddess Dancing in the Boston area advertises that it delivers "belly blessings". Dhyanis, based in the San Francisco area, sponsors an annual production at the time of the Summer Solstice called *The Living Goddess*, which features dance portrayals by a wide variety of artists, many of whom come from the local belly dance community.

Many dancers feel a deep sense of spirituality simply from the act of dancing, even when they are not consciously seeking it. A dancer named An. said,

> *I feel that the dance attracts more that just physical spectators. I call them Witnesses. I can almost feel these silent watchful archetypical beings gathering about the circle, called by the drums and the power of the moment. The people in the audience are archetypical as well. Here the Adolescent Man, there the Women Lovers, there the Tribal Elder, and here the Child. Even the Trickster shows as the crying baby or the heckling frat boy or even the toddler who decides a duet is really warranted. Maiden, Mother, and Crone always attend.*

■ *For contact information see: Shira, page 196, Marguerite Kusuhara, page 196, and Keith Drosin, page 195.*

AMBER
Photo by Walter Rasmussen

Snakes

71

The Serpent Dance Journey

By Suzanne Shakti Copeland

THE SYMBOL OF THE SERPENT HAS ALWAYS BEEN REVERED AS THE KEEPER OF A GREAT AND DIVINE MYSTERY, AND THEREFORE SACRED.

Many of the goddesses and gods of ancient times, especially those of India and Egypt, held or wore serpents as symbols of highly developed consciousness and mastery. The pharaohs and queens wore the cobra on the forehead of their crowns to symbolize their right to rule, bestowed by the Goddess herself. The ancient Druids wore serpents tattooed on their forearms as a symbol of their knowledge of the mysteries and powers of the occult. In ancient Greece, Temple priestesses were called pythonessess and consulted snakes to obtain their insights for their spiritual and political rulers. They were highly revered healers and diviners. Many shamanic cultures revere the snake as a healer.

CADUCEUS Even our modern symbol for medicine is the *Caduceus*; two snakes intertwined around a winged staff. Originally, this symbol was for the Egyptian god Thoth or Tehuti, and later was associated with knowledge through the Roman god Mercury. The Caduceus is the Hermetic symbol of medicine, healing, and the understanding of the duality of life. It is also the symbol of the pathway of enlightenment. The symbol is known as the pathway of Kundalini in the human physical and ethereal body of the East Indian philosophies. The symbol of the serpent has always been revered as the keeper of a great and divine mystery, and therefore sacred. This evidence is all around us in symbols and in the art of the ancients.

The snake is a living transformer, a generator like a crystal, or electrical conduit, a gift from the Goddess of nature. The snakes can take us deep into trance and show how to move our bodies to invoke the energies of the Goddess within. We begin to feel the undulation of energy pathways through the body. We ride the electric, rhythmic wave of the inner Goddess. The serpentine energy of the dance gently creates a heightened awareness and sensitivity. This allows us to shed the skins of old thought forms of negativity and fear, in order to make room for giving birth to a new consciousness.

The snake's energy helps us to stay grounded and earth-connected while experiencing increased states of energy frequencies. They are the keepers of the Earth knowledge and secrets. It is this grounded and centered state which gives us the courage to transform by connecting more deeply to the inner feminine knowing of the Goddess within.

■ *For contact information see: Shakti Center for Transformation, page 196.*

7 2

The Serpent Dance Journey

Ssssane Ssssnake Handling

By Marguerite Kusuhara

A SNAKE IS NOT A PROP, IT IS A LIVING ANIMAL
THAT YOU WILL HAVE A RELATIONSHIP WITH FOR
THE DURATION OF ITS LIFE.

Dancing with a snake can add a high degree of drama to a performance. Dancers who decide to work with snakes must seriously consider a number of issues before committing to this unusual dance partner. The most important thing to know is that a snake is not a prop. It is a living creature worthy of great respect. Keeping that in mind, there are other factors that must be addressed.

Some questions I ask of dancers are as follows: Are you an amateur or professional? Can you care for and handle the animal adequately? Most importantly, do you have proper insurance?

WORKING WITH A CLIENT

Clear and well-documented communication with clients is essential. Be polite and positive with your client about all aspects of the show before you accept a deposit on a booking. Keep written records of negotiations and phone calls from the beginning, and a contract if possible. Always make the deposit non-refundable even though you may think you know your client well. It is important to find out whether or not guests will be comfortable with such a presentation. Be sure that the client has informed the guests that live snakes will be part of the performance. When dealing with the public at large, dancers should be aware that both snakes and the art of Oriental dance could have deep symbolic meanings for many groups. These meanings may either be negative or positive.

MARGUERITE
KUSUHARA
Photo by Keith Drosin

74

SNAKE SELECTION/CARE

Having decided to work with a snake, a dancer must consider the types of animals available that would be good choices for this purpose. Though there are many different snakes with varying behaviors, which could work well for dancers, I will mention only three in this article.

A medium sized (5-8 ft.) brightly colored snake is usually a good choice, as it is easier to work with than a larger variety in regards to transportation, housing and care. Corn snakes are slender-bodied, can be brightly colored and grow to about 6 feet in length. They are not exotics, which make them easier to feed and keep. This snake makes an enchanting dance partner for both the audience to observe and for the dancer to handle. Children will be drawn to their beauty and temperament like a magnet. Corn snakes can frequently be useful when it comes to dispelling fears about reptiles.

Many dancers will choose a ball python to work with, because this variety of python is mature at about 7-8 feet. They are a medium to small bodied snake, can come in marvelous though pricey color variations, and do not attain the girth of the Burmese python. The ball python is an exotic reptile and comes from Africa. Care must be taken to give it a consistent 75-80 degree environment with clean water. According to three snake handlers consulted, it is advisable to place a heating pad underneath the cage to warm the entire environment, a thermometer inside to monitor it, and a grow light. Other lights may be necessary for warmth in the top of the cage depending on enclosure size.

A large albino Burmese python, which is commonly a cream color with brilliant yellow markings, makes a wonderful visual statement on stage. These snakes are arboreal, meaning they live in trees. Water is very important to their survival, and they should be allowed a fair amount of water in a large container for their optimum comfort. Large crockery dishes available from pet stores in half to three-quarter gallon sizes will accommodate snakes under five feet. Ideally, for a snake six feet and over, a small pool should be installed, though most keepers agree that the crockery bowl or a twice-weekly soak in the tub (snake willing) will do.

Burmese and ball pythons are constrictors who will wrap around and cling to a warm-blooded mammal (even though they are not hunting for a meal) as part of their survival behavior. Cold-blooded creatures like to warm themselves any way they can, and will respond to body heat. Burmese pythons are also exotics, heavy bodied (though the male who can be identified by the spurs next to his vent, is more slender than the female) and usually have gentle natures. Please be aware that although certain types of snake may be gentle in general, individual animals will vary in temperament.

Most snakes should be fed approximately every two weeks, and handlers should be aware that they never really stop growing. Some handlers feed them less often and keep them in smaller enclosures to slow their growth, but this is not advised. Be aware of the potential size that your snake will achieve when fully grown. Once they get beyond six or seven feet long, they can be hard to maneuver, become injured or cause injury if they are mismanaged. Do not select a snake that will become too large for you to safely handle.

The Facts of Lunch

Remember, snakes are not vegetarians nor were they ever intended to be so. Although snakes may get used to warmed up, previously fresh frozen mice or rats, the larger Burmese will require larger animals for their food. Some snakes never accept anything other than live animals for their meals. Though we will not cover it here, the process of feeding must also be carefully monitored when giving a snake larger live mammals or birds that will struggle and fight back.

7 5

Ssssnake Sssources

Many reptile sites exist on the Internet, which will specifically interest the snake fancier, with many different varieties for sale. There are also magazines available with more extensive information on different types of snakes, snake care and many listings concerning equipment, animals, and food sources, such as Reptiles Magazine.

SENIOR EDITOR JENNI RECOMMENDS: *http://www.kingsnake.com for snake related information on the Web.*

Larger, well-built habitat-style wooden cages with secure closures are needed for Burmese. These types of cages are easier to get into for cleaning. Never put cedar chips in the reptile's cage or use particleboard in its construction, as these materials will poison the snake. Cages must be cleaned regularly, or the snake will get mites. These parasites may cause lethargy, inhibit the immune system, and bring about the death of the snake. Mites are extremely noticeable on albino color phases.

Attend reptile shows to compare your choices and ask questions. Before purchasing a snake, be sure that the one you choose is the appropriate variety for your needs, that is has a calm nature, and that it will have a good home for the remainder of its life. Dancers often find that once they buy an animal and the novelty wears off or it grows too large, that they cannot bear to feed it, or give it the attention it needs in order to be comfortable with them and their customers. All unwanted animals can be a problem for both the community and the environment. Thousands are destroyed every year.

Once you have purchased your snake, keep the snake in an area where it sees constant movement so that it will not associate general movement with its feeding behaviors. Shower or wash your hands after petting, playing with or handling other warm blooded animals, especially ones that the snake recognizes as a food source. Desensitization to animals other than its food sources is possible, but this may be a long process. It is important to be patient and aware of your snake and its natural instincts.

Always keep the reptile warm and covered when not on your body. Also, the snake should not be left in the sun or someplace that is too hot. Do not leave the snake unattended in a vehicle. Even a corn snake, indigenous to the American Midwest, likes to be warm when it is snowy or rainy outside. In the wild, these creatures hibernate underground in order to avoid very sudden temperature changes. Extreme temperature fluctuations may make the snake sick, or kill it. A must for an exotic snake is to carry a heating pad for the reptile's transport case when you will be near an outlet, or obtain several self activating heat packs and test them on yourself to be sure they are not too hot or do not produce too little heat before using them with the exotic snake. Self-activating packs are available from a number of different sources.

Another option to buying a snake is to rent or borrow one from a willing and responsible herpetologist or collector in your area who is receptive to you, if you are properly insured. Some experienced (please be sure about this) reptile people who put on shows for parties, schools, and larger events may even train you or hire you as an assistant for their own events. Always ask questions of any expert source that will speak to you, and politely thank those who will not.

While dancing with a snake, never loop it around your neck or waist, but instead
drape it over your shoulders (if it is a larger snake) so that the tail is supported up
one arm, across the back of the shoulders, and down the other arm with the head
or neck in one hand. Never let your snake wrap itself around a customer, leave it
unattended with a customer, or even give it to a customer to hold. There have
been lawsuits against animal handlers and their entertainment agencies due to
irresponsible behavior on the part of the handler. Inexperience is not always the
reason for such an incident, unfortunately. Professionalism is necessary. Insurance
is a must. You should obtain an entertainer's insurance policy. Every dancer must
begin somewhere, but you will place yourself in jeopardy if you do not take
particular care while working with the public and live animals. If you work a
lot with larger animals, try to prevent your customers from touching the snake.
Always be aware of where the snake's head is during your show, and hold it away
from the customer if they are close to you. Stay on stage if possible.

If you hold a snake out in front of you, support it in both hands or allow the
length of its body to brace itself against your arm (for smaller snakes only).
Do not let it dangle from one hand, as this may injure the snake. While performing
with a larger snake (7-8 ft) these positions are important for your safety, as well
as for that of the snake. Snakes also will be comfortable braced against your body,
though make sure you know your snake well. Spend time with it before the show,
and remember where the head is at all times. Do not come toward the snake's
head with your hand so that it can see you. This will startle the snake. Grasp the
head from behind or underneath. Do not put the snake up to your face or close
to your eyes.

77

So... You Want to Hire a Snake Dancer?

For the client interested in hiring a dancer to perform with a snake, be sure that the majority of your guests or the guests of honor do not have serious sensitivities or any other extreme feelings about these reptiles. If this is not investigated before your event, or before you place a deposit on reserving your dancer, it can cause you and your performer serious embarrassment, plus both loss of face and financial loss for the dancer and yourself. Buyer Beware. Often you will get what you pay for, and an inexperienced or irresponsible performer may place you in a dangerous or embarrassing situation.

Always feed the snake at least several days before the show or it will be hungry and agitated. Try to place it in a container other than its living space for feeding activity so that it will not associate its living space or your incoming hand with food. Give it a warm bath several hours before you dance with it so that it will defecate in the water and not on you or your customer's property. Rinse the snake with a light solution of antibacterial soap, and let the animal soak in clear, clean lukewarm water for a while, taking care to let it keep its head above water.

Do not dance with your snake or borrow one while it is shedding. A snake that is ready to shed will have cloudy eyes, the skin color will change, and temperament may become nervous, as the snake will then be blind.

Do not wear a costume that will injure the snake. Cloth or lightly/smooth beaded belts and tops with minimal three dimensional decoration are a good choice, as metal, jagged beadwork, rhinestone mounts or coins may cut into the snake's or your skin under the added weight. Loops hanging from the costume will be grasped by the reptile during a show, and may cause an awkward moment.

If you do decide to work with a snake after carefully considering all of the factors, be sure you have practiced with your partner often before any performances. Try to get a feeling as to how your particular snake likes to wrap itself during your movement patterns both standing and in floor work. Get the snake used to you gradually. Do not make abrupt or sudden moves with it until you are certain your snake is comfortable with you. Like dancers, some snakes will become dizzy and agitated when you spin, and some may enjoy the experience. In this movement, make sure the snake is well supported. Agitated snakes will writhe and jerk vigorously, or hiss constantly. Some may bite or make yawning motions.

If your snake does bite you, do not pull its head away from the bite since snake teeth are curved inward toward their throats. Push the base of the jaw together on both sides with your hand or fingers and push forward and hopefully (no 100% guarantees) the snake will release.

All snakes move differently, even within the limitations of each variety of snake. It will take time for you both to get used to each other's movement patterns. Do not press the weight of your body onto the snake during floor work, let the snake fall to the floor or drop down on top of it, as this will injure the animal. For best results, practice in a warm room, taping yourself on video, or in front of a mirror on a regular basis.

If you have friendly gatherings of other dancers at your home or go to various events that are dance oriented, this may be a good place to begin gradually testing your snake's dance and social skills. You will find that the animal will also respond to your emotions, which it will be able to sense when it is close to you.

For the serious dancer as with any other performer or animal owner this last bit of information will be the most important one to remember when working with a snake or any other animal. A snake is not a prop; it is a living animal that you will have a relationship with for the duration of its life.

■ *For contact information see: Marguerite Kusuhara, page 196, and Keith Drosin, page 195.*

Props For Oriental Dance

By Shira

◆ ZILS ◆ CANE ◆ VEIL ◆ SWORD ◆ CANDLES ◆ TAMBOURINE ◆

Props can add variety and appeal to your performance. They spark audience interest, and give a new look to your dance moves. Depending on which prop you choose, it can lend either a folkloric flavor or a glitzy "show-biz" mood to the show.

FINGER CYMBALS

There is a long tradition of dancers wearing percussion instruments on their hands, which has endured into modern times. Dancers often refer to finger cymbals as *"zils"*, because the Turkish word for cymbal is *zil*. It would be more correct to call them *zilya*, which is the plural in Turkish. The Arabic name for finger cymbals is *sagat* or *zagat*.

History

Cymbals were originally sacred instruments. Their name comes from the goddess Cybele. Cymbals resembling those in use today are represented on Babylonian and Assyrian reliefs from around 1000 BCE and a number of actual instruments have been found at Nimrud, a city in northern Iraq.

Zils were used throughout the Middle East and North Africa: from Persia, through Turkey and Arabia, to Morocco. Archeologists have found accounts in Egypt of contracts with a "cymbal dancer" dating to the first century CE. There was also an account of a young boy who died after falling from a wall, who had been attracted by the sound of the cymbals and wanted to see the dancer.

Records dating back to the Roman Empire mention dancers using *castanets,* which occasionally were made of metal instead of wood. Lithographs, paintings, drawings, descriptions, mosaics, and other artwork going back many hundreds of years depict female and male dancers alike performing with finger cymbals.

80

The historical roots of today's flamenco dance lie in an Andalusian dance form called *Zambra Mora* ("Moorish party") dating back to the 1400s, which was performed in bare feet with finger cymbals and sinuous movements. Even today, flamenco dancers still perform a dance they call Zambra Mora using finger cymbals instead of castanets.

Finger Cymbals Today

In Turkey, most dancers still use zils, and these remain an integral part of the Oriental dance performance.

According to Egyptian dancer Nadia Hamdi, the musicians and dancers of Cairo's Mohammed Ali Street district believe that a dancer who cannot play the zils is not a true artist. Despite that, many Egyptian dancers no longer play finger cymbals in their shows. One reason is because most of the readily available zils sold in Egypt today yield poor-quality sound and are suitable only as tourist souvenirs. Also, many dancers now rely on hired musicians in their bands to play for them. This began when Badiaa Masabni, the owner of the Opera Casino nightclub in Cairo in the 1930s and 1940s, loved to play finger cymbals, and would sit in with the band to play for the dancers. It led to the custom of hiring a musician dedicated to playing zils as part of the orchestra. Now only those Egyptian dancers who are highly skilled at playing finger cymbals are likely to use them in their shows.

Selecting Finger Cymbals

If you are new to belly dancing, you will probably prefer using smaller zils. They weigh less than the larger ones and the sound is not as loud. A good size for beginners is 2-inch diameter. Professional dancers often use larger cymbals that are loud enough to be heard over a band or sound system.

Choose the style with two slots side by side, like the one on the left in the illustration. Avoid the ones with a single hole in the center! The single-hole kind is difficult to control, and harder to play. The kind with two slots gives you much more control.

If your cymbals come with the round cord elastic, replace it immediately—it makes cymbals much harder to control! Use flat braid elastic that is about 1/8 or 1/16 inch wider than the width of the slot. Black elastic does not appear soiled over time.

Tips For Using Finger Cymbals

A drawstring zil bag made of velvet or another pretty fabric is handy for carrying your finger cymbals between home and class. Some belly dance supply vendors sell them, but they are also easy to make.

Most dancers use slightly bigger elastic loops on the thumb cymbals. Sew 2 or 3 tiny rocaille beads the same color as your elastic on the thumb zils, at the part of the loop that goes over your fingernail. Even in a dimly lit backstage area you can then quickly identify by touch which cymbals to place on your thumbs.

Use brass polish to brighten your tarnished brass zils.

Make sure that any elastic, safety pins, or buttons inside the cups of your zils are tiny enough to not interfere with the sound. If a cymbal does not ring, adjust it to remove the obstruction.

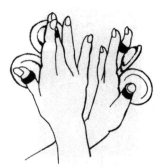

MODERN
FINGER CYMBALS
(ZILS OR SAGATS)
Illustration by K. Harding

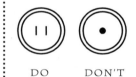

DO   DON'T

81

Props for Oriental Dance

CANE

The Arabic name for the traditional Egyptian cane dance is *raks al assaya*. *"Raks"* means "dance", and *"assaya"* refers to the cane.

History

In the Said (southern Egypt), men practice a martial art called *tahtiyb* that involves battling with sticks. Each stick, known as an asa, is about 45 inches long and 3¹/₂ inches in circumference. The movements involve a series of attempts to hit the opponent and parry his blows, similar to the quarterstaff fighting of European tradition. The roots of tahtiyb go back many centuries—tomb paintings from ancient Egypt depict men fighting with sticks.

The tahtiyb inspired the women of the Said to create their own "stick" dance. The women's cane dance is a playful parody of the men's martial art. The women's raks al assaya movements are playful, feminine, and flirtatious.

Sticks And Canes Today

Today, there are dancers both in Egyptian folkloric troupes and in the Western world that have put the men's tahtiyb movements to music and portray it as a dance. Although it is not the way the movements were originally used, the stick dance has now become a standard element of folkloric Egyptian dance repertoire. Dancing with a tahtiyb could be effective for a male dancer, either as a solo performance against an imaginary opponent, or as an ensemble number.

In Cairo, a nightclub performer usually begins her show wearing a sequined bra/belt/skirt costume and dances to modern-day orchestral music. After completing an entire routine, she leaves the stage and changes into a folkloric costume. She returns to the stage for her next act, which is a traditional-style dance. Often, for this folkloric portion, she will opt to use a cane and dance to music that has a strong Saidi flavor.

Because the United States does not have this costume change tradition, the cane is more likely to be integrated into the dancer's complete routine. She might enter with it to medium-speed or fast Egyptian music, dance with it for the duration of one song, and then set it aside as she continues with her show. Alternatively, she might place the cane off to one side of the stage before her show, perhaps propping it up so that she won't have to bend down to pick it up. During the course of her show, the Egyptian song will cue her to retrieve the cane and dance with it.

The cane is particularly popular as a prop with artists who like to portray an ethnic or historical style of dance because of its origin in the rural villages. When worn with a traditional Egyptian-style dress, and danced to traditional Saidi music, the cane dance works well in a folkloric performance.

A cane routine can spice up a troupe performance. With multiple dancers on stage, the choreography can include segments where the dancers do their own mock fighting with the canes, clashing them against each other. If your troupe is inclined to perform comedy dances, canes present endless comedic possibilities!

Selecting A Cane

Belly dance vendors sell special canes intended for dancing, although you are not required to use one of those. The good thing about the canes sold for dancing use is their light weight. Some have glittery paper wrapped around them, while others are plain wood, sometimes decorated with a carved design.

It's best not to use a utilitarian cane of the type sold in medical supply outlets. Many of these have a "foot" on the bottom to better grip the floor, and their sturdy design makes them too heavy to twirl effectively.

Dance canes do not vary much in their length. Some may be slightly longer than others, so taller dancers may want to look for a longer one. Thin canes are easier to twirl than thick ones, but if a cane is too thin it will warp and become impossible to balance on your head. A cane that is about $2^{1}/_{2}$ inches in circumference works well.

Tips For Using A Cane

- When twirling a cane, hold it just a few inches in from the straight end. Do not hold it in the center, baton-like, while twirling.

- If you plan to balance the cane on your head during the course of your dance, put some hair spray on the top of your head. This will provide a sticky surface, and the cane will be less likely to roll off. You may also wear a turban to prevent rolling.

- When attending a cane workshop, consider wearing a thin latex glove (available in any beauty supply store) on the hand that will be holding the cane. After a three or four hour workshop, you may get a blister on your hand if you do not protect it.

- When not dancing with your cane, either hang its hooked end over a hook on the wall, or lay it flat on a surface large enough to hold the entire cane. If it stands propped up in a corner or lies across a smaller surface, it may warp.

- If you perform with a troupe, place a small sticker somewhere on the shaft of your cane so you can easily identify which one is yours after a performance. Place it about halfway along the shaft so that it won't rub off when you handle your cane.

VEIL

Dancing with a veil adds a touch of elegance to an Oriental dance performance. If done to a slow song using the rumba/bolero rhythm, it also provides a soft, sensuous mood change, which can contrast beautifully with the faster, more exciting entrance music and follow-up music. The veil is made of about three yards of fabric, usually sheer, which flows beautifully with dance movements.

Styles of Veil Work

Today, Oriental dance enjoys two entirely different styles of dancing with a veil— the style developed in Egypt, and the style developed in the United States.

In American-style veil work, the dancer makes her entrance wearing her veil tucked into her costume. These veil wraps customarily hide much of the top half of the dancer's body, and are draped artfully to look appealing in their own right, the way a loose-fitting blouse might look. Throughout the opening song, which is typically either medium speed or fast, the veil remains tucked in. As that song draws to its end, and the opening strains of slow rumba-bolero music begin, she begins the veil work section of her dance. Undulating gracefully in time to the music or spinning slowly, the dancer removes the veil and begins to dance with it. The movements chosen may involve wrapping the veil around her body in various ways, hiding the lower part of her face with the veil while doing head slides, or holding it elegantly behind her as a frame for her spins and undulations. As the song winds to its close, the dancer discards the veil.

In Egyptian-style veil work, the dancer makes her entrance to fast or medium-speed music holding the veil behind her in both hands. It is not tucked into her costume at all. She occasionally swirls her arms, walks with it, and spins with it. About a minute or less after her entrance, she discards the veil and finishes her opening song without it.

There is no tradition of veil work in Turkish Oriental dance. However, some modern-day dancers in Turkey have begun to copy the Egyptian-style veil entrance.

8 4

History

Many people mistakenly believe that the veil entered Oriental dance through the "Dance of the Seven Veils". In fact, there is no such historical dance tradition in the Middle East. The Biblical reference to the death of John the Baptist neither identifies the dancer by name nor describes what props she may have used. In 1896, Oscar Wilde fired French imaginations with his play *Salomé*. Inspired by Wilde's play, Richard Strauss then created the opera *Salomé,* which introduced the "Dance of the Seven Veils" to the world.

The veil actually came into use in Oriental dance in the 20th century. Its use as a dance prop is not related in any way to the Muslim custom of veiling. Egyptian-style and American-style veil work evolved independently of the other, and these separate origins help explain the significant difference that exists between the two styles today.

American veil work originated in the late 1950s and early 1960s in the ethnic nightclubs. At that time, there were not enough skilled dancers to fill all the jobs that were available, so club owners resorted to hiring people who looked good in a costume but did not know how to dance. These performers strode onto stage and did their best to hold the audience's attention through poses and slinky walks. They discovered that carrying a 3-yard length of sheer fabric offered a new way to fill time and hold the audience's attention. Over the following decades, innovative dancers have evolved American-style veil work into a beautiful, unique art form.

In Egypt, the idea of carrying a piece of fabric on stage was made popular by a well-known Egyptian dancer named Samya Gamal, who starred in many Egyptian movies during the 1930s and 1940s. A famous Russian ballerina and ballet teacher named Ivanova instructed Samya to carry a piece of fabric for her entrance to improve her arm carriage. Ivanova adopted this practice from a Caucasian dance, perhaps from Azerbaijan. Samya's practice of entering with this prop became popular in the Egyptian theaters. She performed it on tour in the United States and in a movie entitled *Ali Baba and The Forty Thieves* which was then exported to other countries. Over time, other Oriental dancers copied the idea, and many Egyptian dancers today continue to carry a veil for their entrance.

SUSANNE POTEMPA
Photo by I. Skytte

Veils Today

Veils remain popular as an entrance prop for Oriental dancers in Egypt. They have not been adopted in Turkey.

The North America fashion of wrapping a veil before entering and then "dancing it off" has not caught on in the Middle East. It looks too much like stripping for the taste of Middle Eastern audiences. It has been spread to other Western countries by American dancers who have traveled abroad to teach or by locals who discovered it when they visited the U.S.

Selecting A Veil

Veils usually come in two different shapes: rectangular and semicircular. Their lengths range from $2^{1}/2$ to 3 yards. Certain veil movements work best with certain shapes of veil. For example, double veil works best with semicircular veils.

The best fabric for a veil is sheer silk. Other good choices are single georgette or chiffon. Nylon tricot is acceptable for an inexpensive student-quality veil, but doesn't move as well as the other fabrics.

Pick up a veil that you are considering, and hold it behind you with your arms outstretched. At least 12 inches of extra fabric length should extend beyond each hand. If there is less than that, the veil is probably too short and will be difficult to use.

You can either select a veil that matches or contrasts your skirt. If you opt for a veil that contrasts, try to choose one that has some decoration in the dominant color of your skirt to tie the ensemble together.

Tips on Using a Veil

- Always sew trim to the edge of a veil. When dancing with it, this trim will make it easy to determine when your fingers have found the edge and prevent you from accidentally dropping it. As a bonus, when the trim catches the light it will sparkle and add pizzazz to your dance.

- If you plan to do an Egyptian-style entrance, sew a 1" length of narrow elastic onto the edge of the veil at each of the points where you plan to hold it. Loop the elastic over each ring finger when you enter with the veil so your other fingers remain free for playing finger cymbals.

- If making a semicircular veil, sew a narrow trim on the straight edge and a wider trim on the curved edge. This will make it easy for you to determine simply by touch which edge of the veil lies under your fingers.

- Sew a few tiny rocaille beads on the edge of the veil at the points where your fingers will be when you are holding the veil with your arms outstretched. This will make it easier to tell by touch where to grasp the veil when you're in a dark backstage environment.

CAROLENA NERICCIO OF
FATCHANCEBELLYDANCE
Photo by Marty Sohl

SWORD

Raks al sayf ("sword dance") can be powerful and dramatic. As performed by most dancers in Western countries, the sword dance typically involves balancing the sword on the head, shoulder, hip, or other parts of the body. Audiences are fascinated when the dancer initially produces a sword, wondering, "What is she going to do with it?" When she balances it on her head or elsewhere, they watch intensely to see if she will drop it.

History

There is a traditional martial dance in Egypt called *el ard,* which is performed by men wielding swords. In this dance, the men carry the swords upright, ready to fight, as they perform the dance.

However, there is no widespread history in the Middle East of female dancers using swords in any way. A tantalizing oil painting titled *An Almeh Performing the Sword Dance* by Jean Léon Gérôme dating from about 1870 portrays a dancer balancing one sword on her head and holding another in her hand. This suggests that perhaps there were some individual dancers who may have used swords. There is really not sufficient documentation to suggest that sword dances by women were a common sight, despite the isolated postcard or two.

Dancers in Egypt, Turkey, and other Middle Eastern countries today do not balance swords as part of their acts. They may balance other props, such as the elaborate candelabrum known as a *shamadan* (see page 90) that has become a traditional part of a wedding celebration.

Sword Dance Today

Even though there is no authentic traditional sword-balancing dance, Western dancers appearing in Renaissance Faires and folk festivals find that audiences readily accept the sword as a folkloric prop. Sword balancing has become popular among North America dancers who strive to add a historic flavor to their performance.

Swords are equally at home in a restaurant or nightclub setting. Farouche, of San Jose, California, performs a dramatic sword routine in which she brandishes two flaming swords and balances them while still flaming.

Selecting A Sword

Heavier swords will stay in place more easily than lightweight ones. If you are new to balancing, a heavier sword is better. A slightly curved blade, such as that on a saber or scimitar, will balance much more easily than a straight blade.

Balance the sword on your hand before you buy it, to make sure that it does balance properly. It should stabilize into a completely vertical position, and not lean toward either side. Do not buy a sword that does not balance properly on your hand. If the merchant cannot get it to balance while you're standing there, chances are you won't be able to fix it after you get it home.

Some swords come in scabbards, while others do not. You do not really need a scabbard for dancing with your sword, but if you have one you can make a dramatic production out of unsheathing the sword.

Beware of chromed swords—they look beautiful, but the chrome is slippery and will make the sword more likely to slip off your head. If you succumb to a chromed sword, practice extensively with it before using in a performance.

SA'IDA (LEFT)
IN ASSUIT WITH
CAMEL TASSEL BELT
—
LU'SYNDA (RIGHT)
IN THOBE
—
NUMAIR WASIM
(MIDDLE) IN CAFTAN
FROM EGYPT,
AND SWORDS

88

- Clean hair is slippery. Put a little hair spray onto the top of your head where the sword will rest before you begin your performance. This will make your hair a little sticky and the sword will be more likely to stay in place. For traditional or tribal styles, head scarves and turbans also help.

- To prevent your sword from rusting, always keep it coated with a thin layer of oil. If it does rust anyway, use brass polish to restore the shine.

- Keep an inexpensive votive candle in your dance supplies. Before going on stage with your sword, rub the candle back and forth across the part of the sword's edge that will rest on your head. This will help prevent the sword from slipping while you're dancing.

- Some swords have a knob on the end of the handle that screws off. If yours does, use O-rings, which are sold in the plumbing department of hardware stores, to ensure a secure fit.

- If you are dancing outdoors, consider wearing a headdress. The slightest breeze can blow your sword off balance! For best results, choose a headdress that is made of cloth rather than chains or coins, and the thicker, the better. Make sure it is firmly anchored in place—if your headdress slips while balancing your sword, your sword will slip with it!

- Avoid the temptation to make any permanent alterations to your sword (notches, glued-on sandpaper, etc.) to make it easier to balance. If an audience member gets hold of the sword and sees these modifications, they will assume that's the "trick" that makes it possible to balance it, and they will not appreciate the real skill that it takes to balance a sword even with these assists.

- If traveling on an airplane with your sword, you will not be able to carry it on board. Place it in a rifle case to protect it when you check it with your luggage.

- Make a cloth carrying case with a shoulder strap for transporting your sword. This leaves your hands free to carry other props and open doors. Put extra padding in the end where the point will go.

- When carrying your sword, press a cork into the point to prevent the sword from accidentally poking other people.

- If the sword starts to rotate on your head as you dance, look at the tip of it with your eyes, being careful not to tilt your chin. The sword should quit rotating when you look at it.

- A sword is a great prop to use when doing bellygrams and other private parties in people's homes. It captivates the audience, and lends variety to your show.

CANDLES

Candle dancing mesmerizes audiences with its illuminative beauty. The flickering shadows of the flames add mystery and drama to the performance.

History

In Egypt, *raks al shamadan*, ("candelabrum dance") has become a traditional part of wedding celebrations. The family hires a professional dancer to do a performance that involves balancing a large, heavy, 3-tiered candelabrum with 13 blazing candles on her head. It is not a folk dance, because "folk dance" usually refers to participatory dances that were done by the common people in rural villages to celebrate special occasions. That is not the origin of the candelabrum dance. Rather, professional performers invented raks al shamadan for entertainment purposes.

The originators of raks al shamadan were Zouba el Klobatiyya and Shafiyya el Koptiyya, back in the early part of the 20th century, around 1910-1920. Zouba el Klobatiyya balanced a *klop* (large oil lamp) on her head. Shafiyya el Koptiyya, so named because she was Coptic, was the first to balance the 3-tiered *shamadan*. Other dancers, including Nazla el Adel, Najia el Eskandrani, and her sister Dawlett, learned it from them. Dawlett el Eskandrani passed it on to her granddaughter, Nadia Hamdi. Raks al shamadan is typically performed wearing an elegant full-length evening gown decorated with beads and sequins.

In Turkey, there is a traditional folk dance in which the dancers carry two candles, one on the palm of each hand. They move their arms in different poses in time to the music.

Candle Dance Today

Until recently, raks al shamadan was a popular traditional element of the *zeffa* (procession) for an Egyptian wedding celebration. The dancer, with the candelabrum balanced on her head, would lead the bride and groom into the reception hall. However, during the 1990s a small group of Islamic extremists arose who threatened violent interference with weddings that featured a female dancer. This has led many families to hire troupes of young men instead of professional female dancers to perform for their zeffas. The dances done by the young men may vary—they might be folkloric Egyptian men's dances such as the tahtiyb and el ard, or they might consist of dances resembling an ensemble scene from a Broadway musical. In any event, the popularity of the traditional raks al shamadan has declined with this societal change. Families just aren't willing to risk violence at their celebrations.

In the United States, some dancers have mastered use of the Egyptian *shamadan* and incorporated it into their performances. Another option popular with U.S. dancers is to balance a single candle in a simple candleholder. Often, they will incorporate it into the floor work portion of their dance. A performer may start with the candle balanced on her head, then go into a backbend and move the candleholder to her stomach. While still in the backbend, she may do stomach rolls or flutters.

Dancers wishing to portray a Pharaonic mood may hold a small glass globe in each hand, with a votive candle inside. Using dramatic music, the dancer may pose in ways that are reminiscent of Egyptian tomb paintings, doing arm poses.

Selecting A Candle Holder

If you plan to dance with an Egyptian-style candelabrum with the cap that fits around the head, try to buy one in a setting where you can try it on first. Not all caps are the same size, and you will want to choose one that feels right for you. It should have padding inside the metal band that passes in front of your forehead. Also test the balance—if you cannot balance it before you buy it, there is no guarantee that you will be able to make it balance later.

Even a much simpler candleholder with a single candle can be a real audience-pleaser. Try to select one that has a low center of gravity, which will balance better than a tall one.

Another effective way to use candles is to purchase two small globe-shaped glass candleholders that fit in the palm of the hand, with short votive candles. These can be held on the palms while you do different arm/hand movements. If possible, choose ones with designs molded into the glass because that will enhance the flickering effect of the candles.

Tips For Using Candles

- Practice many times in private with an unlit candle in the candleholder before you appear in public. Do not practice with an empty candleholder, because that will balance differently from one that has a candle in it.

- Tear a scarf over your hair, under the candelabrum, to prevent any wax that drips off the candles from entangling your hair.

- Glue small mirrors to your candleholder. They will reflect the light of the flames and intensify the overall effect.

- Place short candles in the candleholder to keep the center of gravity low and easier to balance.

- Permanently keep two books of matches (or two lighters) in your dance bag. As soon as one is empty, replace it.

- If your candleholder starts to tarnish, use brass polish to make it shine again.

TAMBOURINE

The tambourine, known as *riqq* or *def* in Arabic, introduces a level of excitement into a dance performance.

History

Dance researchers have not been able to find historical documentation that proves the tambourine was ever used as a dance prop in the Middle East. They have found some old postcards that show a woman posing with a tambourine, but the photographer could easily have asked the dancer to borrow one from a musician to make the resulting photograph more interesting.

Tambourines belong to a family of instruments known as frame drums. A frame drum consists of a skin stretched over a ring of wood and secured into place. These come in various sizes, from the large *tabla baladi* used by Egyptian folkloric musicians to the small riqq with cymbals attached to its rim.

91

Thank You

I would like to thank the dance researchers who have devoted time and effort to investigating the history of this wonderful dance form. In particular, I would like to profusely thank Morocco for freely sharing what she has learned in her 30+ years of firsthand field research into the dance traditions of the Middle East and North Africa. All the historical sections of this chapter are built on information that she has generously passed on to the dance community— it could not have been written without her! I would also like to thank Tarik abd el Malik and Donna Lapré for sharing their research on the history of finger cymbals.

Tambourines Today

Performers in the Middle East do not dance with tambourines. It is common to have a musician playing one in the band. A tambourine in the band brings richness to the overall sound of the percussion. In a small musical ensemble, the riqq player may be the only percussionist.

Many dancers in North America incorporate tambourines into their shows for variety, especially for troupe performances. This prop is particularly popular with troupes that wish to portray a Gypsy fantasy style. Even though there is no traditional tambourine dance among the Roma, the image of a Gypsy dancing around a campfire with a tambourine in her hand is widely accepted by Western audiences.

Selecting A Tambourine

If possible, consult with a local musician for advice on how to purchase a tambourine that will sound good. Avoid selecting one that produces a dull thud.

Some tambourines are made of real skin, and others have synthetic skin. Real skin expands and shrinks with changes in temperature and humidity, which leads to changes in the tonal quality. If you expect to use your tambourine outdoors frequently, choose one with synthetic skin.

Tips for Using a Tambourine

- Don't wear any rings on your fingers when dancing with a tambourine. A ring can damage the skin of the tambourine.

- Do not just swat your tambourine on the musical accents. Take some tambourine lessons from a local percussionist, and learn some basics of how to play it as a musical instrument. When you incorporate the musical technique into your performance, your audience will appreciate your multiple levels of talent.

- Tie colorful ribbons that match your costume onto your tambourine at each of the holes around the edge. This will add visual excitement to your dance.

- Glue sequins or small mirrors onto the edge of your tambourine, next to the cymbals, to give it added sparkle as you dance. Do not put these decorations on the section where your hand will grip it.

■ *For contact information see: Shira, page 196, Joyful Dance Designs (Karol Henderson Harding), page 197, Oasis Band & Dancers, page 202, Morocco, page 199, Tarik abd el Malik, page 200, Mishaal, page 203, and School for Oriental Dance (Susanne Potempa), page 202.*

MELEAH
Photo by Kathleen Thompson

Make-Up

93

Henna Body Art in Belly Dance

By Sally Phillips

...ENHANCE THE MYSTIQUE OF THE DANCER...

Henna body art, or *mehndi* as it is called in India, is a form of adornment found in many cultures throughout the Muslim world. It is used by peoples of seven different religions in regions where the plant is grown. In Morocco, henna is often seen on the hands and feet of dancers. In Berber culture, the art form of tattooing is dying out, however the use of henna and other temporary vegetable-based forms of adornment is more readily accepted. While henna may not be exclusive to dance, both the traditions of belly dance, and of body adornment are seamlessly enmeshed within these cultures.

Henna is a natural vegetable dye that is applied topically to the skin as a paste. When removed after several hours, it leaves a rich reddish brown stain that can last up to three weeks on the skin. Many dancers favor the traditional application of henna to those areas of the body that stain the darkest: the hands and feet.

94

Most dancers can find henna body artists in their area by looking on the Internet, and there is always at least one henna artist at every belly dance event or festival! There are also several good henna kits and books out for those who wish to apply henna themselves. Some troupes or groups of dancers may favor hiring a henna body artist for a party. This is a wonderful opportunity for women and men to come together for Middle Eastern music, dance and body adornment in a festive and creative atmosphere.

SELENE (HAND)
Photo by Sally Phillips

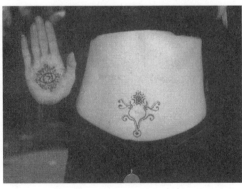

Henna body art can play a vital part in the costuming of the individual dancer or belly dance troupe. In American-Middle Eastern and Tribal belly dance, the application of henna ranges from the decorative to the symbolic. It can be utilized purely to enhance the mystique of the dancer, to draw attention to a specific part of the body, or to create an impression of sacredness and ritual.

JETARAA
Photo by Sally Phillips

There are several different styles of design, all of which can be found in the many books about henna. The Berber people of North Africa create henna designs that are largely comprised of bold geometric patterns, while those of India feature patterned weavings of ornate flowers, birds and paisleys. Arab Emirate designs contain strongly defined swirling vines and flowers. Here in the West, henna artists not only adhere to traditional patterns, but also create their own designs. In the world of belly dance, it is not unusual for the dancer and the henna painter to create particular designs together.

■ *For contact information see: Henna Dreams (Sally Phillips), page 195.*

Henna Body Art in Belly Dance

Stage Make-Up: The Facial Costume

By Meleah

Illustrations by Alan McCorkle

YOU CAN CHANGE THE MOOD BY CHANGING THE COLOR.

Make-up worn during a performance differs from ordinary make-up. Stage make-up must make the face visible and dramatic to the audience. Careful application will complement the dancer's costume and highlight the facial features. The right make-up will enhance the image the costume creates.

This is an introduction to stage make-up technique. With practice, an average application should take 15 to 20 minutes. Allow a few extra minutes for additional steps to keep the make-up in place. Other decorations and effects, such as *bindis,* also add time.

MELEAH

Photo by Kathleen Thomson

SETTING UP THE STAGE MAKE-UP KIT

Stage make-up should be kept in a designated case, separate from daily make-up. If necessary, purchase duplicate items for stage and daily wear. This saves time and makes it harder to forget things. Keep your kit organized and manageable.

Padding protects against breakage. Products should not move within the case during transport. Wrap delicate items, such as eye shadow, in tissue. Keep brushes and sponges in a separate plastic bag for cleanliness.

9 6

FOUNDATION

Proper use of foundation insures the success and durability of the make-up. The right foundation can solve problems, such as inconsistency of color tone. Foundations may contain varying degrees of SPF. Some foundations contain moisturizers. Use additional moisturizer under foundation if needed.

Types of Foundation:

Dual-Active Powder provides minimal coverage. Apply with a sponge. It can be dusted on with a brush to double as a setting powder.

Skin types: smooth, oily, young, or for heavy perspiration. Smoothes uneven tones. Prevents shine. Does not cover under eye circles, acne or blemishes.

Other uses: Body make-up. Smoothes freckles and evens chest tone. A darker shade gives tanned appearance. Good for blending neck color into body color.

Tinted Moisturizer provides minimal coverage. Apply with hands like a lotion. Set with powder.

Skin types: All skin types, smoother texture with no coverage needs.

Other uses: Body make-up. Gives tanned appearance.

Liquid Foundation provides light to medium coverage. Apply with sponge. Set with powder.

Skin types: All skin types with light to medium coverage needs. Oily skin will need more powder. Does not cover acne or blemishes. May cover circles.

Other uses: Body make-up. Provides tint.

Mousse Make-Up provides medium to heavy coverage. Apply with sponge, set with powder.

Skin types: Oily skin. Has excellent oil controlling power. Uneven and rougher textured skin.

Stick Make-Up provides medium to heavy coverage. Blends well. Apply with fingertips or sponge. Set with powder.

Skin types: All skin types. Smooth to rough textures. Can be applied sheer to heavy. Can be used as cover stick in spot areas. Covers razor burn, acne, freckles, scars, under eye circles.

Other uses: Body make-up. Evens chest tone, covers freckles, veins, scars, some tattoos.

One face can have many textures and colors. Using different formulas can solve many problems. For example, liquid foundation may be used all over as a first step. Stick make-up may then be used for areas needing extra coverage such as nose, chin and under eyes.

Foundation Basics

Foundation must be used. It prepares the skin for the rest of the make-up.

When choosing a color, the tone should blend evenly with skin tone. To determine the proper shade, apply foundation to the jaw. Blend with fingertips and wait five minutes. If it turns another color, it does not match. It should disappear, leaving a smoother, natural tone.

Avoid pink bases. They look chalky. Good shades have a yellow base. Yellow warms the skin and looks natural.

97

CONCEALER

Concealer is often misused. Proper use of foundation may eliminate the need for concealer.

Due to its thickness, concealer may cake on the skin and accentuate lines, especially around the eyes. Use it sparingly over foundation, and only when absolutely necessary.

A thicker stick foundation under the eyes will lessen cracking. Avoid concealer and stick foundation around the outer eye where crow's-feet will be accentuated.

Dot on concealer and blend with fingertips on the inner eye only and over severe breakouts. Soften the edges with a sponge and set with powder.

Avoid raccoon eyes by never using a white concealer. White is unnatural and only lightens slightly, leaving a ghostly hue to the skin. Choose a color two shades lighter than skin tone with a yellow or amber tone. Yellow erases redness and leaves a natural tone.

TRANSLUCENT POWDER

Translucent powder is designed to set face and body make-up and keep it from moving. It will help to hold back perspiration during performance. Use a translucent shade with a yellow undertone. For best results, press on a generous amount over foundation with a large velour powder puff. Brush off excess with a powder brush. Powder your chest and stomach to smooth the texture. The more you put on, the longer your make-up stays in place. Use a loose powder in a jar at home. Pack a compact in kit for touch-ups.

If under-eye looks too dry after powder, gently pat on a dot of moisturizer with fingertips. Let the moisturizer soak in and soften the lines.

BLUSH

A soft, natural cheek smoothes the overall appearance and allows the eyes and lips to be the focal points. The slashed style cheeks of the 1980s are gone.

Apply blush directly on the cheekbone, at an angle. Keep it on the outer half of the face to pull the eyes up and out. Use a dome top brush to brush in reverse from sideburns inward. Avoid blush directly on the apples of the cheeks to avoid "chipmunk cheeks".

Choose a warm neutral peachy brown or a cool dusty rose depending on skin undertones and eye color. Choose a shade two shades darker than skin tone to contour just under the cheekbone in a curve to add more definition.

Only contour if the sides of the face are flat with little definition. For prominent cheekbones, contour can look too hard. Blush that is too strong can look cheap and painted.

Eyebrows frame the eyes and give expression to the face. A properly shaped brow is like a mini facelift, taking up to five years off the face.

Brows should be $^1/4$" - $^3/8$" thick at the widest part and taper to a pointed tail. The ideal brow arches up, just past the center of the eye in a straight line, then angles down in a straight line. To determine the correct shape, line up a pencil on the side of the nose to these points: 1) straight up through the tear duct, 2) through the pupil, 3) through the outside corner of the eye. These points mark the beginning, the arch and the end. Use a pencil to lightly connect the points. Eyes will appear more prominent.

1. *Nose through beginning of eye—corner*
2. *Nose through pupil—arch point*
3. *Nose through cornder of eye—tail*

Now tweeze excess hair. Clean out unwanted hair between the brows. Clean out under the brow to where the hair grows denser. Tweeze in the direction the hair is growing right at the root. Pull gently. To numb the pain, either ice the brow or take a hot shower. Tweeze two or three hairs on each brow at a time to stay even on both sides.

Once the desired shape is achieved, fill in with eyebrow pencil where skin shows through the hair. For everyday use, match hair color. For stage and blondes, go a shade darker and extend the tail of the brow up to $^1/2$" longer. Apply a matching matte eye shadow with a tiny slanted brush to set and hold, and to look more natural.

Make-Up Tools

Brushes
three to five for brows, eyes, cheeks, powder, lips

Sponge
latex wedge

Velour Puff
for powder

Tweezers
for stray hairs

Tissues

Washcloth
for blotting perspiration

100

EYES

Eyes allow for a lot of creativity.

There are basically three steps to the eye: 1) *Highlight* 2) *Contour* 3) *Definition*

There are many choices for placement of these three colors. There are several ways to do each dancer's eyes.

The following plan works for most eyes. Keep this in mind for the stage: be bigger than life, more dramatic, less subtle.

Preparation: Include the eyelid when applying foundation and powder. This prevents creasing.

Step 1: Highlight Cover the entire lid from lash line to brow bone with the lightest shade of choice. Good choices are creamy white, light pink, gold, silver, and light yellow. Mature skin should stay with matte shadows and avoid frost.

Step 2: Contour This technique creates a crease and lifts the brow bone. Looking straight ahead, apply a medium shade to crease just behind the eyelashes. This should be applied somewhere halfway between lid and brow. A little higher is better for stage.

Follow the crescent shape of the bone and extend out beyond the corner of the eye. Use medium taupe, chocolate, charcoal or plum. Match your hair or eye color if appropriate. A neutral shade deepens the eye.

Step 3: Definition This technique defines the desired eye shape such as catlike, Egyptian, almond, round, etc.

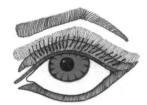

Almond

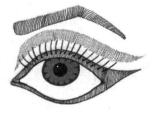

Catlike

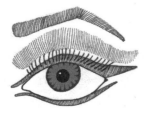

Egyptian

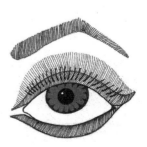

Round

Using waterproof pencil, softly line the lash on the upper lid. Stop at the corner of the lid. Open eyes and determine where the line should end. Make a dot. Now close the eye and work backwards, connecting the ending point to the corner point. This will insure the desired angle and keeps both eyes even. The best angle is found by lining up a pencil from the nose edge through the outside corner of the eye. Follow this angle for the most lift. Be brave. Extend the line up to $1/2$" or more. It looks great on stage.

Under eyes often look too hard with a solid line, so try a smudged line. Line the under eyes and smudge them a bit. Extend the lower line by connecting it into the upper line or running parallel, leaving a space that can be filled in with highlight color.

Black, soft black and navy are good colors for lining. Waterproof pencils are good because they are easy to use and blend. To set and smooth the line, apply a matching matte shadow over liner with a tiny moist brush. This locks in the line against running. Liquid liner dries shiny, does not blend, and looks too hard. Use it only on a large stage with strong lighting and a theater audience. When dancing closer to people, liquid liner appears crackled, aging the face.

MASCARA

Black mascara is best for everyone. Lashes need to be strong. They finish the eye. Apply three to four light coats, alternating eyes. Mascara builds gradually, rather than all at once. Layering prevents clumping. Let each coat set a minute. Roll the brush up while applying, extending to the tips and working the brush left to right. This deposits extra on the tips. Lower lashes only need 2-3 coats closer to the roots. Long lower lashes may touch the face when perspiring and smear. Pull excess mascara off the lower tips. For dancers who perspire heavily, use waterproof mascara, but keep in mind that waterproof mascara is like tar. A good remover is necessary.

Curl lashes first if they don't curl on their own. Apply extra mascara to the outside lashes to give a more exotic look. Another option is to apply two to three individual false lashes to the outside quarter of the lid.

Make-Up Checklist

Foundation
a darker and lighter shade

Concealer
one or two shades lighter than the foundation

Translucent Powder
one loose in a jar, one in a compact

Blush
two colors: one softer, one darker for contour

Brown Color
powder and/or pencil

Eye Shadow
three or four shades from highlighter to black, brown or charcoal

Eyeliner
pencil and/or powder

Black Mascara
one regular, one waterproof

Lip Pencil
three shades, medium to dark

Lipstick
three to five shades that work with costume or hair color

Moisturizer

101

LIPS

There are options for lips. They can coordinate with the costume or with the dancer's personal coloring, such as hair color. Experiment to see which complete the total picture. Lipstick is the final accent. Changing the color changes the mood.

Some costumes in the orange, red, wine and pink families look great if coordinated with a matching lip color. Costumes with more gold or silver may need a frosty metallic. Multicolor costumes may need a light nude to avoid confusion.

Keep in mind a few facts regarding color. Light or bright shades make lips appear larger. Deep and brownish shades make lips appear smaller. Frost or shine reflects light and makes lips appear fuller. Matte recedes light and makes lips appear smaller. You can adjust lip size accordingly with a lip pencil. Red is considered a neutral if it is a true red. There are warm reds and cool reds. Hair color will determine the appropriate tone of red.

Foundation and powder applied under lip color hold the color. Apply lip pencil just over the edge of the lip line. Fuller is better. Slightly color in to stain the lips. Apply lip color with a lip brush for maximum staying power. Blot with a tissue; brush on a light dusting of translucent powder, and re-apply lipstick. This layering with powder trick locks on the color. To save time, try applying lipstick first, then lining. It is much faster and avoids the heavily outlined look.

Keep your lip outline clean, but curved. A hard angular mouth looks smaller and firmer. Soft curved lips are more approachable. Again, fuller is better.

Avoid wet and glossy products. They wear off quickly and hair gets stuck more easily. Look for long lasting formulas with a glow. Try a highlight in the center with a gold or silver glitter or eye shadow.

This is an introduction to stage make-up. The information on make-up is endless and changes seasonally. Enough information is provided here to get started and experiment.

Remember one final point. A dancer needs to be seen clearly from the audience's perspective. Standing 10 to 20 feet away from the mirror, make sure all features can be seen and that everything is in proportion. Deepen colors or elongate lines if necessary.

■ *For contact information see: Meleah, page 196.*

DINA — THE COSTUME
GODDESS
Photo by Keith Drosin

Costumes

103

Killer Gold and Noisy Ankles

A Whirlwind Tour of Ethnic Jewelry

By Michelle Morrison

TUNISIAN MEN CAN RECOGNIZE THEIR WIVES
BY THE TONE OF THE TRADITIONAL ANKLETS
RESTING LOW AGAINST THE FOOT.

MICHELLE MORRISON

A
n old piece of jewelry reflects the history of the woman who wore it, and is a symbol of her people. It is often difficult to ascertain much about an item being purchased. Is the necklace an authentic piece or simply a reproduction cast from pot metal? Could that huge pendant with the thick hook possibly be an earring? A little bit of history can help immensely when purchasing ethnic jewelry.

COINS

Coins are an inherent part of traditional Middle Eastern jewelry. They signify wealth, and to a lesser extent, make a pleasing ornament with their soft jingling sound. Most jewelry available now has the coins soldered to a link, which enables them to be attached to a necklace or headdress. The *Ouled Nail* of Algeria sewed such coins to long black ribbons that they looped across their chests or draped in vertical strips from collars. Women of Afghanistan trimmed their blouses and bodices with coins. In Egypt, *Ghawazee* dancers would sew coins onto an *anteree* (a bolero-style jacket). Often a garment would be completely covered with coins. A late 19th century advertisement for Turkish cigarettes shows a young woman wearing a short vest bedecked with coins.

Ouled Nail

Tribe that lived in Algeria, near Biskra.

These ornamental uses of coins led to the modern coin bra. The modern coin belt also has its roots in Morocco, where girls in the early 1900s would sew coins on skirts and hip wraps. Alternatives to coins are bells, which are used in mass profusion on Indian jewelry. Bells range in tone from a delicate tinkling of tiny silver bells to the louder clang of brass bells.

ANKLETS AND BRACELETS

Authentic anklets (*redif* in Morocco, *khekal* in Tunisia) and bracelets (*swar* in Tunisia) are wonderfully heavy, chunky affairs—not bits of thin wire or delicate chain. They are often hinged, and closed with a straight pin or fashioned as cuffs. The anklets fit snugly against the ankle or wrist, yet still make sounds with movement. Tunisian men can recognize their wives by the tone of the traditional anklets resting low against the foot. Spiked bracelets are common and intended to protect the wearer, although many are hollow and lightweight, indicating that the protection may be more spiritual than physical.

NECKLACES AND PENDANTS

The type of traditional necklace most easily found today is the choker, bedecked with coins. The choker is inlaid with lapis or colored glass and may boast upwards of twenty strands of coins. A well-made piece will be backed with heavy fabric to prolong the life of the metal. The fabric is often beaded around the edges.

Another common style is a simple coin necklace reminiscent of the Ouled Nail drapes. Rows of coins are suspended from a simple woven neckband. A band woven through the upper row of coins will identify a neckband as authentic.

The torque is popular in Africa, the Middle East and India. Called *hansli* in India, they often illustrate the influence of Greek design, which first appeared with Alexander the Great.

Pendants and amulets bear more meaning than simple wealth. They are often religious in nature or worn for a specific purpose. For example, cylindrical amulets, called *hirz* or *tumar,* often contained verses from the Koran. Other amulets were filled with carnelian to protect expectant mothers. Intricate silver boxes could also contain Koranic verses, love tokens, or other small personal possessions.

Often items that a Westerner would assume to be pendants are headdress ornaments. Tunisian women wore long dangling silver ornaments while an Uzbeki woman may have worn a gold and turquoise ornament on their forehead.

EARRINGS

Again, often pieces that might appear to be pendants actually turn out to be massive earrings *(halaq).* Not all earrings are worn through pierced ear lobes however. Many of the heavy or large earrings are actually fastened with hooks to the side of a headdress. Women of Oman sometimes suspend the earrings from their necklaces and Moroccan women support the weight of large earrings with hooks attached in their hair.

FARAH

Photo by Michael J. Monson

Killer Gold and Noisy Ankles

DISCERNING AUTHENTIC PIECES FROM REPRODUCTIONS

Without being a trained expert on folkloric Middle Eastern jewelry, it is difficult to determine whether every piece is authentic or a modern reproduction. There are several clues, however, which can help.

The color and weight of the metal are great determining factors. Many folkloric pieces are silver. A piece that is heavily tarnished and heavy to lift probably contains a great deal of real silver. If it is a shiny bright white color and feels light or flimsy, the amount of silver is minimal. It is most likely made of cheap pot metal (random bits of metal melted together). Many reproduction pieces, specifically the choker-coin necklaces, come from India. These are most often made with light pot metal, what some jewelers call "new silver." The coins are thinly stamped discs and the inlay is lightweight colored glass that cracks easily and chips. Real silver is desirable in pieces from India. Although real silver may appear tarnished, it can be restored to its shining luster, while the silver finish of pot metal will eventually rub off, never to return.

The stones may help to authenticate a piece as well. Turquoise is used in ethnic pieces from Saudi Arabia. The Bedouin favor red coral because it symbolizes life; the Berbers revered it for its healing properties. Carnelian is said to protect expectant mothers and horses. Lapis is common in Afghani pieces. Although these stones can be a determining factor in authenticity, colored glass is also common in traditional jewelry.

Determining a piece's country of origin is an equally difficult task. Dowry jewelry was popular because it was easily portable by the nomadic tribes that traveled all over the Middle East. As women married away from their tribes, they took with them their style of jewelry.

The Middle East has long been a popular tourist spot. Viking sailors came down the Volga. The Roman Empire stretched its influence across the Mediterranean. Nomadic tribes and powerful kings warred against each other. Each traveler brought with him his native style of ornament and returned home with a foreign one. Norwegian and Tunisian women alike closed their aprons with *fibulas*—the original safety pin. In Tunisia they are called *hillal*, in Algeria *ibzimen*, and in Morocco, *tizerzai*. They are often linked with amulets for protection, and the size and workmanship of the fibula reflect the wearer's social status.

The use of gold in the Middle East was popularized by the influence of the Greeks and Romans. Beautiful gold jewelry is indicative of Saudi Arabia and India, although gold filigree is often worked onto silver pieces throughout the Middle East and Africa. As gold is non-corrodible, some believed that it contained a life of its own which had the power to kill. Others called gold the metal of the sun.

The purity of gold was quite high until trade with Europeans after the fifteenth century. Demand increased to the point that local craftsmen would dilute the gold with brass and silver. Before this became a common practice, however, gold was used extravagantly. A common practice in India involved inserting gold foil between a stone and its mount to add brilliance to the gem while concealing irregularities.

106

A Sampling of Traditional Jewelry

Top: *an earring (halaq), the style of which dates back to Etruscan times.*

Middle: *an amulet, of a design found all across the Middle East and the Orient. (This one originates from India.)*

Bottom: *an Afghani necklace with colored glass and real coins. It is backed with heavy cloth that has been beaded around the edges.*

■ *For contact information see: Michelle Morrison, page 199, and Michael J. Monson, page 196.*

How Much Glamour is Too Much?

If you enjoy dressing over the top—wearing the biggest hairdo, the gaudiest colors, the tightest skirt, the highest slits, the shiniest fabric, the deepest cleavage, and the bluest eye shadow— be very confident that you appear, in spite of all this, tasteful and beautiful.

Designing a Cabaret Costume

Text and illustrations by Dina

Digital renderings by Kate Reed

BE REMEMBERED AS AN ORIGINAL.

What is a cabaret costume? A magical vision of the glamorous, exotic belly dancer was popularized by Hollywood decades ago. In glittering bra and belly-baring skirt, draped with diaphanous veils, she undulated and shimmied to the accompaniment of her jingling finger cymbals. This cabaret style of costume and dance is flashier, more theatrical and more revealing than the many historic, ethnic styles of Middle Eastern cultures.

THE COSTUME PIECES

The cabaret costume usually consists of fringed hip belt, ornate bra, skirt and/or harem pants, and one or more veils. A fitted gown sometimes replaces bra and skirt. Decorative arm coverings, headpieces, and shoes are optional. Jewelry completes the ensemble. See "Cabaret Costume: The Pieces", page 118.

WHY DESIGN?

Ready-made cabaret ensembles are expensive. If they are mass-produced, the choices of size, style, and color are limited. They often fit poorly and alterations are difficult. The purchase may prove to be a costly and disappointing compromise.

Making your own costume is challenging and labor-intensive, but fun. The result is an original work of art that gratifies your creative urge, displays your talent, flatters your figure and generates amazed and envious compliments.

If you lack sewing skills, you may be able to find an expert who is willing to instruct you, trade, or work for hire. If that's not feasible, the following analysis and design process will give you a clear idea of what you should know before you shop for a costume.

GOOD TASTE IN COSTUME

It's not hard to step over the line that separates theatrical and scintillating from garish and tasteless. Belly dancers must make a special effort to avoid any suggestion of vulgarity in their dress or manner, burdened as we are with that annoying public perception that compares us to other "exotic dancers."

108

The belly dancer's dazzling costume need not be too revealing, and has many options for modesty and camouflage. Accept and love your body as it is, yes; but use good judgment in your display of bare skin. The lighting in many venues is far from kind. You don't want the audience to be distracted from your artful dance moves and charming stage persona by a stark view of loose flesh, fat rolls, stretch marks, buttock cleavage, spider veins, dimply knees, or bouncing bosoms.

CHOOSING COLORS

The correct costume color enhances your natural beauty; the reverse is true, as well. If you don't know what colors flatter you, ask a friend or teacher. Time spent with some fabric samples, a mirror, and various lighting effects (natural light, florescent, and incandescent) will help you decide, as will the books on this subject in the beauty section of your bookstore. A few guidelines might be helpful:

- If your coloring is bold—dark hair and light to dark skin—you are able to wear stronger and brighter colors without being overwhelmed by them. White and black are dramatic against dark hair, as are such intense colors as hot pink, red, electric blue, and violet.

- Against very dark skin and hair, black and midnight blue may not provide enough contrast. White may provide too much. Any of the brighter colors would be fine.

- Against pale skin, lighter hair, and delicate features, black, white, and bright colors can be too overpowering, as if the costume is wearing the dancer. Soft-to-medium shades of rose, peach, aqua, ivory, and lavender would be better.

- If your coloring is somewhere in the medium range, any shade that's not too extreme could work with suitable make-up and accents.

- Consider warm versus cool. Many redheads, golden blondes, and warm brunettes look good in shades of gold, orange, vermilion, and bronze. Many dark brunettes with olive or brown complexions look better in silver, turquoise, blood red, magenta and purple.

- Solid gold or solid silver will reflect the most light, and will be dramatic.

- Florescent colors, such as lime green, neon orange, and screaming pink do not flatter most complexions, and occupy that zone between gaudy/theatrical and gaudy/tacky. They may not be the wisest choice.

- Costumes generally have gold or silver accents to reflect light, and sometimes a second or third costume color: red and black with gold, for example, or blue and violet with silver. Other options include several shades of one color, or multi-colors.

Your stage persona is an artistic projection of your personality. If you're new to dancing, you may not be sure what your style is.

Friends and teachers might perceive this more clearly than you do. Some are comfortable in full flashy cabaret style. A cabaret dancer is at liberty to express her taste, personality, and artistry through her many costume choices.

Your costume suits your persona when it gives you pleasure and inspires your dance. Don't be afraid to innovate and improvise. Classic cabaret is popular, but modern variations inspired by other sources (flamenco, Indian, Art Deco, ancient Greek) are perfectly appropriate too.

Designing a Cabaret Costume

Trace a figure from a picture that resembles yours, or trace a full-length snapshot of yourself taken in leotard, striking a graceful pose. Use this as a guide when you sketch designs. By now your imagination is flowering; there are thousands more ideas in books, websites, silent movies, Italian fashion magazines, rock concerts, and temple carvings...

THE DANCER'S FIGURE & THE ART OF ILLUSION

Most women are aware of their figure proportions that will be discussed shortly, and best and worst features. It may still help to ask a fashion-conscious friend or teacher for an honest evaluation. The artful use of veils, drapes, layers of fabric, glittering accents, jewelry, and accessories can create illusions that enhance a dancer's beauty and camouflage less-than-perfect features.

Exercise A

List your three favorite features.
Examples: graceful hands, big blue eyes, small waist.

1. _____

2. _____

3. _____

THESE ARE THE FEATURES TO EMPHASIZE. BUT HOW?

- Bare skin: Any bare skin (tummy, thigh, arms) revealed on stage will attract the eyes of the audience.

- Cosmetics: Black eyeliner, false lashes, nail polish, etc. Cosmetics are a must on stage, and will enhance any especially attractive features.

- Jewelry: Jewelry can be placed to call attention to favorite features: lots of rings and bracelets for the hands, for instance, forehead pendants for the eyes, chains for the waist.

- Sparkle: Light-reflecting details, such as body glitter, sequins, and rhinestones, will catch the viewer's eye.

- Moving parts of the costume: fringe, tassels, dangling coins. Wrist tassels will draw attention to the hands.

- Details: Decorative trim, curved or angular edges, cutouts. A dress with cutouts at the waist says, "Look at my waist".

Exercise B

List three least favorite features.
Examples: large hips, scar, mousy hair.

1. _____

2. _____

3. _____

THESE ARE THE FEATURES TO DE-EMPHASIZE. BUT HOW?

 AVOID the "emphasize" tricks in these areas. If at all possible, cover the disliked feature.

Cover with concealing makeup, if possible (scars and blemishes).

Cover with costume or jewelry. Example: an Egyptian headpiece covers short or drab hair.

Cover with veils. Example: Veiling the abdomen could cover a surgical scar.

If it's not possible to cover the unappealing feature, create illusions and distractions with design. The "Do's and Don'ts" illustrations clarify the design principles outlined below and how they create a more flattering silhouette for these figure types.

Designing a Cabaret Costume

Costuming Do's and Don'ts

▪ ▪ ▪ THE WELL-PROPORTIONED DANCER ▪ ▪ ▪

Do take advantage of the many costume options that flatter your figure.

Do show off a nice figure with a tasteful form-fitting or skin-baring costume.

Do

Don't wear a costume too revealing to be appropriate.

Don't

▪ ▪ ▪ THE ROUNDED DANCER ▪ ▪ ▪

Do disguise excess pounds with multiple layers of sheer skirts and harem pants, and gracefully draped veils.

Do add center details, such as a cluster of jewels in front and back of belt and bra, to draw attention to the center of your body for a narrower look. Place fringe in center back and front for the same reason.

Do consider wearing a lovely *beledi* dress for maximum glamour with minimum bareness.

Do emphasize pretty hands, hair and face with sparkly details and dramatic, but tasteful make-up and jewelry.

Don't wear overly revealing or too-tight costume pieces.

Don't exaggerate girth by wearing contrasting belt and skirt, or horizontal design lines across belt and fringe.

Do

Do

Don't

112

Costuming Do's and Don'ts

Do wear a skirt with horizontal stripes or border, or full harem pants. Cover bony collarbones with jewelry, arms with sleeves.

Do wear extra layers of veil and hip scarves to round out your silhouette. Add large details to your bra and belt such as coins, horizontal fringe, round beads, thick cording, and side tassels.

Don't wear a costume that's too bare.

Do

Don't

■ ■ ■ THE PEAR-SHAPED DANCER ■ ■ ■

Your lower torso appears much wider than your upper torso.

Do balance your proportions by wearing more detailed costume pieceson your upper half. Examples: headpieces, jewelry, extra bra fringe, shoulder fringe, wide shoulder straps. Pretty bloused sleeves or gauntlets will balance a small top half better than bare arms.

Do use bra padding, if appropriate.

Do minimize your lower width with small-to-moderate-sized angled belt and center details such as jeweled medallions and center tassels.

Don't wear a large belt with a horizontal line across the belt or belt fringe.

Don't wear a belt with insufficient curve that gaps at the top.

Don't wear a skirt in fabric that reflects the light, such as satin, lamé, or sequins; this will call attention to large lower half.

Don't wear a tight straight skirt or a circle skirt, for the same reason.

Do

Don't

Costuming Do's and Don'ts

■ ■ ■ THE SHORT DANCER ■ ■ ■

Do make sure your skirt, harem pants, sleeves, and veil are the proper proportions for your height.

Do keep the eye-catching details on the upper half of your costume.

Do wear matching colors on top and bottom.

Do use center details, such as jeweled motifs, on belt and bra.

Do use curved and angular lines for belt.

Do break up your fringe into clumps or tassels.

Do wear a skirt with a pointed or curved hem, and vertical details such as seams, trim or center ruffle.

Do keep harem pants slim.

Don't wear a heavy, over-designed costume that overwhelms your small frame.

Don't wear contrasting color on top and bottom.

Don't wear a circle skirt, or any skirt with a horizontal hem, border, ruffle or stripes; it will make you appear shorter.

Don't wear wide harem pants.

Don't wear a belt with an upper edge that is cut straight across.

Don't wear thick horizontal fringe.

Do

Don't

114

Costuming Do's and Don'ts

▪▪▪ LARGE BUST ▪▪▪

Do wear a supportive, well fitting bra. If necessary, use two sets of straps, or wider straps, to distribute weight evenly. Keep fringe or coins on bra to a minimum.

Don't wear a flimsy, ill-fitting bra that allows breasts to bounce, sag, or spill over.

Do

Don't

▪▪▪ LARGE ARMS ▪▪▪

Do cover soft, chubby, droopy or lumpy arms with full or draped sleeves.

Don't leave arms naked

Don't wear upper arm bracelets.

Do

Don't

FLAT BUST

Do use a slightly larger bra cup with padding, if more bust curve is desired.

Don't add lots of fringe, coins and decorations to bra.

Don't use a much-too-large, ill-fitting bra and attempt to pad it.

THIN ARMS

Do cover bony arms with fitted sequined or beaded sleeves, or full sleeves.

Designing a Cabaret Costume

Varieties of Tummy Covers

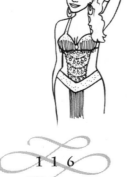

■ ■ ■ PROBLEM TUMMY ■ ■ ■

Do disguise protruding tummy, stretch marks, and surgical scars with belly draping jewelry, beaded covers, colored mesh, body stockings, and veils.

Do, if tummy protrudes only slightly, wear belt lower rather than cutting flesh with tight high belt.

Don't leave tummy bare or cover with body glitter.

Do

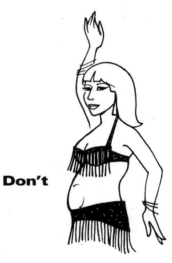

Don't

Do, if tummy protrudes considerably, consider wearing a dress instead of a bra and skirt.

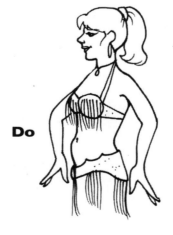

Do

Don't

116

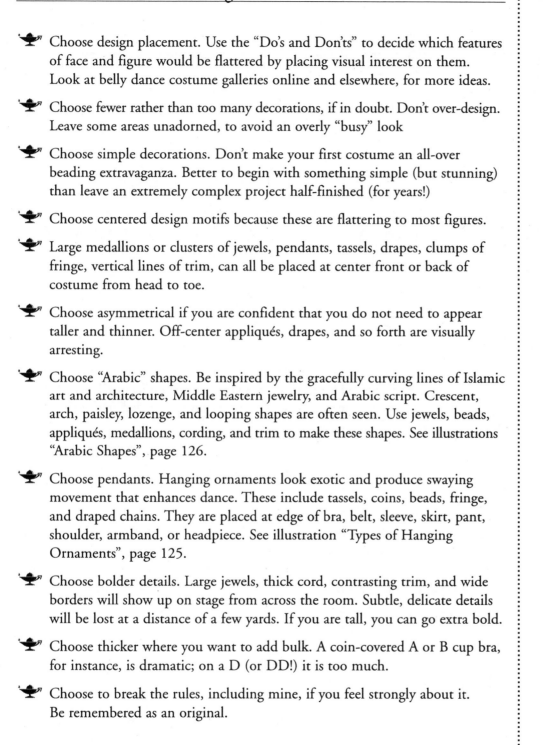

- Choose design placement. Use the "Do's and Don'ts" to decide which features of face and figure would be flattered by placing visual interest on them. Look at belly dance costume galleries online and elsewhere, for more ideas.

- Choose fewer rather than too many decorations, if in doubt. Don't over-design. Leave some areas unadorned, to avoid an overly "busy" look

- Choose simple decorations. Don't make your first costume an all-over beading extravaganza. Better to begin with something simple (but stunning) than leave an extremely complex project half-finished (for years!)

- Choose centered design motifs because these are flattering to most figures.

- Large medallions or clusters of jewels, pendants, tassels, drapes, clumps of fringe, vertical lines of trim, can all be placed at center front or back of costume from head to toe.

- Choose asymmetrical if you are confident that you do not need to appear taller and thinner. Off-center appliqués, drapes, and so forth are visually arresting.

- Choose "Arabic" shapes. Be inspired by the gracefully curving lines of Islamic art and architecture, Middle Eastern jewelry, and Arabic script. Crescent, arch, paisley, lozenge, and looping shapes are often seen. Use jewels, beads, appliqués, medallions, cording, and trim to make these shapes. See illustrations "Arabic Shapes", page 126.

- Choose pendants. Hanging ornaments look exotic and produce swaying movement that enhances dance. These include tassels, coins, beads, fringe, and draped chains. They are placed at edge of bra, belt, sleeve, skirt, pant, shoulder, armband, or headpiece. See illustration "Types of Hanging Ornaments", page 125.

- Choose bolder details. Large jewels, thick cord, contrasting trim, and wide borders will show up on stage from across the room. Subtle, delicate details will be lost at a distance of a few yards. If you are tall, you can go extra bold.

- Choose thicker where you want to add bulk. A coin-covered A or B cup bra, for instance, is dramatic; on a D (or DD!) it is too much.

- Choose to break the rules, including mine, if you feel strongly about it. Be remembered as an original.

Tools and Supplies

General Handsewing

- *Sharp small scissors*
- *6" ruler*
- *Long straight pins and safety pins*
- *Variety of needles (sharps)*
- *All-purpose thread and heavy buttonhole thread or beading floss*

Belt Construction

- *Handsewing tools*
- *Dressmaker scissors*
- *Buckram (stiff, heavy woven interfacing)*
- *Medium to heavy non-woven interfacing (such as Pellon®)*
- *Felt yardage (not 12" squares)*
- *Skirt hooks and eyes, the large size*
- *Velcro® snaps*

Pattern Making

- *Several yards of pattern paper, which is printed with a grid. If that is unavailable, large sheets of plain paper or even paper bags*
- *Measuring tape and ruler or yardstick*
- *Scotch tape and straight pins*
- *Pencil and felt-tip pen*

A description of the cabaret costume pieces will help you understand their construction and function before you begin to design and make your own.

Belt

The belly dancer's belt fits around her hips, leaving the waist free to perform undulations and belly rolls. The belt usually has hanging fringe, tassels or coins on it that emphasize the movements of the hips.

The belt is reinforced with layers of stiffening to support the weight of the beaded fringe or coins. It is covered with sequins, beads or decorative fabric and often further embellished with jewels, appliqués, heavy cording, or ornate trims. It may have a straight edge, or may be curved, angled, or scalloped in some way. Usually the bottom edge of the belt dips lower in the back to allow fringe to dangle freely from derriere. The belt closure may be front, side or back.

The variety of possible shapes and ornaments makes the belt fun to design.

Bra

The dancer's bra does not resemble lingerie. It is reinforced all over to support the weight of beaded fringe or coins on the cups and band. Any elastic is covered with decorative fabric or trim, and the cups are covered with sequins or fabric, as well. It matches the belt in its decorative details: jewels, tassels, beaded appliqués, and so on.

The bra may be further adorned with draped chains, coins, or beaded strands that reach to the waist or abdomen and shoulder fringe.

Veil

The classic veil is three yards of sheer or featherweight fabric. It will float most weightlessly if unadorned, but decorative borders are often used. The veil can be draped and wrapped around the dancer in a number of ways, and is then unwrapped and manipulated during the veil section of the dance routine.

Accessories

Accessories include matching armbands, wristbands, headbands, and neckbands, scarves, face veils, headdresses, and jewelry.

Cover-Up

A loose, pretty cover-up, preferably with front closure, is worn before and after a performance.

Beledi Dress

The *beledi* dress is an alternative for those not wishing to bare the midsection. It may be semi-sheer; loose fitting with flared sleeves, or form fitting and slit to the thigh. Usually it is accented at the hip with beaded scarf or fringed belt.

Velcro is a registered trademark for Velcro USA's brand of hook and loop fasteners.
Pellon is a registered trademark of Freudenberg Nonwovens.

Skirt

A cabaret classic is the circle skirt: one and a half or more circles of gauzy fabric gathered on to a band to create the most voluminous folds possible, making it suitable for floor work and veiling effects. The cost of the 6 to 10 yards of fabric, and the fact that it's not flattering to some figure types, makes it a less than ideal choice for a first skirt. A one-circle skirt would be a variation that is still flared, but less voluminous.

Many skirt styles are now seen in cabaret costume.

The **sheath skirt** is cut close to the body: straight up and down or slightly tapered at the bottom. Long side slits allow for leg movement. Variations have an overlapping ("petal") edge with curved hem, or draping at hipline. This skirt is not full enough to allow for floorwork.

The **handkerchief skirt** is a square of fabric, and falls gracefully in four points. It can be layered under a second square, making eight points.

The **mermaid skirt** is close-fitting to the knee, then flares out gracefully. The skirt can be all one piece with flared seams, or have a separate ruffle.

The **ruffled skirt** is a one-circle skirt with a ruffled border, which may be fastened to hipline at side or back for a different look.

The **feathered skirt** consists of fifteen or more overlapping strips sewn to a band. This works well with harem pants.

The **multi-pointed skirt** is a flared or tiered skirt cut into points along the hem.

1 1/2 circle
"classic"

sheath

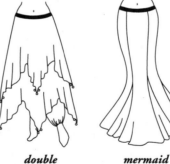

tulip hem
draped sides

double
handkerchief

mermaid

multi
pointed

gathered ruffled
mermaid

circular ruffle
arranged vertically

tiered with
ruffle border

multi
feathered

Bra Construction
- *Handsewing tools*
- *Grosgrain ribbon, a yard or so in widths from 1/2 to 1"*
- *Skirt hooks and eyes*
- *Non-roll elastic (width varies)*
- *Bra pads and/or stiff sew-in bra cups (if necessary)*

Decorating
- *Handsewing tools*
- *Beading needles (extra long and thin needles)*
- *Beading thread: heavy button thread to fine beading floss or nylon invisible thread, depending on bead size*
- *Jewel glue, made to adhere costume jewels to fabric*
- *Tacky fabric glue for quick adhesion of non-jewel items*
- *Fabric paint, glittering and iridescent colors*

Making Costume Items with Seams
- *Handsewing tools*
- *Sewing machine*
- *Serging (overlock) machine (which finishes raw edges) optional*
- *Dressmaker scissors*
- *Iron & ironing board*

119

Sleeves

Sleeves may be attached to the bra, but often are separate pieces called gauntlets. They may reach to the elbow, or nearly to the shoulder, and secured with elastic. The sleeves may be fitted, often with fringe along the seam, or they may be full gathered or bell-shaped sleeves.

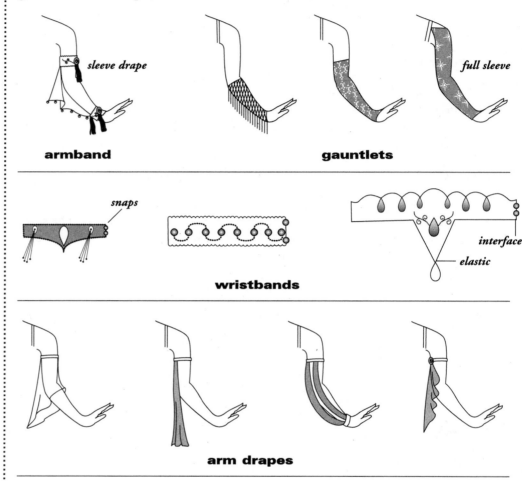

sleeve drape

full sleeve

armband   **gauntlets**

snaps

interface

elastic

wristbands

arm drapes

Harem Pants

Classic harem pants are full, and gathered at the ankle, but may be modified to make them slimmer. They may be open at the side or not, may be sheer or not. For cabaret, they are usually worn under a skirt. The pants allow maximum modesty when performing spins and floorwork, which can reveal too much leg.

classic full harem   *open sides*   *turkish pants (traditional, not cabaret)*   *slim style pants*   *with triangular scarves*

pant styles

COSTUME FABRIC CHOICES

Fibers are either woven or knitted together to make fabric. Keep in mind that knits are better for beginners to use. They do not ravel much on the cut edges and have some degree of stretch, making them easier to handle and fit around curves.

Buy the best fabric that you can afford. A poor quality fabric will make your costume appear amateurish, no matter how you fashion it.

Knits

Stretch velvet and velour have a nap (fuzzy texture). They are good for skirts, belts and bras, but may be too warm for harem pants and sleeves. The matte surface makes an elegant background for glittery costume parts. Remember that the pattern pieces must be cut in the same direction, especially panné velvet, which is pressed flat and sometimes appears shiny depending on the angle of light.

Metallic knit has shiny threads running through the fabric. Make sure these threads aren't too easily snagged. If the fabric is scratchy, the costume piece may need a lining between fabric and skin.

Glitter dot fabric has reflective dots fused to the fabric. Use a minimum of seams because the gluey residue causes the sewing needle to stick and need frequent cleaning or changing. It has a short dance life, due to the effects of friction, cleaning, etc., but is suitable for a dramatic caftan cover-up or headpiece.

Liquid lamé has a slick, shiny surface. It too has a short dance life and is difficult to sew, so use the simplest possible draped and wrapped shapes.

Stretch lace is excellent for snug pieces such as fitted sleeves or dress, and the open texture allows some ventilation and a glimpse of skin. Glamorous sequined lace is expensive, but you can spend some time sewing or gluing on sequins, beads, or light coins yourself.

BELEDI DRESS

Mesh and net are stretchy and semi-sheer. They are used for fitted sleeves, cutouts, and tummy covers; may be flesh-colored or not, plain or glittered. Power net is a less sheer, heavier weight net that can support the weight of jewels and beaded fringe.

Sheer knit may be striped, glittered, or otherwise decorative. It can be lined or not for use as skirts, pants, and dresses. May snag easily: test first!

Designing a Cabaret Costume

Check Out

*http://www.saroyanzils.
com/offset/coins.htm
for online costume coins.*

Wovens

Silk is available in a range of weights (momme or mm). Chiffon (or gauze) (4mm) is a sheer fabric often used for the veil and circle skirt. The fine fabric can be gathered into a small fraction of its original width, creating voluminous folds. Featherweight silk (5mm) is ideal for a veil because of its lightness and dense weave. It floats and billows like no other fabric. Usually this is white and must be dyed to match a costume. It is worth it. Lingerie- or blouse-weight silk (7-8mm), sometimes called charmeuse, has fluidity and sheen, is suitable for a skirt, harem pants, or lining, but it stains and creases easily, and must be dry-cleaned.

Synthetics, such as polyester, are often substituted for silk when cost and easy care are considerations. These include chiffon, georgette (a heavier gauze), and soft lingerie satins. Avoid stiff, heavy satins.

Sequined chiffon is suitable for unstructured skirts and dresses. The sequins dull the needle quickly, which will need frequent changing.

Metallics are flashy, but again, test for snagging and scratching. The best quality are brocades; the least expensive, gaudy tissue lamé, is popular with beginners, but it is stiff and amateur looking.

Lace, plain or glittered, does not ravel and makes nice sleeves and ruffles, but sharp ornaments such as rhinestones with prongs can get caught on it.

Velvet (see under knit) may be solid or woven in patterns on a chiffon background, which is elegant and not as uncomfortably warm to dance in.

Cotton and Linen and easy-care synthetic blends, and are available in a wide variety of patterns, stripes, and florals, from sheer batiste to heavy textures. These are suitable for less formal ethnic and folk costumes: vests, Gypsy skirts, peasant blouses and Turkish pants.

CABARET COSTUME DECORATION

The decoration possibilities in costuming are limited only by the designer's imagination. After the important design choices of color, fabric, and shape, decorations give the costume its unique character.

Materials

Some frequently used materials:

Coins are attached to a garment edge, draped from a chain, or sewn in rows to cover an entire bra and belt. The coins create an "ethnic" look. They must be sewn securely, but loosely, in order to dangle freely and touch each other to produce a jingling sound. Attractive costume coins of aluminum or brass are available in costume or import shops. Real ethnic coin pieces are more difficult to fashion, and best left to experienced specialty costume-makers.

Bells, usually silver, are sold loose or on chains to be worn as jewelry or sewn to a costume piece.

Trims are sold by the yard and include round cording, twisted and braided patterns, metallic and sequined varieties, decorative ribbons, rhinestone strings, beaded bands and fringe. They decorate and cover edges and seams, or outline designs.

Beads come in many varieties. They're used to make fringe, tassels, strands, and flat motifs. For costume, glass beads are recommended for their sparkle and durability. A practice or beginner's costume could use lighter and less costly plastic or metal beads, but these eventually dull with wear.

Beaded fringe swings from the bra and belt, and sometimes the sleeves and shoulders of a cabaret costume. It is made of tiny round rocaille beads, or short to long bugle beads, which reflect the light best due to their tubular shape. This fringe can be bought in plenty of colors by the yard in lengths usually from 2 to 12 inches—even custom-made.

Round beads make thicker fringe and tassels, and long strands of them can be draped from a bra, belt or sleeves. Using lightweight by-the-yard pearls and metallic beads is a quick and inexpensive way to do this.

Sequins and paillettes are inexpensive flat metal or plastic shapes that reflect light like mirrors. They might cover a costume for maximum flash, or add sparkle on a hem or sleeve. Sequins are circular and sewn through the center, available loose or in strands, trims, and stretchy strips. Sequined fabric is available by the yard. Paillettes may be round, oval, or other shapes. They are sewn through a hole near the edge to dangle freely.

Appliqués are flat, decorative shapes made of sequins and beads, which can be sewn onto a costume.

Chains are another "ethnic" detail. They are draped from a bra or belt edge and may be hung with coins or bells. Tassels can be made from fine chains as well.

Patient bead-stringers can make their own fringe, tassels, and strands.

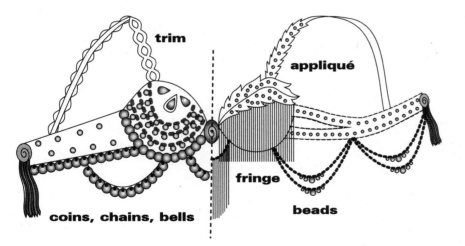

Jewels are available in many shapes, sizes and colors. They are sewn or glued to a costume piece. Acrylic jewels are light, inexpensive, and quite acceptable, but glass jewels have more sparkle and durability. Real rhinestones reflect the full dazzling spectrum.

Found items that can be fashioned into decorations include necklaces for drapes and forehead pendants (two coin necklaces make back and front drapes for a belt), ankle bells (for tummy drapes and fringe), jeweled buttons and pins, chain belts, pendant earrings, silk flowers, shoe clips, and bits of beaded lace.

■ *For or contact information see: Dina—The Costume Goddess, page 201, and Kate Reed, page 195.*

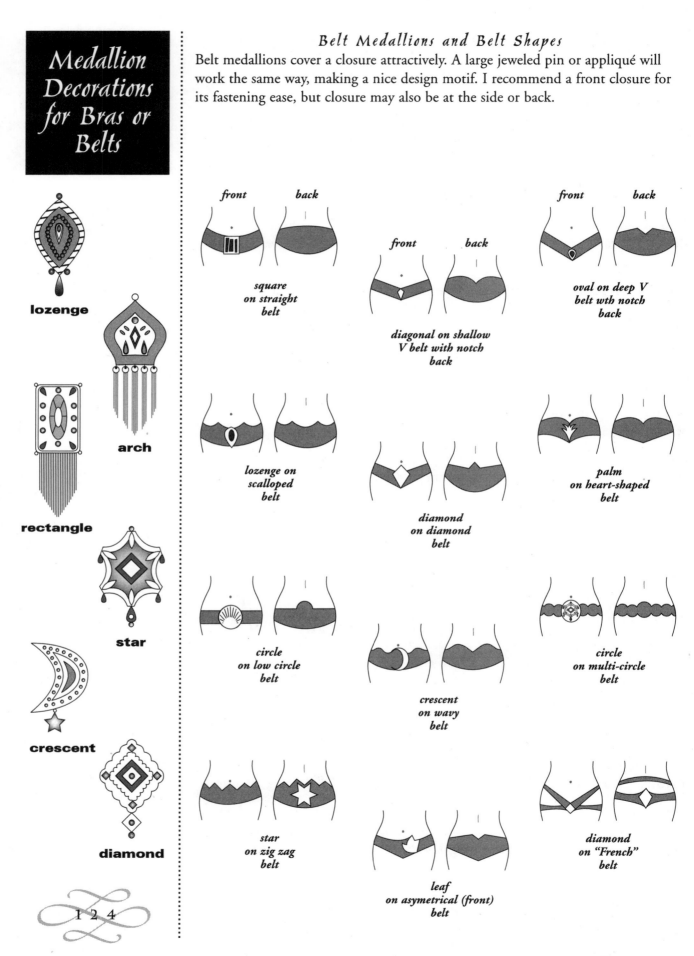

Belt Medallions and Belt Shapes

Belt medallions cover a closure attractively. A large jeweled pin or appliqué will work the same way, making a nice design motif. I recommend a front closure for its fastening ease, but closure may also be at the side or back.

Medallion Decorations for Bras or Belts

lozenge

arch

rectangle

star

crescent

diamond

1 2 4

front   *back*

square on straight belt

front   *back*

diagonal on shallow V belt with notch back

front   *back*

oval on deep V belt wth notch back

lozenge on scalloped belt

diamond on diamond belt

palm on heart-shaped belt

circle on low circle belt

crescent on wavy belt

circle on multi-circle belt

star on zig zag belt

leaf on asymetrical (front) belt

diamond on "French" belt

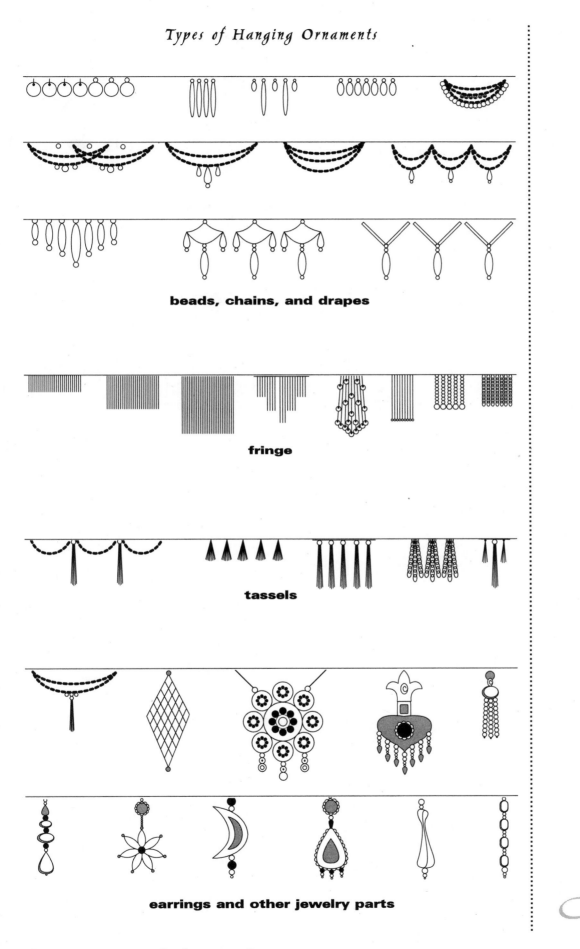

beads, chains, and drapes

fringe

tassels

earrings and other jewelry parts

Designing a Cabaret Costume

lettering

dagger

tiles

arches

domes

motifs

containers

Easy First Costume

Text and illustrations by Dina

EXPERIMENT UNTIL YOU ACHIEVE A PLEASING LOOK.

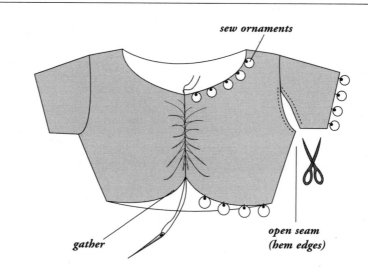

sew ornaments

gather

open seam (hem edges)

I f you have never made a costume before, and have some basic sewing skills, start with this easy ensemble. It is relatively simple, but pretty enough for performance.

Top is a purchased snug-fitting sleeveless or short-sleeved top, midriff length, in a dressy fabric such as stretch velvet or stretch lace. A leotard may be used, if you prefer to cover the midriff and abdomen.

The center front may be drawn up with a running stitch, as illustrated, to produce a gathered effect at the bust and a curved hem. Ornaments (coins, beads, tassels or paillettes) are sewn along the hem, sleeve and neckline, spaced an inch or two apart.

Important: To preserve stretch on the edge, sew ornaments individually, or connect them with zigzag stitches.

If the top has sleeves, the seam may be opened under the arm to allow freedom for overhead arm movements, and prevent top from riding up. (The open seam should be finished off nicely with a narrow hem, bias binding, or trim.) Strings of beads, fringe, or jewelry chains may be draped at lower edge as shown. Now you have an "Arabic" top.

Skirt is a handkerchief-style skirt. See "How to Make a Handkerchief Skirt", p. 133.

Harem pants are optional under the skirt. They are easy to make, but if that is too much of a challenge, even a loosely fitting, longish pair of metallic, silky or cotton gauze dress pants would work. Cut the purchased pants several inches lower at the waist to make "hip-huggers", and add a casing for elastic at waist and ankles. Add decorative trim to ankle and/or side seams if desired.

"Arabic" top

basic belt

handkerchief skirt

harem pants worn
under skirt

easy first costume

Try using a pair of
pull-on pants several
sizes too large for you,
if you can find some in
a suitable costume-like
fabric (not doubleknit!),
perhaps in a secondhand
store. (If you have a
prominent abdomen, the
pants may hang better
if worn backwards.)
After adjusting the leg
length and cutting the
waist lower, sew a casing
as described below at hip
and ankle. Adjust elastic
until you get a satisfactory
fit. Trim if desired.

Belt Alternatives

A purchased beaded hip scarf, or one that you've decorated with rows of coins, beads, or fringe may be substituted. Fastening the scarf with a decorative pin (through all layers) will prevent possible damage from knotting, and secure the scarf better.

If you have a purchased coin belt, it may be worn alone, over a hip scarf, or be tacked to your belt edge, but reinforce your trim belt underneath with stiff interfacing to support the weight of the coin belt. Line with felt.

Easy tip: *Two coin necklaces may be sewn on front and back of belt to make coin hip drapes.*

The Basic belt is a piece of sequin trim or any sturdy, ornate trim you like about two inches wide and darted at center front to produce a pointed shape. The hooked or snapped closure is on the side, or center back if you prefer. If trim needs more body, back trim with non-woven interfacing, sewn invisibly through all layers, and line with felt for a neat finish.

Tip: Quick-drying fabric glue keeps ends of trim from raveling. Let glue dry, then trim ends neatly, turn under and sew.

Costume jewels, pins, and other baubles can be sewn to the belt, following its pattern if it has one, with coins or tassels along the edge of the belt. One or more draped swags of chains and coins, fringe, or beaded strings on the front and back of the belt add a lot of action to the dance movements.

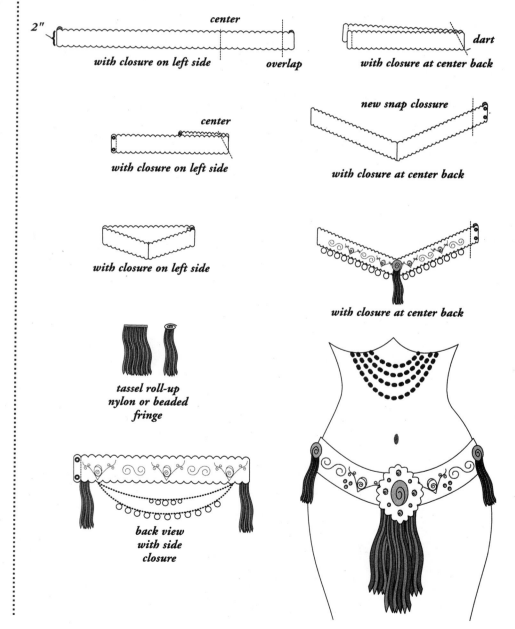

2"

with closure on left side   center   *overlap*

with closure at center back   dart

center
with closure on left side

new snap closure
with closure at center back

with closure on left side

with closure at center back

tassel roll-up nylon or beaded fringe

back view with side closure

1 3 0

Alternative Design

Classic harem pants are worn under a skirt, or worn alone with a bra or top. Typically they are full, measuring six to twelve inches one and a quarter to two times larger than measurement of hip and thigh. Each leg is a single piece with no side seam. Fullness is gathered into elastic casings at ankle and hip.

Often the front and back are exactly the same. My version has a slightly smaller front that dips an inch lower than the back. But if you have a prominent tummy, cut the front of pants to match the back.

Variations: The side may be slit to leave an opening, which may then be outlined with decorative trim, and the two halves connected with beaded strands or other decoration. Cuffs may be used instead of casing with ankle elastic.

Level: Easy. Once your pattern is perfected, the classic pants require only two seams and two casings.

I suggest starting with a generously sized pattern piece—the pants can always be taken in if you wish. Another possibility is to make a mock-up of the pants in cheap muslin, perfect the fit, then use this muslin as a pattern for your costume fabric.

harem pants with triangular scarves

Considerations: Slimmer, rather than fuller, pants flatter the more petite figure. Beware a balloony look! A taller or long-legged dancer can wear the fuller pants gracefully.

The pants keep the legs (and underwear!) covered during floorwork, spins, and outdoor breezes, as well as for those who prefer to cover legs for whatever reason. Even sheer pants appear more modest than bare legs.

Fabric suggestions: For the classic harem pants, soft fabrics such as chiffon, georgette, metallic sheers, metallic knits, lace, cut velvet on chiffon, lingerie satin, or blouse-weight silk. For a more folk-loric look, sheer to medium-weight soft cottons., and lightweight brocades. The finer and more sheer the fabric, the fuller the pants can be cut. Avoid stiff fabrics such as bridal satins, thick velvets and heavy brocades. The slim style pants can use a slightly more firm fabric, since they don't need to drape.

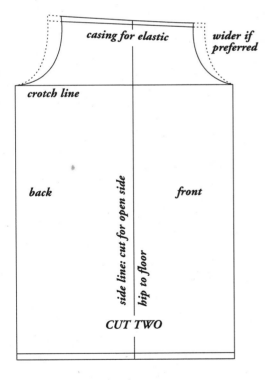

casing for elastic   *wider if preferred*

crotch line

back   *side line: cut for open side*   *hip to floor*   *front*

CUT TWO

optional side slit or seamless side

—

elastic at hip and ankle

—

front hip 1" lower than back

trim one half   *cut square in half*

sew

triangular scarves

Design Tip

For open side:
Cut pattern along side line. Sew a ¹/2" seam to connect front and back at top and bottom 2¹/2" from top edge to dot, and 2" from bottom edge to dot, leaving remainder of side open. Turn under this raw side edge and finish nicely, then cover this edge with trim or decoration. Make seams, casings and add elastic as in steps 6-9. Fasten the side front and back at top inch or two and bottom. Connect the remainder of slit every few inches as desired, a half-inch to two inches apart, with ribbon, trim, or strands of beads. Experiment until you achieve a pleasing look.

132

Yardage: Depending on size and height:
    1-1¹/4 yards of 60" wide fabric OR 2-2¹/2 yards of 52" or 45" wide fabric.

Materials: Measuring tape, pins, pattern paper, all-purpose thread, dressmaker scissors, ¹/2" elastic for ankles, one inch elastic for hip.

1. Tie a piece of ¹/2" elastic around abdomen snugly. Move this elastic higher or lower to decide where on your hip you would like to wear your belt, from navel down to barely legal. Measure this line, using the measuring tape. This is your **belt line.** See "Measurements", page 143.

Measure from this line to the floor. This is your **pants length,** or **skirt length,** for costume purposes (leaving allowing an inch or so for hem). Add two or three inches for blousing.

Measure the largest part of your hip, probably several inches lower. This is your **hip measurement.**

Measure the largest part of your thigh. This is your **thigh measurement.**

Sit on a chair and measure from the beltline to chair. Add one or two inches for roomier pants. This is your **crotch depth.**

2. Start with a rectangle of paper the measurement of your pants length, plus 2" for casing and blousing at ankle and 1¹/2" for casing at hip. For classic harem pants, add ten to thirty or more inches to hip and thigh measurements for the width—depending on how loose full you want your pants. For slim harem pants, add 6-10" to hip and thigh measurement.

Remember that the pattern piece is one-half of belt line at top, but a full leg.

3. Use diagram to adjust your rectangle. Note that the beltline is curved one inch lower at front. This is optional.

Remember that 1¹/2" is allowed at the top for casing for one-inch elastic, ³/4" at bottom of leg for ankle elastic, and ¹/2" for seam allowances.

4. Pin pattern to fabric and cut.

5. Sew center seams, then inseams.

6. Finish edges of casings nicely with ¹/4" turn under, overlock, or zigzag, then turn under 1¹/4" at top and ³/4" at ankles, and topstitch. Leave small opening for elastic.

7. Using a safety pin, thread elastic through casings, to body measurements, pin the elastic shut, then try on the pants. Pull elastic to adjust the size of the openings. Elastic should be snug but not uncomfortably tight. Pants should blouse slightly at ankle, but not enough to touch floor. If pants seem too long or beltline seems too high, pin out the extra length, pick out the stitching, trim edge this amount, then repeat.

8. When fit is correct, sew ends of elastic and sew shut opening in casing.

9. Add a line of trim up the side, if desired.

The handkerchief skirt is a simple narrow-hemmed square the width of the fabric (45 to 54 inches) with a circular hole in the middle slightly larger than hips. (If you are tall and/or plus-sized, you may need 60" fabric, or sew fabric together to make a 60" square).

The four corners fall in graceful points and can be decorated with paillettes and trim. For a layered effect and eight points, two squares can be overlapped as shown, and attached at the opening, or separate and worn together.

Use a soft sheer fabric such as chiffon, or a soft silky non-sheer. Avoid stiff or heavy fabrics, or fabric that is easily snagged, raveled, or creased.

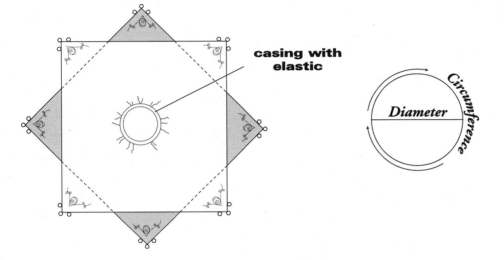

casing with elastic

You may remember from your basic geometry that the circumference of a circle is about 3.14 times the diameter. Thus a 12" diameter circle would produce a 39¹/2" opening—okay for a 37-38 inch hip; a 13" circle would work for a 38-39 inch hip; a 14" circle for a 40-42" hip; and so on. Enlarge or reduce the circular opening accordingly. Use a pencil on a string to draw the opening, or trace a large dinner plate. Leave a ¹/2" seam allowance. Staystitch the seamline and clip to stitching to allow the curved seam to lie flat.

The opening will be sewn to an elastic band to gather it to your beltline (hip area where the skirt and belt are worn). Make a casing for a 1" elastic with a matching 3¹/2" wide strip of costume fabric one inch longer than skirt opening. (This works much better than attempting to fold under the curved edge of the opening to make a casing.) Seam this strip to make a circular band. Press under ¹/2" on each long edge.

Enclose skirt edge inside folded casing to staystitching line and stitch close to folded edge, catching both folded edges in stitching, and leaving a 2" opening to insert elastic. Thread the elastic into the opening and through the casing, and adjust to fit beltline snugly, then fasten elastic and close opening. Decorate as desired.

■ *For contact information see: Dina—The Costume Goddess, page 201, and Kate Reed, page 195.*

Creating a Custom Belt

Text and illustrations by Dina

THE BASIC PATTERN CAN BE COPIED AND VARIATIONS MADE IN THE SHAPE.

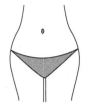

average

high curves

low curves

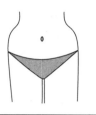

straight

The basic belt pattern is a curved shape that duplicates the shape of your hip. You may copy this pattern many times, changing the style by redrawing the outline, but the belt will fit the same way. (See "Belt Medallions and Belt Shapes", page 124.) The help of a friend is useful.

HOW TO MAKE A CUSTOM-FITTED BELT PATTERN

If your backside or hip has a "high" curve, it requires darts at top only. These will have to be duplicated in the belt construction. How can you tell in you have a "high" curve? If the darts in your paper pattern extend from top to bottom of pattern, they can be converted into a flat curve as above. If the darts are short, mark them, open them, and cut pattern flat. Duplicate the darts in belt interfacing and covering.

1. Begin with a strip of pattern paper about 10 inches wide and the measurement of your lower hip plus 3 inches. Plain paper will do.

2. Wrap the strip around hips so the lower edge fits snugly around largest part of hip, then tape or pin shut, lining up vertical edges. Don't attempt to angle the edges. The belt is now cylindrical like a tuna fish can, and will gap at the top. The closure may be front, back or side. Line up edge of paper where you prefer closure. Mark center front and center back lines. (Line them up with navel and spine!)

3. Make darts in belt to fit it to hip, beginning at sides. To dart, pinch out extra paper, crease flat, and tape or pin closed. No dart should be more than $1/2$" wide folded (an inch total). Make more, smaller darts rather than a few large ones. This way, the shaping is evenly distributed to make a smooth curve.

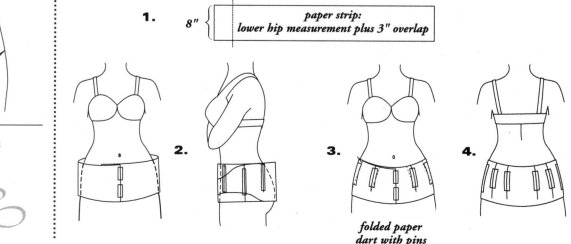

1. 8" { *paper strip:*
lower hip measurement plus 3" overlap

2.

3.

4.

*folded paper
dart with pins*

4. Continue darting at front and back, making darts symmetrical. The back will probably need two darts on each side, as shown.

5. Now the paper pattern fits, but covers too much of your body. Mark the shape you want with a pencil, using the belt shapes illustration as a guide. The bottom edge of belt should be cut an inch or two lower in the back so fringe dangles freely. Belt should curve up at sides, and dip slightly at front, as shown. The top edge should be cut slightly lower in the front; it's more flattering. A notch in center top back edge is more flattering than a horizontal line, as well, but the design can be fine-tuned later.

6. Cut along this marked line, then try on belt again, making sure you like the shape. Ask you friend to provide feedback.

7. When the shape pleases you, fold the belt pattern in half (at center back line, if closure is at front), making sure darts and edges are symmetrical. If not, make adjustments. One side will have a 3" overlap. Leave this to make future enlargements if necessary.

8. The finished belt pattern, folded and taped, can be placed on a new strip of paper and cut out again. The darts and seams have been eliminated, converted to a curved shape that conforms to your individual contours. A narrow hip figure will have a slightly curved pattern; a "hippy" figure will have a more curved pattern.

9. The basic pattern can be copied and variations made in the shape.

5.

6.

7.

8.

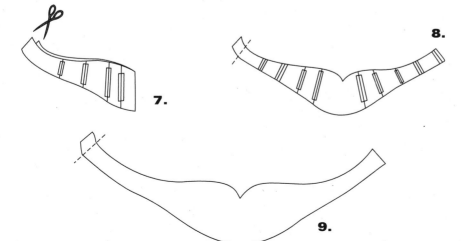

9.

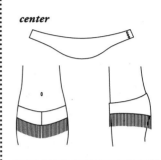

center

slim

center

average

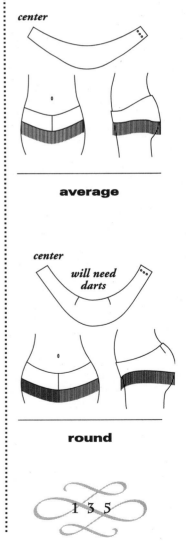

center

will need darts

round

Now that you have your belt pattern (See "How to Make a Custom-Fitted Belt Pattern", page 134), the next steps are constructing a stiff interfacing and covering it with suitable fabric. (See "Costume Fabric Choices", page 121.)

You will need approximately 1/2 yard of 45-54" fabric and lining. Of course, you could cut up a vintage dress or any garment with enough yardage. For lining, choose lightweight lining fabric or stretch lingerie tricot.

When your belt interfacing is covered with fabric and closure completed, it is ready to be decorated with fringe or coins, jewels and trim. (See "Cabaret Costume Decoration", page 122.)

Making Belt Interfacing

The belt stiffening must be strong enough to support the weight of heavy beaded fringe or coins.

1. Lay pattern on buckram, making sure that center back or center front line is on straight grain, pin and cut out. If opening is center front then place center back on the grain. If opening is center back or side, place center front on straight grain.

2. Cut out a second layer.

3. Cut out 2 layers of non-woven interfacing in any direction.

4. Cut out one layer of felt in any direction.

5. Pin the 2 layers of buckram together and sew by hand, curving them slightly as you sew.

> **Tip:** The purpose of curving as you sew is to keep multiple layers, from bunching and buckling when fitted around body, as they can do when sewn flat by machine or hand. A round wastebasket can help you do this.

Trim 1/8" off edges so that buckram will be slightly smaller than non-woven interfacing.

1.-4.

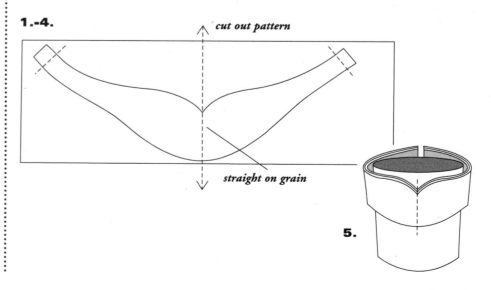

cut out pattern

straight on grain

5.

6. Pin the 2 layers of non-woven interfacing on each side of buckram, again curving the layers, and hand sew. No buckram should be visible at edges.

7. Pin felt on one side, again curving the interfacing, and hand sew.

8. If sewn properly, the interfacing should curve slightly and fit smoothly around body, and closure edges will be slightly uneven. Trim these edges even.

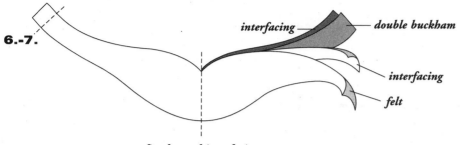

6.-7.

interfacing — double buckham

interfacing

felt

five-layered interfacing

Covering Interfacing with Costume Fabric

1. Mark centerline of folded fabric to determine straight grain.

2. Open fabric flat.

3. Lay pattern on fabric, making sure center back or center front is on straight grain of fabric.

4. Cut out fabric, leaving generous 3/4" margins around belt pattern.

5. Place fabric over interfacing, pinning smoothly around edges.

6. Turn over belt, pull fabric margins smoothly over interfacing edges and pin. (These raw edges will later be covered by lining.) Clip corners and curves, where necessary.

7. Hand sew fabric margins to felt layer. If trim or decoration will cover belt edges, you may sew through all layers, leaving tiny stitches on outside of belt. Check frequently to make sure that fabric lies smoothly over interfacing, with no rippling or bunching.

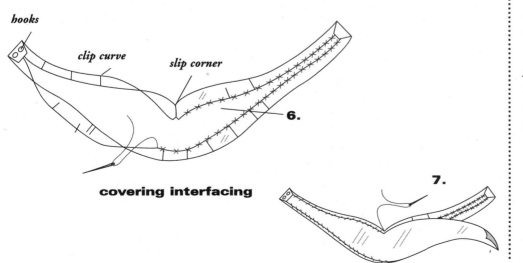

hooks

clip curve   slip corner

6.

covering interfacing

7.

For belt cover fabric, a medium-weight knit (Examples: sequined knit, metallic knit, stretch velvet) will be easier to fit over curves and angles than a woven fabric. (Examples: metallic brocade, non-stretch velvet). Choose a sturdy fabric that will be able to take a lot of wear. Avoid sheer or fragile fabrics.

A double layer of buckram (stiff woven interfacing), sandwiched between two layers of non-woven interfacing and a layer of felt. You will need about a yard of each. The purpose of the non-woven interfacing is to keep the sharp buckram edges from rubbing directly against fabric edges, which will eventually cause wear. The purpose of the felt is to provide an extra layer on the inside that will absorb sweat and is easy to pin through.

8. Try on belt and mark line where edges overlap. Sew skirt hooks and eyes on these lines. (This closure may be covered; see "How to Construct a Medallion", page 139.) Try on and check fit.

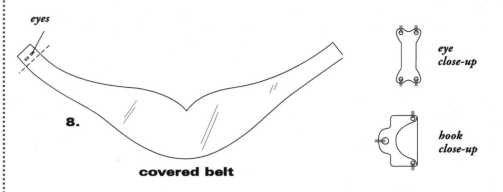

covered belt

eyes

eye close-up

hook close-up

9. Belt is now ready to be decorated. When you sew trim and decorations to belt, sew through all layers.

Tip: Fringe will swing more freely if it is sewn to top layer of belt, not underside, where it can bump against your body. Cover unattractive edge of fringe with trim, beads or coins.

10. When all decorating is complete, belt may be lined to cover all stitches. When the lining shows wear, it can be easily removed and replaced.

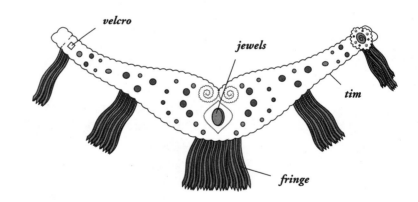

velcro

jewels

tim

fringe

Lining Belt

The purpose of the lining is to provide a layer to absorb sweat and finish the inside of the belt attractively. (When the lining shows considerable wear, it may be replaced.)

1. Cut out lining as for covering fabric.

2. Pin lining to inside of belt, tucking under seam allowances. Hand sew lining 1/8" from inside edge, clipping corners and curves where necessary.

You may wish to make a medallion to cover closure edges, allow for minor size adjustments in future, and create an attractive motif.

1. Design a shape for the medallion, slightly larger than belt closure edges. Cut a paper pattern.

2. Using the pattern, cut out a layer of interfacing, a layer of felt and a layer of fabric (the fabric with an extra seam allowance of $1/2$ inch).

3. Pin the fabric over interfacing and hand or machine sew around edges.

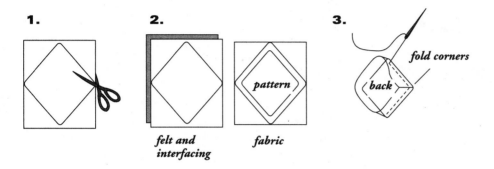

4. Pin felt on back of medallion to line it and sew all layers.

5. Your medallion is ready to decorate. (See "Medallion Decorations for Bras or Belts", page 122.)

6. When decoration is complete, sew medallion to right belt edge, lining up centers. Medallion will protrude over centerline.

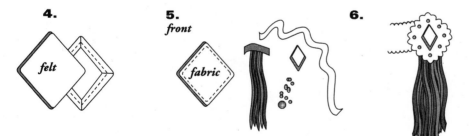

7. Use Velcro® to adhere medallion to under layer of belt.

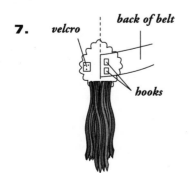

■ *For contact information see: Dina—The Costume Goddess, page 201, and Kate Reed, page 195.*

How to Cover a Cabaret Bra

Text and illustrations by Dina

Digital renderings by Kate Reed

Materials

- *3/8 to 1/2 yard (depending on size) of sturdy knit or woven costume fabric (see "Costume Fabric Choices", page 121.)*

- *1 1/2 to 3 yards of 1/2" to 1" grosgrain ribbon*

- *about 1/8 yard of heavy woven interfacing*

- *skirt hooks and eyes; bra pads (if applicable), and varying amounts of decorative trim*

START WITH A WELL-FITTING, WELL-MADE UNDERWIRE BRA.

A lingerie bra goes through some dramatic changes to transform it into a well-constructed costume piece. It must be covered with costume fabric, reinforced, and ornamented.

A ready-made velvet-covered or satin-covered bra such as those made by Victoria's Secret® is a suitable substitute for those who find the following instructions too much of a challenge, but it may still need reinforcement.

This method uses a two-piece cover for the bra cups, which is easier than attempting to cover cups using a single fabric piece.

Construction

1. Start with a well-fitting, well-made underwire bra. If you plan to add padding, you may start with a cup that is one size larger than you normally wear. If cups seem slightly too close together or too far apart, make a seam or extension in center front to correct this. The cups should be as sturdy as possible, to support the weight of any fringe or coins you add. If the cup seems soft, it needs to be lined with a stiff bra cup such as those made for swimsuits.

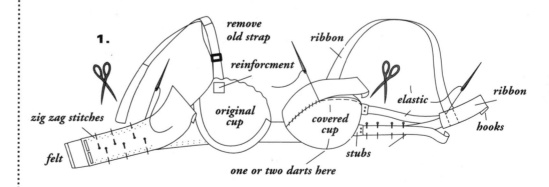

2. Add bra pads, if you wish more fullness and have allowed for a slightly larger cup size. The pads are usually placed at outside or bottom half of bra for push-together or push-up effect. Tack pads to bra lining. Do not overpad bra: this will cause it to stand away from the body.

3. Replace elastic shoulder straps with grosgrain ribbon or a double layer of heavy woven interfacing. The ribbon or interfacing will be covered with costume fabric or decorative trim. Try on bra, with ribbon safety-pinned in place front and back. Make sure the straps are tight enough to be supportive. (A second set of straps, or wider straps, may have to be added if finished bra is particularly heavy with decoration, or bust larger than average.) Mark attachment point on cup, midriff band, and strap with safety pins; add an inch to front of strap and an inch to back for underlap. Remove straps. Hand or machine sew a reinforcing 1" square of folded interfacing on backside of cup at attachment point, through all layers, to avoid future strap disasters. If converting to halter, mark center back of neck on straps; add an inch on each strap for overlap and a half-inch to turn under for extra strength.

4. Cover shoulder straps with costume fabric or matching trim, tucking under seam allowances neatly so no raw edge is visible underneath. Lining straps with felt will add comfort. If you are beading straps or attaching jewels, it's convenient to do it before attaching straps.

5. Sew straps to cups securely with heavy button thread, through all layers. If using halter straps, cut to proper length, and sew hooks to back neck. Leave straps unattached at back, until midriff band is completed.

6. Reinforce midriff band. If you prefer no stretch at all in your midriff band, like many large busted dancers, reinforce (or replace) entire band with ribbon at top and bottom edge. If you prefer a degree of stretch for comfort in the sides, reinforce band only across back for with ribbon to provide strength for closure and shoulder straps. Either way will make the strap tighter, so try on again and adjust fit. Leave two or more inches of overlap at center back.

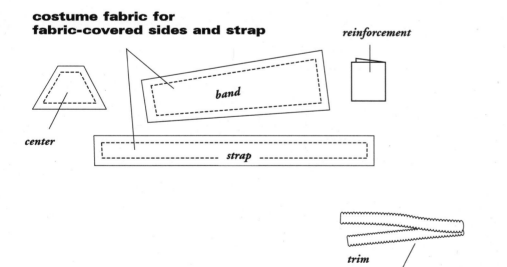

costume fabric for fabric-covered sides and strap

reinforcement

band

center

strap

trim

trim-covered sides and strap

7. Cover back and side strap. If you have opted for no stretch, use instructions below using straight instead of zigzag stitches, disregarding references to stretch. If you have opted for stretch in the sides, they can be covered several ways, as illustrated:

For a solid, covered strap, cut a piece of fabric the size of stretched strap, adding $1/2$" all around to turn under. Pin fabric to strap, stretching elastic as you do. Seam allowance should be tucked under between outer surface and elastic, so no messy edge shows on the inside of bra. (That way, you need not line bra to cover raw edges.) Handsew fabric to midriff strap with zigzag stitches, which expand and contract with elastic. (Straight stitches will prevent elastic from stretching and result in a too-tight fit.) The stitches should appear long and slanted on the inside of bra and small on outside. If sewn properly, the finished strap will appear slightly puckered on the side and will expand smoothly when worn.

For a double side strap, cut off original side strap, leaving elastic stubs. Replace lingerie elastic with $1/2$" or $3/4$" non-roll elastic, stitching it securely to stubs of lingerie elastic or bra cup, and to reinforced ribbon at center back. Try on and adjust fit. It should be snug, but not stretched to the max. Cover these elastic straps with elastic trim such as stretch sequins, or use decorative ribbon or other trim sewn on in zigzag stitch as described above. Overlap the trim where the straps converge and continue across back.

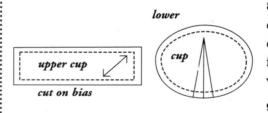

lower

cup

upper cup

cut on bias

8. Sew skirt hooks and eyes to back closure with heavy thread, after trying on again and adjusting fit. Do not leave flimsy lingerie hooks. Do not secure with safety pins!

9. Attach straps to midriff band with heavy thread, after adjusting fit once more.

10. Cover cups, starting with bottom half. Cut a generous oval bigger than bottom half of cup. Top edge of this piece should be slightly higher than apex of cup. Pin, folding and adjusting dart (or two darts, for large size cups) until piece fits smoothly over cup. Trim, leaving a $1/2$" seam allowance all around. Baste raw edge flat across top (this will be covered by upper piece). On the underwired edge, tuck under seam allowance (clipping, if necessary, to flatten it) and sew, using small stitches. Again, don't leave a messy raw edge on underside of cup, unless you plan to line it.

11. Cover top half with a rectangular strip cut on bias (if using woven fabric) or stretchy grain (if using a knit) to allow some give. The seam line should be at apex of cup. Pin to fit, trim and tuck seam allowances under, and sew as above. If sewn properly, the cup should be smoothly covered with unobtrusive seams and nearly invisible stitches.

12. Cover center of bra with costume fabric, if it will be visible under ornament. Your bra is ready to be decorated. (See Cabaret Costume Decoration", page 122)

■ *For contact information see: Dina—The Costume Goddess, page 201, and Kate Reed, page 195.*

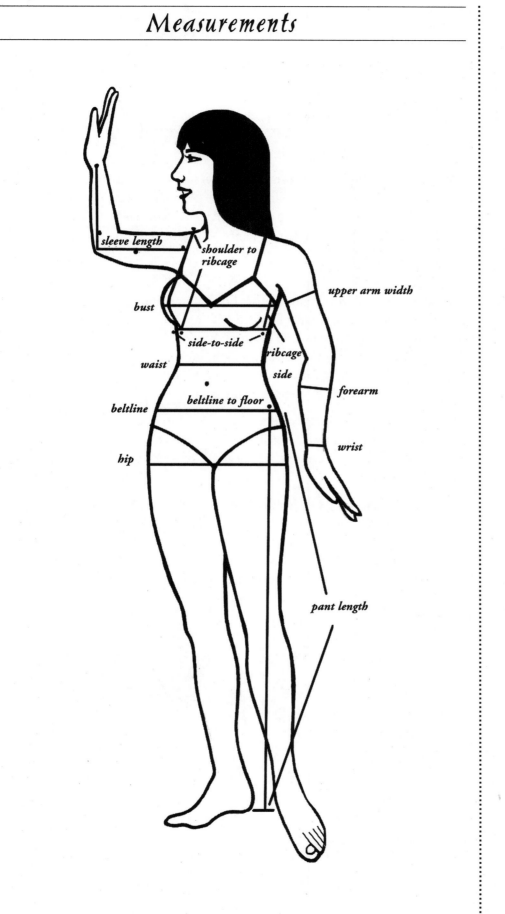

sleeve length

shoulder to ribcage

upper arm width

bust

side-to-side

ribcage side

waist

beltline to floor

forearm

beltline

wrist

hip

pant length

Creating a Custom Belt

- *Cut the choli back low, but still covering the bra back. Use two sets of ties or fasten choli in front instead of back.*

- *Wear a ghawazee vest instead of a choli, leaving the front of coin bra showing, while back is covered, but still pretty with keyhole cutout or tasseled decoration.*

- *Wear a supportive bra over instead of under the choli, but cover the bra with costume fabric and decoration. Change straps to halter—if it's not too uncomfortable. Change fastening at back to ties instead of hooks—again, if it's comfortable and functions as a bra should.*

- *Cover and decorate back of bra to appear like part of the costume.*

The Choli

Text and illustrations by Dina

SUITABLE FOR: ANY DANCE OCCASION EXCEPT FORMAL CABARET.

othing shows off a female back as exotically as a *choli!* The choli is a blouse of Indian origin that is a popular costume piece for American Tribal Style dance, worn with harem pants, full skirt, or both.

Typically, it is a midriff-length blouse, fitted snugly under the bust, with gathered or darted front bodice, usually fastened with a string across the nearly bare back. A second fastening string behind the neck keeps the blouse shoulders from slipping down. The fitted sleeves may be any length, but most often are just above or just below the elbow, leaving forearms uncovered to display jewelry. Sometimes a coin bra is worn over the choli, sometimes just an ornate necklace.

Variations include a front piece that covers the abdomen, different neckline shapes, and full or bell instead of fitted sleeves. Decorations may include ornate trim around neckline. Coins, tassels, or beads can be sewn to the bottom edge or draped on strings.

The underarm gusset, a wedge of material, is a feature of the choli that makes dancing easier. Adding extra material under the arm allows overhead movement without causing the short blouse to ride up. The top of shoulder looks like a normal set-in sleeve, and the gusset fabric, cut on the bias for flexibility, is hidden in folds of fabric when the arm is down.

A choli of stretchy fabric may have enough "give" to make gussets unnecessary, but one of woven fabric will need them, most likely, if it has fitted sleeves.

Another debated choli-related issue is underwear. The backless choli seems to preclude the wearing of a bra, since it would be visible to the audience. The large-busted dancer has to be concerned about the noticeable and possibly uncomfortable lack of support, while the small-busted dancer may feel she appears flat-chested.

HOW TO MAKE A CHOLI

Description: Midriff-length top with cut out back. Set-in fitted sleeves with gusset under arm. Bias binding around lower edge extending into ties. Bias binding around neck, extending into ties. Bias binding around back edge.

Variations: Stretchy choli is form fitting; non-stretch choli slightly roomier, with larger gussets. Gussets may be left out for open Arabic-style sleeve. Sleeve length may be long, 3/4, below elbow, above elbow, or short. Front neckline may be scooped, v-neck, high neck, or gathered. Center back may be completely cut out or scooped low to cover bra. Front stomach drape may be added.

Decorations, such as beads, coins, and tassels may be added in almost any fashion.

Level: Intermediate

Suitable for: Any dance occasion except formal cabaret.

Fabric suggestions: For the non-stretch choli: sturdy, medium-weight plain or decorative woven fabrics such as cotton, velveteen, or sand-washed (matte) rayon. Avoid stiff fabrics such as heavy brocade or satin, or light and fragile fabrics such as silk.

For the stretchy choli: stretch velvet, stretch velour, or cotton & lycra blends. Avoid shiny, obviously synthetic fabrics such as spandex—at least, if you want an ethnic look. Dark colors are popular because they make a nice backdrop for jewelry. (See "Fabric Choices", page 121).

Directions are for non-stretch fabric. Stretch fabric allows for a closer fit, so seams should be adjusted on the body. For both types, I recommend the use of a mock-up garment in a cheap fabric to perfect fit and choose style variations before cutting costume fabric.

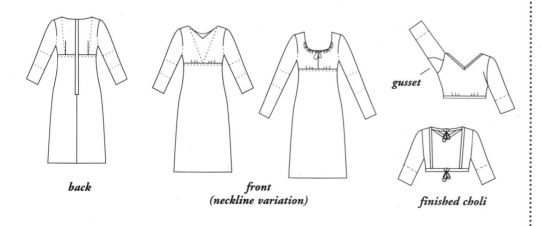

back

front
(neckline variation)

gusset

finished choli

Choli Notes

Shortcut: *Use ready-made bias binding in cotton, velveteen or satin if available, and if it looks good with your costume fabric.*

Economize: *If you're really short on fabric, you may make the long ribcage binding out of fabric cut on the straight grain instead of the bias.*

Are gussets much of a challenge? *Get around that by using fuller sleeves, ; or leaving the lower armhole open in Arabic style, and finishing edges neatly, perhaps outlined with metallic trim.*

A last choli-related thought: *Make sure the choli is not too short— at least an inch below your natural breast line. Fallout is embarrassing, to say the least.*

The Choli

Materials

- *Dressmaking tools (See "Making Costume Items with Seams", page 119.)*

- *1 to 1 1/2 yards of 45-60" fabric, depending on pattern size, sleeve length, and seaming of bias strips. (More yardage means less piecing.)*

- *Butterick® pattern #6333 (check envelope for size) or any dress pattern with empire waist.*

I've chosen Butterick® pattern #6333, a high-waisted dress with neckline variations. Using only the bodice pattern pieces, I added gussets, and made alterations to the pattern pieces as described below. My simplified construction technique eliminates the use of facings and interfacing. Instead, the garment edges are finished using bias binding.

Any pattern with a seam below the bust could be altered similarly.

Measuring and Altering

1. Take these measurements: front bust, ribcage, shoulder to ribcage, upper arm, forearm, shoulder to sleeve hemline (after deciding on sleeve length.) See illustration "Measurements", page 143. If you plan to wear no bra under choli, then do not wear one to measure.

2. Compare measurements to pattern. I found that after choosing a pattern size according to the body measurements on envelope, the size of the garment was roomier than I wanted. That's okay—you can always reduce a slightly too large pattern.

3. Add an inch to shoulder-to-ribcage measurement. The front pattern piece between shoulder seam and lower edge should be this measurement. (Edges of bodice (neckline, bottom, back) won't need a seam allowance because they will be enclosed in the bias binding instead of seamed or hemmed.) If you're tall, large-busted or low-busted, you'll have to add to the pattern length. If you are tall, but not large-busted, lengthen back pieces the same amount.

4. Add an inch to front bust measurement. This should be the width of front bodice, between side seams. Again, if you are large-busted, you may need to add width at center bodice by slashing pattern vertically.

5. Use shoulder to sleeve hem measurement to shorten sleeve pattern, allowing an inch or so for hem.

6. Add about three inches to upper arm measurement. This should be the width of the sleeve just below the armhole seam. Measure armhole seam lines of sleeve and bodice with tape—they should still match. If not, alter the sleeve. Add one inch to your forearm measurement (for 3/4 sleeve). This should be the width of sleeve at lower arm.

7. Add 22" to ribcage measurement. This is the length of midriff bias strip (which extends into tie ends). Measure front neckline of pattern and add 22". This is the length of neckline bias strip (which extends into tie ends). Measure the back edges from top to bottom. This is the length of each back bias strip.

8. Cut the pattern back vertically at dart line. This eliminates center back of garment.

Note: Yes, this is a lot of measuring! It's to achieve that custom-fitted look. The choli is not "one size fits all". All these measurements are my preferences. Adjust the finished prototype to your own.

To subtract from the pattern piece, make a fold in it (rather than cutting). To add to the piece, use pattern paper taped or pinned to the pattern piece.

Cutting

Arrange the altered pattern pieces on folded fabric as closely together as possible. Cut out pattern pieces.

Note: Velvets and all napped fabrics must be cut with pattern pieces facing in the same direction. The smoother nap running UP will appear as a darker, less-shiny tone. Make the bias strips full length if possible, but shorter pieces may be seamed neatly to make a longer strip.

Cutting Tip

Cutting the sleeve on the bias (for woven fabric) will add a degree of stretch that may make the gusset unnecessary. Cutting the sleeve on the crosswise stretchy grain will do the same for knits.

Choli Pattern Pieces

front variations

1/2 armhole

gusset

back slice

1/2" wide

sleeve

bias tape close-up

Construction

1. Staystitch all edges (³/₄" from edge) to prevent stretching.

2. Make two parallel rows of long stitches across lower edges of front and pull up bobbin threads to form gathers. Finished measurement should equal one half of ribcage.

3. Fold and press the two back bias strips as illustrated: fold and press long edges under ¹/₄", then fold strip in half, and press so that one half is slightly wider. The smaller side is the top side (to be topstitched), and the wider underside will be caught in topstitching. The finished strip should measure ³/₈" to ¹/₂" wide.

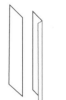

fold and press bias

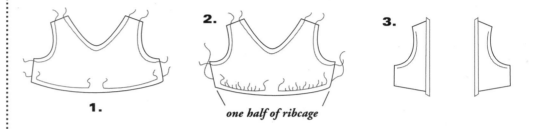

1.   **2.**   **3.**

one half of ribcage

Pin folded bias strip over and under center back edges of choli, enclosing raw edge. (Short edges of bias will be covered in following steps.) Baste close to the edge of seam binding, through all layers, making sure the wider under layer of bias is stitched through. Machine stitch. Press.

4. Right sides together, pin and sew shoulder seams.

5. Right sides together, pin side seams. If front piece (which you may have lengthened) is longer than back, ease in fullness with gathering stitches as with the bust gathers above. If front is an inch or more longer than back, try making a dart at side instead. Pin the dart in first to make sure it is positioned properly.

Note: The original pattern did not include a side bust dart or gathers, but if you're average to large busted, it will fit better with one.

6. Right sides together, stitch front to back at side seams.

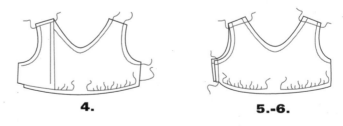

4.   **5.-6.**

7. Safety-pin some ribbons to lower edge and neck edge to simulate finished ties. Try on choli. Seamline of armhole (allow for ⁵/₈" seam allowance) should be at top of shoulder, not dropping off edge. I found the shoulder seam of this pattern to be very wide, so trim it if necessary. Check that the front length is correct, covering the bust plus an inch, and the gathers are symmetrical.

8. Make a binding from the long midriff bias strip as above. Mark center. Pin bias binding over the choli lower edge, matching centers. The measurement between the two side seams is one half of ribcage. Baste.

9. Machine stitch the whole tie close to edge. Press.

10. Try on, adjusting shape of neckline lower if desired. Trim to desired shape. Staystitch $1/4$" from edge.

11. Fold and press neckline bias binding as above. Mark center. Pin over neckline front, matching centers, and covering raw edges of back bias binding, then letting tie ends extend. Baste.

For curved neckline: press in the curve, stretching edges slightly.

For V-neckline or square neckline: clip V or square angle of bodice neckline to stitching, so that it will open flat. Pin and baste binding on angle as if on a straight edge. Machine stitch. Then make tiny dart at center of bias binding to create a sharp angle.

enter front dart in binding

8.-9.   **10.-11.**

12. Try on, fastening ties and checking fit before sewing on sleeves.

13. Sew sleeve seam, press.

14. Measure halfway around front armhole and back armhole and mark with chalk or thread. Sleeve will be set into choli armhole only at top half of armhole between these marks.

15. Pin sleeve into armhole between marks. Baste, if necessary. Machine stitch, backstitching at marks.

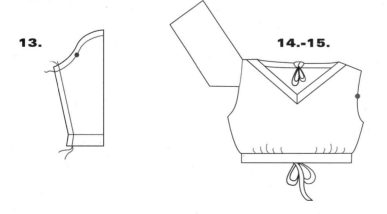

13.   **14.-15.**

16. Try on choli. Make sure top of shoulder seam is at natural shoulder line. Lift arm overhead. The open underarm edges widen considerably to allow this movement. If you are leaving armhole open, finish edges with neat narrow hem or bias binding.

The Choli

Decoration Options

- *Trim on sleeve, neckline, and lower edge*

- *Appliqués sewn on bodice*

- *Draped chains with coins along lower edge*

- *Tassels or ethnic beads*

- *Mirrored embroidery*

- *Coin bra*

- *Necklaces and multiple bracelets (See "Costume Decoration", page 122.)*

17. For gussets: Measure the distance of open underarm, with arm overhead.

The gusset will provide this much extra material. Five inches wide was sufficient for me. The gusset is shaped like a football as illustrated. Each curved edge measures one half of armhole seam, plus ¹/2" seam allowance all around. It is cut on the bias for flexibility (important!)

18. Pin one edge of gusset to lower bodice armhole, clipping armhole curve if necessary. Baste if necessary, and machine stitch, breaking and backstitching at marks, making sure seams meet exactly, leaving seam allowances free.

19. Pin remaining edge of gusset to lower sleeve armhole. Baste and stitch as above. If stitched correctly, the three seams will begin and end at the same mark, leaving seam allowances inside free, and all seams will be smooth and unpuckered.

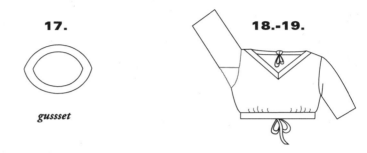

17.

gussset

18.-19.

20. Pin sleeve hemline to desired length. Press. Hand or machine stitch.

21. Trim and knot ends of ties, or leave unfinished.

Wearing Tip: Fasten neck ties so shoulder seam is centered properly, then leave neck ties fastened, to save time when dressing, and slip head through opening.

■ *For contact information see: Dina—The Costume Goddess, page 201, and Kate Reed, page 195.*

Business

Chasing Butterflies
How to Survive Stage Fright

by Aziza Sa'id

FORTUNATELY, BEING ON STAGE IS NOT USUALLY A LIFE-THREATENING EXPERIENCE.

Anyone who has ever been in front of a group has felt it: sweaty palms, racing pulse, light-headedness, that distracted feeling. No, it's not love. It's stage fright. People are more afraid of being on stage than anything else. It is believed that the fear of speaking or performing in front of a group is even more prevalent than the fear of death! Even career performers feel it; Frank Sinatra said he still had stage fright before every show.

Despite the fact that stage fright is natural there are some things you can do to manage it. Let's look a little bit at what stage fright really is.

Different people have different physical and mental responses to the fear of performing in front of a group. Some people react with clammy hands, pounding pulses, and rapid, shallow breathing. Others get butterflies or an upset stomach. Some people shake, get hiccups or feel distracted and anxious. Many people's minds go "blank" or run an endless chatter of what-might-go-wrongs and what-will-people-thinks.

So what causes all this upset? The physical responses are caused by a chemical reaction in the body. When the brain senses danger, either real or imagined, it prepares for action. Adrenaline dumps into the bloodstream, causing the fight-or-flight response. The result is a whole symphony of symptoms and feelings. Sweating, butterflies, shallow breathing and rapid pulse are a part of that survival response.

Interestingly enough, the physical response to excitement is exactly the same. The only difference between fear and excitement is the way you interpret your reaction. When your pulse jumps because a car in front of you nearly causes an accident, we call it fear. When it jumps because you are reunited with a dear friend after a long absence, we call it excitement.

Fortunately, being on stage is not usually a life-threatening experience. Unfortunately, the physical response can interfere with your ability to execute your performance as planned. Your mental response also affects your performance. If you expect to be afraid and nervous, then that's how you'll feel. If you expect to be excited, then you will feel excited.

How you expect to feel is, in part, determined by how you have felt about similar situations in the past. If you have had bad experiences on stage, you are more likely to be afraid than if all your experiences have been good. Often, people are afraid because they don't know what to expect. Human beings instinctively fear the unknown. Some mental preparation can help in reducing the amount of stage fright you feel.

So what, exactly, can you do about it? I've used the following fear management techniques for years. They take practice, but they're easy to do and I've had great success using them when preparing for shows, competitions and auditions.

GETTING READY

Know your material and give yourself as much time to practice as you can. If you are using choreography, rehearse until you can do it end to end without thinking. Knowing your performance thoroughly makes you less likely to go "blank" on stage. If you are not using choreography, practice and listen to your music until you know every phrase by heart.

Practice in your costume. Knowing how your costume will behave when you dance can make you feel more secure about your performance. Make sure you take care of any mending in advance and check your hooks to be sure they're in good shape and securely sewn on. There will be enough stage fright without last minute costume failures to worry about.

Write out a list of all the things you need to take with you to the show. Put together a "spares" kit with extra safety pins, earring backs, hooks, and a sewing kit. Pack everything the day before the show, then double check the list before you head out for the performance, especially if your show is far from home! Knowing that you will have everything you need can quiet a lot of nagging anxieties.

Be aware of your thoughts and words. Listen carefully to what you say to yourself and others about how your performance will go. If you spend a lot of time thinking, "I'm always so nervous before I go on stage. What if I forget my routine?" then you will be nervous when it comes time to dance and you might go "blank" on stage. If you tell people, "I never do as well on stage as I do when I'm practicing", then that is how it will probably happen. On the other hand, you can program in a more positive result by saying, "I still get nervous, but with each performance I feel more confident," or "I've worked really hard on preparing this routine and I'm going to give it my best tonight!" Your words have the power to create, be mindful of what you say.

Fear of failing is the flip side of the desire to do well. After all, if you didn't care about giving a good performance, you wouldn't be afraid of doing poorly. Give yourself credit for the work that you've put into the performance and give yourself some room to make mistakes. Many of us are too critical of ourselves. Be as patient and encouraging with yourself as you would be with someone else. Remember, dancing is supposed to be fun!

Give Yourself a Purpose

My goal for this show is:

☑ *to have fun and remember to smile.*

☑ *to reach out to the audience.*

☑ *to keep my posture at its best.*

☑ *to do the best show I'm capable of doing.*

HANDLING THE MENTAL RESPONSE

Writing your purpose on paper will help make it even more effective. Tape it to your make-up mirror where you'll see it as you are getting ready. Having a goal in mind helps you stay focused and calm.

Visit the location of the show in advance if possible. Dancing in an unfamiliar environment can make you feel tense and anxious. If you can see the area in advance, walk around the stage and checkout the changing room. You'll be a lot more comfortable at show time. If you can, arrange a time to practice on the stage using the lights and sound system that will be used during the show. Knowing what the stage looks like will also help you visualize.

Visualize yourself getting ready for the show, feeling prepared and calm. Notice that even though you are excited about performing, your mind is clear and you are happy and relaxed. Visualize yourself dancing. Close your eyes and "watch" yourself going through your entire routine flawlessly. See it as if you were a member of the audience watching you dance. Notice how relaxed and confident you look. Visualize it again as it will look from your viewpoint while you are dancing. Use your imagination to make everything as vivid as possible. Be sure to use all of your senses. See the stage, the seating, the curtains, and the audience. Hear the music, your zils, and the applause. Feel the floor under your feet, the weight and movement of your costume, the heat of the overhead lights on your face. Smell the perfume you'll be wearing and the dusty, woody smell of the stage. See yourself after the performance enjoying the applause and feeling pleased with how you did. If you are dancing in a competition or auditioning, see yourself winning. The more clearly you can conjure up these images and feelings, the better your performance will be. Use this technique as often as you can; the more you use it, the clearer and easier it gets.

Plan for the unexpected. It can be unsettling when things change at the last minute, but sometimes it happens. For instance, you are scheduled to dance third when suddenly you are asked to dance first! You scurry off to get in costume with no time to prepare. Decide in advance, and tell yourself, that you can calmly handle anything that comes up. That way, no matter what happens, you'll be able to give your best performance.

HANDLING THE PHYSICAL RESPONSE

What happens when stage fright gets the better of you and you find yourself hyperventilating backstage in a cold sweat? Here are some things you can do to manage the physical symptoms of fear before you go on stage.

Remember to breathe. (Does that sound silly? How can you forget to breathe? It happens!) Spend a few moments noticing how you are breathing. Are you holding your breath? Is your breathing slow and deep or quick and shallow? Rapid breathing can cause you to hyperventilate, making you feel light-headed and dizzy. Focus on and regulate your breathing: inhale slowly and deeply and fill your lungs completely, then exhale the same way. Using the abdominal muscles and diaphragm has a particularly calming effect. Inhale, exhale and hold your breath out for an eight-count before taking your next breath. If you are light-headed, breathing into a paper bag may help.

Burn up the adrenaline. A little adrenaline is a good thing, but too much of it can make you feel overwhelmed, anxious and queasy. You can burn off some of the excess by using the large muscles in your legs—they're especially good at eating up adrenaline. Running hard in place or a quick sprint really helps reduce the excess, but in case you don't want to dash around the block in your beaded costume, there are some other things you can do: Try clenching the big muscles in your legs and buttocks as tight as you can, then holding them clenched until they begin to shake. Release the muscles and then clench them again. Three or four minutes of clenching can burn off quite a bit of adrenaline and will help you feel calmer and more in control.

Notice which muscles are tight and shake or stretch them gently to get them to relax. The shoulders, neck, back and jaw are most common, but people can get tense just about anywhere. Do an inventory of your body. Start at your head and move down to your toes, relaxing each set of muscles as you go. Is your jaw tight? Your neck? Are your shoulders hunched up around your ears? Are your fists clenched? How about your stomach muscles? Your legs? Are you standing with your knees locked? Go through your regular dance warm-up routine. Walking around can help you loosen up and helps keep you warmed up too.

Check in with your stomach. Some people feel best if they eat something light about an hour before show time. Others do better if they haven't eaten anything for several hours. Experiment and let your body tell you what works best. Be sure to drink enough fluids early on the day of the show so you don't get dehydrated, even if you aren't eating. A dehydrated body runs out of energy quickly.

Meditate or use self-hypnosis to calm down and relax if you know how. If not, you can just sit in a quiet place for ten or fifteen minutes. Focus on breathing slowly, relaxing your muscles, and making your brain as still and quiet as you can.

MAKING STAGE FRIGHT WORK FOR YOU

Remember that stage fright is natural. Most of us start out by wanting to "get rid" of our stage fright, but it's a normal part of performing and can be used to your advantage. Adrenaline prepares you for the demands of a fight-or-flight situation by providing a burst of energy, increased alertness and improved reaction time. Those same changes can help you create a better performance.

Use the extra energy to boost your performance level. Use the increased alertness to pay attention to your music, your choreography, and your audience. The altered mental state that adrenaline creates can be used to create a transcendent performance.

Your stage fright may never disappear completely, but once you learn to manage it, stage fright can become a valuable part of your performance skills. Use the excitement to your advantage. As with other aspects of your dancing, the more experience you have with it, the more familiar and less frightening it will be.

■ *For contact information see: Aziza Sa'id, page 194.*

From Student To Pro

By Shira

BEING A "PROFESSIONAL DANCER" REQUIRES MORE THAN JUST DANCING WELL.

Most eager up-and-coming dancers don't realize that dancing professionally is not for everybody. Too many people believe that dancing for restaurants, nightclubs, bellygrams, and other paid settings is the ultimate fulfillment of a dancer's growth. For a small minority of dancers, it is. Many teachers encourage their students to aspire to professional work because that is the direction they took with their own lives. However, up-and-coming dancers need to think carefully about whether that path is right for them.

A dance job can take precious evening and weekend family time away from spouse and children, place the dancer among strangers in potentially dangerous situations, and divert money into a constant drain of manicurist appointments and new costumes. Some club owners treat dancers like dirt. Dancers with day jobs may find that their business travel or long hours prevent them from being able to make a commitment to a regular evening dance job.

SHIRA

At first dancing professionally seems glamorous, but over time it becomes a job like any other. Some people get so caught up in competing for dance jobs, fending off indecent proposals from club owners, embroiling themselves in politics with other dancers, and fighting with club owners over pay that they lose sight of the joy they once derived from dancing. Some marriages have been strained when the spouse has objected to his partner spending every evening away from home.

Before taking the plunge into becoming a pro, each dancer should carefully examine her own situation—both her personal situation and the employment opportunities available in her community — and honestly determine whether it's the right move for her.

156

Once a decision has been made to shoot for the stars, the dancer needs to honestly assess whether she is truly ready to start the professional circuit. It takes more than knowing a few moves and performing in a recital or two to turn a dance student into a professional performer. The following checklist should help a student determine whether it's time to join the pros:

YOUR CHECKLIST

☐ *Your teacher has said that your dance skills are good enough to look at turning professional.*

☐ *You have performed in a variety of student recitals, doing a combination of troupe and solo performances, and tried your hand at both choreographed and improvised dances.*

☐ *You can honestly identify which areas are your strong points and which ones are your weaker areas. If you do not think you have any weak areas, you are probably not ready to call yourself a professional, because you are not able to look at yourself objectively.*

☐ *You have built a collection of music that puts you into the dancing mood, and you own the necessary sound equipment to assemble good-quality tapes for use in your shows.*

☐ *You own at least one professional-quality costume, preferably more.*

☐ *You have attended a wide variety of professional-level performances by your teacher and other dancers, and paid attention to how each of these artists interacts with the audience while dancing. You have also noticed the difference between the type of dancing done for a bellygram, a performance at an ethnic wedding reception, and a restaurant.*

WHERE TO START

Dancing professionally is a business. The first mistake many newcomers make is failing to recognize that. Dancers need to consider income taxes, marketing, record keeping, job-hunting, managing customer relationships, and other business-related issues right from the beginning.

It is important to understand how laws relate to teaching and performing professionally. Dancers need to remember to report income, keep careful records of expenses, and learn which expenses are tax-deductible. They should look at whether sales taxes apply in their community and whether they need any kind of business license. If they are planning to refurbish a room in their homes to be a dance studio, they may want to consider whether zoning laws in their neighborhood could cause problems for them. It may be a good idea to invest in liability insurance, in case a student claims that she was injured by taking classes.

In a perfect world, a dancer's teacher will help her launch her performing career. Some teachers provide advice on how to get started as a professional, invite promising students to accompany them on paid gigs, set up booking agencies and arrange jobs for their talented students, and otherwise help students launch their own careers. However, the majority do not. A student who is committed to turning dance into a serious profession may have to shop around until she finds a teacher who can give her this kind of help. Most students will probably need to figure it all out on their own.

MARKETING

Most dancers love to promote themselves. In gearing up to advertise her services, a dancer should prepare as follows:

Once the dancer has assembled the following marketing materials, she's ready to pound the pavement and promote herself. She can contact each of the local businesses to inquire about job opportunities and offer to audition. She might contact local musicians who play Middle Eastern music to see whether they would consider bringing her in when their own employers ask them to bring a dancer.

Free shows for community festivals, charitable fund-raisers, hospitals, and other worthy causes may be a good way to be seen. At each event, the dancer should take a supply of flyers and business cards to distribute. A dancer needs to be careful when booking free shows—some places such as nursing homes have an entertainment budget and may be willing to pay $30-$50 for performers. A dancer who offers herself for free without first checking whether there is an opportunity to get paid is undercutting both herself and other dancers in the community.

158

PROMOTING YOURSELF

☐ *Create a resumé that highlights your credentials as a teacher or performer.*

☐ *Write a brief one or two paragraph biography that prospective employers can use to advertise performances.*

☐ *Set up a session with a professional photographer, ideally one with experience in taking photographs for other dancers or model portfolios. Have several prints made in various sizes. The 4" x 5"size is well suited to enclosing with a résumé when making initial contact with a prospective employer. This is also a good size for flyers, press releases, and other promotional activity. It is useful to have some 8" x 10" prints made for employers to display when promoting upcoming shows.*

☐ *Print up a supply of business cards. The best ones include a photograph of the dancer in costume, but if finances are tight, a plainer card with artwork will do. Cards should include the name, telephone number, email address and website if applicable, and indication your city or area. It is probably best not to include the home address.*

☐ *Print a supply of flyers.*

☐ *Create a music cassette or CD for auditions. This should be about 10-12 minutes long, and feature favorite songs. The sound quality should be crystal-clear.*

☐ *Research the local employment opportunities. Who are the local singing telegram and balloon bouquet agencies? What about entertainment agencies? Are there any local restaurants that feature Middle Eastern cuisine? Are there coffee shops or lounges that feature live entertainment? Are there local dance clubs that might hire a dancer to hold customer attention while the band is on break?*

About Money

A dancer should always insist on being paid the going rate in her community when applying for a dance job. Offering to dance for less than what other dancers are being paid is a Very Bad Thing. It is unethical, and a dancer who does it is implicitly suggesting that she is not worth as much as the other dancers. It causes employers to see her as someone who has no self-respect, and therefore they will not treat her with respect. People often assume that whatever they paid for something must be an indication of its value.

If a dancer is not skilled enough to win a job on the merits of her dancing ability, then she probably shouldn't be performing professionally.

159

TYPES OF SHOWS

Although there is endless variety in the types of shows that a dancer might do, some of the more common ones include:

The Festival

This is usually an informal outdoor community event. Dancers appear on stages flanked by vendors selling food, handcrafts, and other wares. Audience members come and go during the performance. Although these events offer a setting where dancers who are launching professional careers can display their skill and distribute flyers, more established pros avoid them because there is rarely any pay.

The Bellygram

This was originally inspired by the notion of singing telegrams, which are cheerful "greetings", sent to honor a birthday or other special occasion. A bellygram is typically 10-12 minutes long, and usually involves a "guest of honor" who is the center of attention. Such performances are generally a mixture of dancing and comedy. People who employ dancers for bellygrams generally want the dancer to focus on "entertainment" rather than "artistry".

Most bellygram messengers try to incorporate "photo opportunities" into the show. They'll try to get the host or the guest of honor to dance with them. They might place a turban on his head, or wrap their veil around him. They'll encourage children in the audience to get up and dance. At the end, they might pose for pictures with partygoers.

Some dancers incorporate a gimmick into their bellygrams. They might show up wearing a "bag lady" costume over their dance costume, and then as the show gets underway peel off the outer layer to expose the glamorous sequins underneath. Or, they might incorporate sleight-of-hand magic tricks into their act. In general, such gimmicks should be used only when requested by the employer at the time of the booking.

The best bellygram messengers focus on making happy memories. They realize that what their audiences want to remember in five years is not a sublime artistic moment, but rather the look of surprise on Uncle Ned's face.

The Restaurant or Nightclub

The audience is seated at a series of tables, eating and drinking during the performance. During the performance, waiters continue to move about the tables, serving people. During the 1950s and early 1960s, the nightclub environment was the setting that brought Oriental dance to the attention of the American public and made it a lasting part of American culture.

Although most dancers think of Middle Eastern restaurants as being good prospective employers, there is no need to limit the options. Any restaurant that offers live entertainment may be a candidate for a dance job. Other possibilities could include the lounges of local hotels, bars that feature live dance bands, etc.

160

Private Parties

These differ from bellygrams in that the employer wants a full nightclub-length performance with emphasis on dancing rather than comedy, but in a private setting. Such parties might be corporate events or family occasions such as weddings. These shows usually pay the best rates, but it is harder to break into the private party circuit. Often, performing in the bellygram and restaurant settings offers a dancer the chance to be seen by someone who is planning to hire a dancer for a private party.

The Theater

In a formal theatrical production, the audience is usually hushed and focused on the show. People are usually not eating or drinking in their seats, and no one moves around until intermission. Theatrical shows are generally aimed at either educational or artistic goals. An educational show might involve a portrayal of a historical dance form with ethnically correct music and costuming. An artistic show might involve telling a story, portraying a particular character, acting out an emotion, or celebrating a spiritual theme.

BOOKING SHOWS

"You only get one chance to make a first impression." In most cases, a dancer's first contact with a prospective employer is either a face-to-face meeting or a telephone conversation. If she can present herself as a well-organized, competent professional in that first contact, she will give herself an edge over other candidates.

Smart dancers keep a notepad, pencil, map, and appointment calendar next to the telephone. If just starting out, they may also add a checklist of questions to ask. The dancer who says, "Wait a minute, let me find a pen...no, there's not one here, let me look somewhere else...." gives the impression that she doesn't get this type of call often.

Most dancers do not quote a fee until they know how long the desired show would be, how far they will need to drive to get there, what kind of occasion it will be, and whether there are any special requirements that would require extra preparation or special work.

If applying in person for a dance job, a dancer should style her hair nicely, put on a bit of make-up and wear something a bit dressy. People are not likely to hire someone who looks like a slob for a job where she is expected to project a glamorous image. If the dancer does not care enough to look great for the job interview, then the employer has good reason to wonder whether she will care enough to show up on time, wear professional-quality costumes, work effectively with the band, etc.

161

GOOD QUESTIONS TO ASK WHEN BOOKING A JOB

☐ *What is your name and telephone number?*

☐ *What is your mailing address? (For building a mailing list.)*

☐ *What is the date and time of the performance? (Check against the calendar. If the employer doesn't have an exact time in mind, the best time to perform is about an hour or hour and a half after the party begins, before the guests get too drunk or tired.)*

☐ *Where will the performance be? What kind of facility is it? (Some dancers charge extra if it is necessary to travel a long distance. Knowing the type of facility is helpful in identifying the correct building when arriving.)*

☐ *How long should the show be? (The length of the show will influence what to charge. Bellygrams should be 10-12 minutes in length. Newcomers to performing should not accept a long show, because they may not have the skill to keep things interesting for half an hour.*

☐ *What is the special occasion or theme for the event? (In case of birthday or similar occasion, some dancers like to take along Mylar balloons or greeting cards to give the guest of honor. Some dancers prefer not to accept certain types of bookings, such as bachelor parties.)*

☐ *How did you find out about me? (It is useful to know which advertising/promotion methods are the most effective.)*

☐ *Will the audience include large numbers of any particular ethnic group, such as Middle Eastern? (If the dancer knows in advance that the audience is likely to feature a particular ethnic group, she may try to select music from that region.)*

MORE GOOD QUESTIONS TO ASK WHEN BOOKING A JOB

☐ *What ages of people are likely to be there? (If children will be present, then chances are the performance will be in a wholesome, safe environment. If there will be only adults, it may still be a great audience, but there is a greater risk of drunkenness and rowdiness—it may be advisable to insist on an earlier performance time.)*

☐ *What percentage of the crowd will be men, and what percentage women? (Some dancers prefer not to perform for a crowd of almost entirely men, or they insist on dancing early in the evening before too much alcohol is consumed.)*

☐ *Just to make sure that I deliver the kind of show you're looking for, could you please briefly describe what you're expecting? (People often have stereotypes or expectations in mind when they hire a belly dancer. Asking this question helps the dancer determine whether her kind of show matches what the prospective employer is looking for.)*

☐ *What would you like the greeting card to say? (If there is a guest of honor, presenting a greeting card along with the show offers a nice personal touch.)*

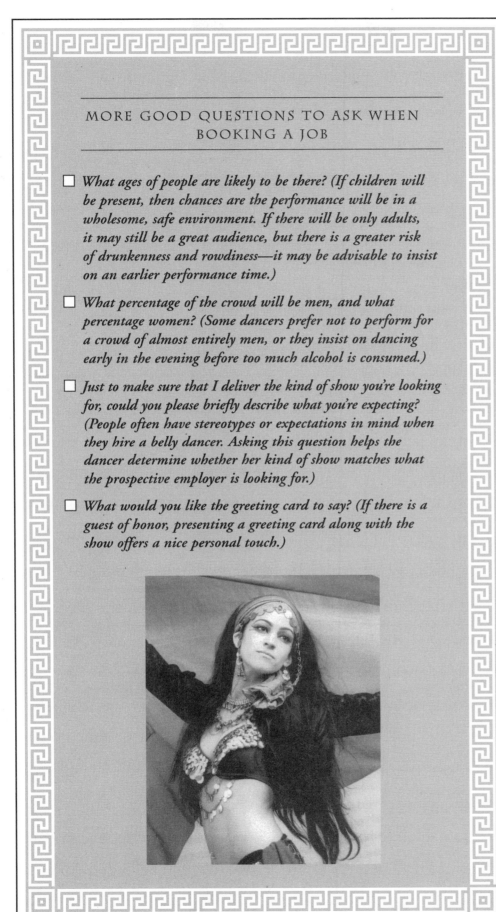

MISHAAL IN TOKYO

Photo by Yuji Kitahara

163

CHOOSING MUSIC

In a perfect world, a dancer will have live musicians available to play music for her; however, there are many performance opportunities where the dancer must rely on taped music. Selecting good music is critical to a dancer's success, because the dance itself is built around the music.

- It is important for a dancer to select music that she likes very much. If she does not particularly care for the music she is using, the audience will probably sense that she is not feeling inspired.

- The nature of the event can impact which music will be most effective. Music played on a synthesizer with a New Age flavor would be a poor choice for a Renaissance Faire, while heavily ethnic music would probably alienate most restaurant audiences.

- For American audiences, keep the songs under 3^1/$_2$ minutes in length. If songs are too long, the audience will get restless—the "Top 40" radio station format has taught Americans to have a short attention span when it comes to song duration.

- If the audience will contain significant numbers of a particular ethnic group, the dancer should consider that when choosing music. People like to hear songs that are familiar to them. Arabic audiences enjoy classic Arabic movie hits like *Tamerhenna,* and newer pop songs like *Habibi Ya Nour El Ain.* Turkish audiences usually appreciate traditional folk songs like *Shisheler* and current hits from artists like Tarkan. Longer songs are acceptable for an ethnic audience—songs played on Middle Eastern radio stations are frequently 4 or 5 minutes in length, and some can be as long as 20 minutes or even more.

- It is good to consider the age of the audience members. Younger people will probably respond best to current pop hits from Arabic artists like Hanan, Amr Diab, and Ehab Tawfeek, or to Turkish artists like Tarkan. This is true even if these audience members are American and not familiar with Middle Eastern music. The bright sound and strong dance beat appeal to young audiences everywhere.

- When dancing for a mostly American audience, it is good to vary the style of music and dance done to it. For example, the dancer might open with a lively Arabic song, and close with a Turkish *karsilama*. In contrast, ethnic audiences might prefer a performance that is not too "busy".

- For a polished ending, dancers will leave a gap of a couple of seconds after the end of the final song for the closing bow or curtsy, then follow that with "get-off-the-stage music". This exit music can be a reprise of the finalé if desired, but something else fast and dramatic could also work well.

- The wise dancer does research to find out what the lyrics of a song are about before including it in her show, especially if she has reason to believe there will be people who speak the language in the audience. She would probably look foolish if she performed a joyous or flirtatious dance to *Lisah Faker* (a classic Arabic song with heartbreaking lyrics about failed romance) or used it for a performance at a wedding reception.

 1 6 4

In the United States, a full-fledged professional restaurant or nightclub performance is about a half hour long, and consists of seven distinct parts:

- **Opening/Entrance**
- **Veil Work**
- **Medium/Fast I**
- **Either Standing Undulations Or Floor Work**
- **Medium/Fast II**
- **Drum Solo**
- **Finale**

This structure is somewhat different from the Egyptian style of presenting the dance. Egyptian dancers do not do American-style veil work, and they don't do floor work because that was banned by law in the 1950s.

If performing a bellygram, which is generally a short 10-minute performance designed to celebrate a birthday or other festive occasion, the dancer will probably perform only 3 of these parts.

Opening/Entrance

The dancer begins the show backstage. The first song usually begins with a few slow, improvised snippets of melody. Then the drums pick up the rhythm, and a medium-speed song fully begins. As the rhythm fully catches hold and the melody gets underway, the dancer makes her appearance. This would be a medium-speed or fast song. Usually, before settling into the center of the stage, the dancer walks along the edge of the stage area to greet the audience. She makes eye contact with them, smiles brightly, and nods or waves to those who seem particularly responsive.

At this point, the dancer is wrapped in a 3-yard veil that covers much of her costume. When she first comes on stage, she does simple walking and arm movements. Bert Balladine, a longtime instructor of Middle Eastern dance in the United States, once made this comment backstage:

> *If a dancer is very good, she will just walk all the way around the stage once when she first enters. If she is very, very good, she will do it twice.*

At this point, the audience is still drawing their attention away from their dinner plates and focusing on the fact that there is now a dancer to watch. They are studying what they can see of the costume, and not ready to appreciate intricate movements.

After introducing herself in this way, the dancer then settles into her performance and begins to dance in earnest to the music. As the opening song winds down, the dancer slows her movements with it and ends with a suitable pose.

Veil Work

The next stage of the American-style routine is the veil work. The music for this is generally of a soft, flowing nature. Usually it employs either the rumba or bolero rhythm.

Initially, as the song begins, the dancer performs some graceful undulations, arm movements, or head slides. Once the rhythm is fully underway, the dancer gracefully removes the veil and dances with it, taking care to avoid the tone of a seductive strip tease.

There are many different styles of veil movement, which can include:

- Using the veil to frame spins, undulations, head slides, and arm movements

- Wrapping up in the veil in artistic ways, then unwrapping

- Handling a heavier, semicircular veil like a toreador's cape

At the end of the song, the dancer discards her veil. If performing a bellygram, she might wrap it turban-style around the head of the guest of honor or drape it around him.

Medium/Fast I

For the third segment, the dancer selects medium-speed or fast music and does a variety of hip articulations, step combinations, and other suitable moves.

Standing Undulations or Floor Work

The music for this section is generally very slow. Often, the melody line will be improvised on a solo instrument. If there is any kind of background rhythm, it is probably *chiftetelli*.

For this section, the dancer uses soft, undulating moves such as hip circles, figure 8s, snake arms, head slides, stomach rolls, crescents, etc. For those dancers who wish to dance with a snake or balance a prop, this is the ideal time in the performance to do so.

Some dancers like to perform floor work, while others do not. Some clubs require it as a condition of employment. Generally speaking, floor work has fallen out of fashion for several reasons:

- Audience members in the back often can't see what the dancer is doing.

- Dancers hate to drag their expensive beaded costumes across a dirty floor.

- Some floor work movements can be hard on the knees.

- Floor work movements are often very difficult to do well.

- Because it has been against the law in Egypt since the 1950s, dancers who attempt to imitate Egyptian style don't use it.

However, many talented dancers continue to be inspired by the artistic possibilities offered by floor work. Performers like Suzanna Del Vecchio and Delilah continue to offer the dance community beautiful examples of how floor work can enhance a performance.

Medium/Fast II

If the dancer is planning to go around to the audience and collect tips, the fifth song is usually the point where she does so. If necessary, she uses the opening strains of the song to discard a prop or get up from the floor, and then proceeds out to visit the tables and greet her audience up close. She returns to the stage by the end of the song.

Drum Solo

This part of the dance features a solo by either a single drummer or a full percussion section. The dancer uses a series of shimmies, hip lifts, hip drops, and other articulations to highlight the accents in the rhythms.

Finalé

Finalé music is typically fast, giving the dancer an opportunity to raise the show's energy level to a peak. It may be a reprise of a song that was used earlier in the show, but does not need to be. If the dancer opts to use a karsilama (9/8) song in her performance, she usually saves it for this part of her dance.

The finalé is usually short. The dancer says good-bye to the audience through nods and bright smiles, does a few dramatic spins on the stage, uses a gesture to acknowledge the band and invite the audience to applaud them, collects her discarded veils and props, and vanishes.

PROPS

Not every prop is appropriate in every kind of show. Experienced dancers determine which props will work well and which will not for a given performance, and choose accordingly. If the show will take place in a private home, then it may be best to avoid props such as canes or veils that take a great deal of space to use effectively. For example, the dancer who likes to end her bellygram by draping a veil around the guest of honor may want to substitute placing a pre-made turban on his head for shows in cramped quarters.

There is always a risk to performing with a new prop or using an old prop with a new costume. No matter how experienced she is in working with that sort of prop, if a dancer has never used a particular prop with a particular costume before, she should try a dress rehearsal before the day of the show. A new sword or tray may balance differently or be more slippery than what the dancer has used in the past. A new headdress or body stocking may make a balanced prop slip off more readily. New finger cymbals might need to have the size of the elastic adjusted. The only way to make sure the new prop or new costume will not cause any bloopers is to practice with that combination ahead of time.

For dancers with the skill to balance a sword with confidence, it makes an excellent addition to a show—it builds suspense as the audience wonders what the dancer is going to do with it, and the talent required to do it always impresses them.

Dancing with Fire

Audiences love performances that use live fire in the form of candelabrum, flaming sword, or hand-held candles. However, if the performance will be in a public place, the dancer should check with her employer ahead of time to find out whether the building where the show will occur will allow it. There is probably not any problem with using fire in a private residence as long as space permits, but if the show will be in a public place such as a restaurant, the dancer might be told to douse her flame. It could be embarrassing to abruptly discover that an integral part of the performance could not be used, and it could disorient her enough to prevent her from putting her best foot forward through the rest of the show.

☑ **Make them laugh.**

☑ **Get them involved.**

☑ **Create suspense or drama.**

SETTING THE PARTY MOOD

In most private party jobs, the employer wants an entertainer, not an artist. Of course, the dancer should be skilled at her craft. But usually the reason for hiring a dancer is to make the party more fun, livelier, and more memorable. The dancer who plans ahead on how best to set a party mood will please her audience and open the door to additional business in the future.

The experienced dancer knows that five years in the future, the treasured picture in the party-goer's photo album will not be of her, a stranger, striking a dramatic pose, but rather of her placing a turban on good old Joe's head. Two years after the party is over, people won't still be talking about her artistic presentation, but they will still be talking about how much fun it was to watch Grandma Smith dance exuberantly with her.

There are several ways to put the audience into a party mood:

Make Them Laugh

Comedy is a favorite technique for bellygrams, although it can also be used in other types of shows. The dancer could insert some funny music into the show, or inject a touch of humor into her costume, but the most common technique is to single out audience members for special attention. If there is a guest of honor, that person can be the one who gets the spotlight. Otherwise, the dancer can select other audience members (including women) who seem to deserve a moment of fame.

When singling out an audience member, the dancer should take care to keep the attention at a family-oriented level of humor. Even if no children are present, it is best to behave as if they were. Seductive, steamy attentions may offend some audience members, leave people remembering the performance with distaste, and even trigger couples to fight if one partner gets jealous over attentions paid to the other. For example, it would be in poor taste for a dancer to place a man's head between her breasts and then shimmy them, ask a man to tuck a banknote into her bra cups, place a skirt over a man's head and gyrate the hips, or shimmy the breasts directly in a man's face. Although it might get some laughs at the time, performers who engage in these practices cause the public to lose respect for the dance and get a reputation for being sleazy. Sexual come-ons could also potentially give some audience members the wrong idea about the dancer's availability as a "full-service" entertainer, and lead to unpleasant scenes.

The following techniques should be effective for setting a light, humorous mood without causing any unpleasant scenes. When there is a guest of honor, of course that person should be the center of some of this attention, but it's also good to spread the fun around to more than one partygoer:

- Throughout the show, occasionally select someone from the audience to get up and dance. Smart performers give women and children equal opportunity to dance with them.

- Put a turban on someone's head and dance around him or drape a veil around him when done dancing with it.

168

- Place someone in a chair in the center of the performance space and lead all the party guests in a simple folk dance in a circle around him or her.

- Pose for pictures with party-goers afterward.

These are all good to do because they draw the focus to various individuals while allowing them to keep them dignity. When going for a comic tone, it is best to focus on light, playful mischief, and to avoid humiliation or seduction.

Get Them Involved

There are different ways to involve the audience. When the dancer gets audience members to take turns dancing with her, she involves not only the "victim", but also everyone who wants to take pictures or shoot video. If the dancing audience member seems to be enjoying the attention, the dancer might lead everyone else in clapping along with the music for that person, or tuck a dollar bill into the person's clothing as a tip.

Sometimes dancers will take a moment to teach an audience how to do the high-pitched Arabic ululation known as *zaghareet*. They can also be taught to shout *"Opa!"* to show their enthusiasm for the fun of the moment.

Another good way to involve an audience, especially at a party where many children are present, is to teach everyone a simple folk dance. There are a number of easy Greek, Turkish, Armenian, and Israeli folk dances that fit well into this type of show. Some Lebanese *debkes* are also reasonably easy.

When Zaina performs at Tasso's in Kansas City, she sometimes recruits several men from the audience to sit in chairs on the stage and gives each a turban to wear. She then draws several women from the audience to dance for them, giving them a lesson on the spot in snake arms and hip lifts.

Create Suspense Or Drama

Props can be useful at creating suspense or drama. At the first sight of a prop, the audience will wonder what the dancer is going to do with it, and they will watch with interest to find out.

Whenever a dancer balances anything on her head, the audience is captivated wondering whether it will fall off. If she puts on a show of acting just a little apprehensive about it, that encourages them to watch with rapt attention.

Certain items have an innate drama about them. Swords carry an aura of danger, and conjure images in audience members' minds of bygone times. Balancing anything with live fire adds a level of danger and excitement that other props cannot match. A Moroccan tea tray is intriguing to look at with its intricate decorations, and audience members enjoy watching the dancer pick up the pitcher and pour liquid into the cups before she places it on her head. Snakes often evoke a primal response in audience members—they are either fascinated or terrified.

Dancers who are adept at spinning can create drama by going into a lengthy, extended spin. At first, the audience will not be impressed. But if the spinning continues, and continues, and continues, people will take notice.

Debke
a folk dance native to Lebanon with intricate footwork, and often some squats. The upper body is held in a proud, upright posture with minimal movement.

1 6 9

Skilled isolations can be dramatic. Una, a dancer in San Jose, California, is well known for wearing a string of beads around her midriff. Accompanied by slow, undulating music, she uses a variety of abdominal moves to roll the beads up toward her rib cage and down toward her hips. Sometimes the beads on just one side move, then the other, then the entire string together. Audiences are fascinated by her control.

TECHNICALITIES

The best performances occur when the dancer's full attention is on interpreting the music and enjoying the audience interaction. When little things go wrong, it can distract her attention from the dancing and the quality of her show will suffer. By smart planning and paying attention to the little details, she will be able to arrive on time and deliver a peak performance.

- The day before each show, a savvy dancer examines the costume she plans to wear to make sure all the closures work properly and are firmly sewn into place, all straps are securely anchored, etc. and makes any needed repairs.

- Whenever she gets a new costume, the experienced dancer practices in it using the same props she plans to use in her next show to get comfortable with how it moves.

- When dancing in a private residence or similar setting where the performer will be very close to the audience, she should not wear a costume that shows a lot of wear and tear up close. Instead, she should pick something that will appear to be in good condition both up close and from a distance. For these occasions, she should also be scrupulous about grooming: well-manicured fingernails and toenails, etc.

- Experienced dancers make two tapes of the music for each show. If one should break or go bad, the other is then available as a spare. If the dancer has access to a computer with a writeable CD drive, then making a CD of the music is also a good backup measure. Dancers have been known to show up for performances at places that have only CD players, no cassette decks and vice versa.

- Before each show, a dancer should check the batteries in her boom box to make sure they still work. A spare set of batteries in the dance bag is always a good idea.

- It is best for the dancer to set the volume on the boom box to the desired level before the show so it won't be necessary to meddle with it after starting to dance.

- The day before each show, the dancer who plans ahead will fill the tank of the car with gas.

- A dancer who does a large number of private parties and bellygrams should always keep maps of the area in her car.

- Before each show, a dancer should check the elastics on her finger cymbals and replace them if necessary.

COLLECTING TIPS

Dancers should avoid jobs where the employer tries to pay a low fee, using the excuse that the dancer's pay will come from collecting tips. Such jobs put the dancer into a position of being a beggar who must go around to ask for money.

However, assuming the employer is paying a decent wage, tips can be a pleasant bonus source of income. Different employers have different policies with regards to tips. Some forbid dancers to collect them. Others require it, because they want their audiences to have an opportunity to see the dancer up close. Some do not have a policy either way. When starting to work for a new employer, the dancer needs to find out what the policy is regarding tips and determine whether she is comfortable with it.

Arab audiences have a couple of charming customs for tipping the dancer. One is to tape together a necklace made of dollar bills, and then hang that around the dancer's neck. Another is to carry a handful of bills to the stage and shower them over the dancer's head while she performs.

The more common custom in the United States is for the dancer to visit each table individually and dance for the patrons there. In a restaurant that has a special stage area, the dancer usually waits until near the end of her show before going around for tips. When visiting a table, the dancer may say hello to the people there, ask if they are enjoying the show, compliment the women on their outfits, and thank them for coming. If the customers are inclined to offer her tips, this is the point when they are likely to produce them and tuck them into her costume.

Dancers usually play their finger cymbals while going around to visit the audience and continue doing subtle dance moves such as shimmies, shoulder rolls, and undulations. This lets the audience see how the dance looks up close. Space between tables is usually limited, but there are still many movements that work within those constraints. A smart performer is careful not to play the cymbals directly in anyone's ears.

Upon accepting a tip, a dancer should always nod graciously, make eye contact with the donor, smile brightly, and say thank-you. Using the *salaam* gesture or blowing a kiss can be a nice touch. It can also be fun to try to get the tipper to dance with her for a few moments.

Different communities have different policies with respect to the tips that the dancer collects. In Egypt, a dancer usually shares her tips with the band, whom she has hired. In the U.S., some dancers share their tips with the bands, while others do not. In some settings, it is assumed that any tips that fall on the floor will be given to the band, while the dancer keeps those that remain tucked in her costume. Each dancer should try to find out the practices for her own community, then make informed decisions on whether to follow them.

Business Tip

Build a mailing list of customers she has worked for in the past, and keep them informed of her latest projects. If they hired a dancer once, they just might do so again some time!

THE PROFESSIONAL TOUCHES

Being a "professional dancer" requires more than just dancing well. It also involves handling oneself with courtesy, dignity, polish, and confidence. It means treating one's dance activity as a business, with attention to marketing, record-keeping, financial planning, ethics, and ongoing training.

A top professional will:

- Always arrive for shows either a little early or on time. She leaves the house 15 minutes earlier than necessary to allow time for unexpected delays *en route*.

- Stay organized. She will have a make-up bag pre-packed with a duplicate set of all her cosmetics. She will have a checklist of items needed for a given show, and consult it when getting ready to go. She'll keep a "survival kit" stocked with necessities like safety pins, a spare comb, hairpins, etc.

- Consider her personal safety. She avoids flirting with strangers who may misinterpret her intent. When possible, she takes an escort with her on gigs, even if it's just one of her students.

- Maintain high ethical standards. She does not try to steal the jobs of other dancers by offering to dance for less, because she realizes that will only lead to everyone, including her, getting paid less than they are worth. She hands out the business cards of the agency that booked her for a given job, rather than handing out her own. She urges her students to buy their own CDs and tapes, rather than making copies of her collection for them.

- Build relationships with other dancers in her community. She cooperates with the others to jointly pressure club owners to pay more, sponsor dance events, and combine their marketing energy to raise local interest in the dance.

- Keep the promises she makes to others.

- Avoid smoking or drinking alcohol to excess when in costume. It creates a seedy image for the dance.

- Wear a cover-up when not actually dancing.

■ *For contact information see: Shira, page 196, Visionary Dance Productions (Delilah), page 201, Oasis Band & Dancers, page 202, and Mishaal, page 201.*

SOME TIPS FOR DEALING WITH TIPS

☐ *Some dancers plant a friend, student, or family member in the audience. When they're ready to collect tips, they go to the friend's table first. The friend then gets the tipping started by planting a bill or two on the dancer's person. This gives the idea to other audience members.*

☐ *Some dancers tuck a couple of bills into their belt before the show, to suggest that tipping would be appropriate.*

☐ *If the tipper is a stranger, the dancer usually directs him to place the tip in either the side of the hipband, an armband, or a bra strap that goes across the back. She avoids letting him place the tip in her bra cups or the center front of her belt.*

☐ *If a customer tries to place a tip in an unacceptable spot, the dancer takes a couple of steps away, wags a scolding finger, and gestures to indicate the side of the belt as a more appropriate spot.*

☐ *A dancer who is not comfortable accepting tips tucked in her costume can carry a tambourine, basket, or hat around with her and indicate that that is where tips should be placed. For extra showmanship, she can balance the basket on her head.*

☐ *In the United States, most tips are one-dollar bills. If a dancer receives a larger bill, she usually moves it to a very secure spot in her costume to make sure it doesn't fall out and get lost.*

☐ *Some dancers who dislike going around for tips place a basket on the stage with a sign indicating its purpose is gratuities. This usually attracts less money than visiting the audience up close, but may make some dancers feel more comfortable with the tipping process.*

☐ *Dancers should never stoop to pick up tips that have fallen on the floor, because it looks tacky. Instead, they usually make arrangements ahead of time to have either restaurant staff or friends in the audience collect their fallen money and give it to them backstage after the show.*

☐ *Begging is bad. Audiences are offended by dancers who stay at their tables waiting for a tip.*

When In Rome…

Respect the local standards of her community and concerns of her clients. If she is given the opportunity to play a dancing Biblical character in a local church pageant, she doesn't flaunt her cleavage just for the fun of being rebellious. She treats her employers and audience members with courtesy, and expects courtesy in return.

173

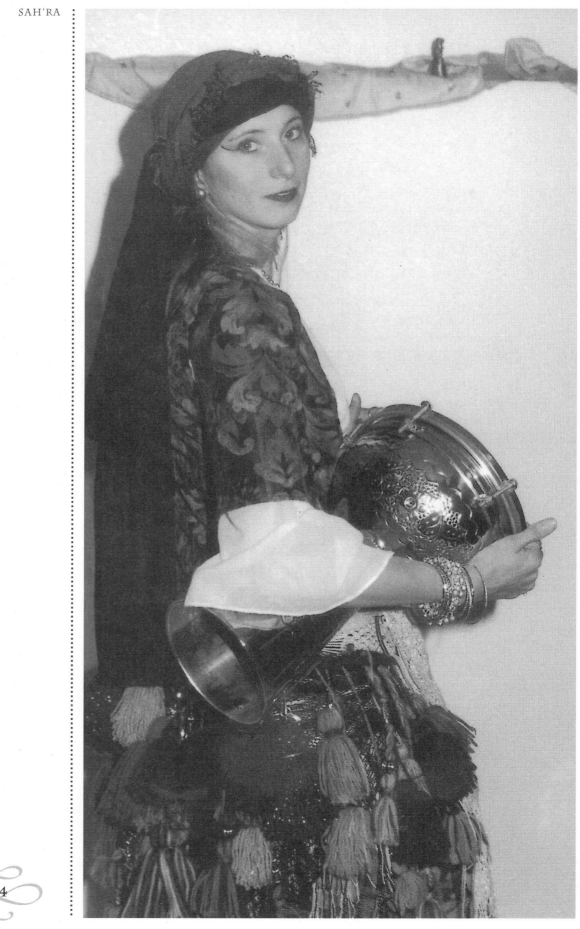

HOSSAM RAMSY
Photo courtesy of ARC Music

Music

Basic Rhythms for a Cabaret Belly Dance Routine

by Mary Ellen Donald

KNOWING THE RHYTHMS IS AN INTEGRAL PART OF BECOMING A FIRST-RATE DANCER.

Dancers sometimes perform with finger cymbals to accompany a drumbeat. It is important to distinguish one rhythm from another, detecting the unique underlying accent pattern of each one. Such rhythmical understanding brings authority and precision to dancing and cymbal playing.

To perform to a cabaret belly dance routine, become familiar with a few major rhythms. A cabaret routine can take many different forms. One common example is as follows:

 **1. Entrance piece:** three to five minutes of complex music containing a number of rhythm changes, stops, and breaks to show off the dancer's expertise.

2. Slow piece: three to four minutes of sensuous music to which the dancer often displays her creativity with the veil.

3. Drum solo: two to four minutes where only percussion instruments are playing, full of syncopation and offbeat accents, providing an opportunity for playfulness and intense shimmies.

4. Finale: usually under one minute of lively exit music. (If going out for tips is appropriate, then lively music would be inserted between the drum solo and the finale piece.)

Baladi, maqsoum, masmoudi, and *malfouf* are rhythms often found in entrance pieces such as *Hani* and *Tamrihinna.*

For dancers and drummers alike, the task connected with performing **entrance pieces** is to know the melodies well, and to know which rhythms accompany each melody. Dancers who perform oblivious to the rhythm changes in their music, or who perform the same cymbal patterns through baladi, malfouf, and masmoudi sections miss an opportunity to bring variety to their performances and to express the variety within the music.

The **slow section** of the dance routine is usually accompanied by either the *bolero* rhythm or the *chifte telli* rhythms. The bolero usually accompanies a lyrical song such as *Erev Shel Shoshanim* and *Norits Karoon Yegav*. The chife telli usually accompanies a melodic improvisation *(taqsim)*, that is, not a fixed melody. For the most part, dancers are playing with veils and not playing cymbals during this section. Nevertheless, it is important for dancers to know the structure of bolero and chifte telli so that their movements can reflect the unique flavor of each.

During the **drum solo,** a tambourine player or a drummer with a deep-toned drum is providing a rhythmical backup, often the maqsoum rhythm, while the lead drummer links a series of fills, often improvised. Usually, these are played two or four times in a row to help dancers have a better chance of catching the accents with their hips. A good way for dancers to prepare for performing to improvised drum solos is to listen to many drum solos over and over so that typical patterns can be recognized.

The **finalé section** (such as *Toutah, Tafta Hindi,* or *Hijaz Finale*) is usually short, often beginning at a moderate tempo, and ending up very fast. *Ayoub* and malfouf rhythms are the main rhythms accompanying this section. If dancers are going out for tips before the finalé, then moderate tempo music accompanied by the maqsoum rhythm is a popular choice.

Knowing the rhythms is an integral part of becoming a first-rate dancer. Knowing the names of the rhythms facilitates better communication with your accompanying musicians. In closing, I'd like to share a bit of inside information, which is probably not much of a secret. Musicians are likely to play better music for dancers who alter their dance steps to adapt to the changing rhythms.

◼ *For contact information see: Mary Ellen Books, page 196.*

TUNISIAN DRUMMER
by Alan McCorkle

MARY ELLEN DONALD

177

Music for Dancing with Props

by Shira

"LAUGH NOW, LIFE WILL SMILE FOR YOU!"

It is said that a good dancer will make the dance fit the music, but a great dancer will make the music fit the dance. Here's a few suggestions for which songs go with which props.

SUGGESTED SONGS FOR CANE

All of the songs suggested below are Egyptian. The recordings should be available from most vendors who specialize in Arabic music.

Folkloric Songs:

Sallam Alay. The lyrics say, "If my beloved calls me, I would forget about my friends and family. I would be happy being close to her." Recordings of this song are available on an Egyptian album called *I Remember Egypt* and also on a CD by the U.S. band Sirocco.

Tfarrak Al Halawah. This was originally recorded by an Egyptian musician named Metkal Kanaawe, but more recently has also been recorded by the American ensemble, The Sultans. This song is an ode to a beautiful woman. The title translates to, "Watch the Beauty." The lyrics say, "Your beauty is a wonder, how pretty your ankle bracelet is! You are beautiful, intelligent, and polite. You honor your cousin. Play hard to get, oh girl with the eyes lined with kohl! Play hard to get!"

Egyptian Al Jeel (Pop) Music:

These songs would be perfect for a nightclub setting with a young Arabic audience that prefers to hear pop music instead of traditional.

Ed Hak. This one was recorded by Hanan, and appears on her album *Testahel.* The song title means "Laugh!" The lyrics encourage you to laugh and be happy, saying, "Oh man! Laugh now, life will smile for you!"

Ya Leylet Ma Gani El Ghali. Nadia Hamdi taught a cane routine to this song on her 1999 U.S. tour. It was recorded by Mohammed Rushdi. The title means, "The Night My Precious Came To Me."

SUGGESTED SONGS FOR VEIL WORK

Bir Demet Yasemen. (Turkish) Many musicians have recorded this beautiful song. The song title means, "A Bunch Of Jasmine." The lyrics mourn the fact that a bunch of jasmine is the only remaining memory of lost love. Some recordings show the title of this song as "Sali." Turkish audience members would instantly recognize and appreciate this song.

Cleopatra. (Arabic) The full song *Cleopatra,* sung by Mohammed Abdel Wahab is 20 minutes long. Dancers usually use only its lovely instrumental opening, which is well suited to veil work. This classic Egyptian love song became famous several decades ago, and remains popular with the Arabic community today. The lyrics say, "Our night is wine surrounded by singing desires…Oh my darling, this is my love's night!"

Erev Shel Shoshanim. (Hebrew) This love song appears on many CD's recorded for belly dancing use. The title means, "Evening Of Roses," and the lyrics state, "Let me whisper a song to you quietly, a song of love." Although the song originated in Israel, it has also been popular among Arabs under the name *"Yarus."* Armenians know it as *"Vartér."* You could use an instrumental version of it with any audience.

Tien Afto. (Greek) The lyrics ask, "What is this thing called love? What is it? What is it?" and end with, "I love you! I love you!"

Mihtagalak. (Arabic) This song is particularly suitable for Arabic audiences who prefer to hear newer, pop music. A well-known vocalist named Warda recorded it in the 1990s. The lyrics say, "I need you more than you can imagine."

Misirlou. (Greco-American) American audiences like this song because it is familiar to many of them. The lyrics say, "Old temple bells are calling across the sand, we'll find our kismet answering love's command. Heaven will guide us as we go hand in hand."

SUGGESTED SONGS FOR CANDLES

Your choice of candle music will depend on what type of candle dance you do. Balancing a candle on your head as part of a restaurant performance will call for a different style of music than doing a Pharaonic portrayal in a theatrical setting. To help you get started, here are some suggestions for specific cuts on popular belly dance tapes and CDs that would work well for candles. Most of these should be available from vendors who sell belly dancing music:

Shamadan

For the large, multi-tiered Egyptian candelabrum, choose bright, happy Egyptian wedding music.

Raks el Hawanem. Played by Jamil Bachir on *Various Dance Melodies From Lebanon.*

Candle Balancing

When balancing a candle on the head or abdomen, most dancers choose slow, undulating music—usually either with free-form rhythm, or with a slow, pulsating chiftetelli rhythm. Usually, the melody is improvised.

Chiftetelli (Isis). Played by Desert Wind on *Kali Ma*. The New Age quality to the sound makes it appealing for Western audiences. (Contact Desert Wind, P.O. Box 3722, Salt Lake City, UT 84110 or see their web site at www.desertwindmusic.com.)

Pharaonic

It is possible to use any slow, sensuous music for a candle dance that involves holding a small candle in each hand. Some dancers particularly like to do this style of candle dance with a Pharaonic theme.

Dance *"Phaedra Pharaonica."* Played by Eddie Kochak, on *Strictly Belly Dancing Volume 6*. (Contact Eddie Kochak, P.O. Box 1141, Brooklyn, NY 11202.)

The Lamentations Of Isis. Played by Ali Jihad Racy on *Ancient Egypt*. Several songs on this CD work well for a Pharaonic performance. Ali Jihad Racy, a prominent Arab musician, composed them in 1978 for the King Tutankhamun exhibit at the Seattle Art Museum to evoke the essence of Ancient Egypt. (Contact Lyrichord Discs Inc., 141 Perry Street, New York, NY 10014.)

SUGGESTED SONGS FOR TAMBOURINE

Tambourines work well with traditional Turkish Gypsy music. Try using your tambourine with one of these entertaining songs. The first two use a fast ayoub beat (2/4), Rompi Rompi uses karsilama (9/8). All of these should be easy to find on recordings that feature Turkish music.

Shisheler. This is a popular drinking song and perfect for setting a lively upbeat mood. The lyrics say, "You drank raki without me? And you fell in the mud too, you aimless…Beloved…Oh Mercy…"

Istemem Babacim. This folk song is a dialogue between a girl and her father. He asks if she wants to marry Ali, and she refuses because he's crazy. Then he asks if she wants to marry Ummer, and she refuses because he's too old. Finally, they get to Zarhosh, the town drunk, and she says she wants to marry him because when he gets drunk he makes love to her.

Rompi Rompi. This popular drinking song is also sometimes called *Çadirimin Üstüne* on album labels. The lyrics say, "Put coffee on the stove, let it boil, let it boil. Let Halime's navel jiggle. Let's sell on credit, let's have nothing left. Let God not take my life. Hey! Rompi Rompi Rompi Rompi! Now it's the time to drink!"

■ *For contact information see: Shira, page 196.*

Recommendations

181

Recommendations

The recommendations section was created to profile some of the great products available to the world of belly dance. Our criteria for selection was simple: What would we, the reviewers, recommend to 10,000 of our closest friends?

This section is the answer.

Note three things:

1. This is not the end-all of quality belly dance products. There are plenty of things out there that we haven't written up.

2. Some of the things here are not belly dance specific. We wanted to give dancers who've seen EVERYTHING something new to look at.

3. We do not accept advertising. Everything is here because we believe it is worthy of being recommended. For that reason, there are not a lot of superlatives in the reviews. If it's in here, it's good.

BOOKS

THE TRIBAL BIBLE
by Kajira Djoumahna

Review by Zenuba

Kajira Djoumahna has written an excellent guide to American Tribal Style dancing. *The Tribal Bible* is a complete introduction to Tribal dancing, with separate chapters devoted to Costuming and Makeup, Musical Choices, Posture and Demeanor, Movement Vocabulary, and Group Improvisational Choreography. There is a thorough discussion of the background, tradition and "herstory" of Tribal dance.

The first edition was published in August 1999 and is sold out. A new edition will be published by early 2001. Kajira says the new edition will include more input from others in the tribal scene, more photos, interviews with John Compton of Hahbi'Ru, musicians and others, photos of the early FatChanceBellyDance and a younger Carolena Nericcio, photo documentation of tribal people in the Middle East and surrounding areas as well as a thorough movement section and much, much more! For more information, contact: Kajira's Black Sheep Bellydance, Books, Bodywork & Bazaar, PO Box 14926, Santa Rosa, CA 95402-6926. Phone: 707-546-6366. Email: Ghaziya@aol.com

THE GOLDEN TRANSLATOR
by George Moawad

Review by Shira

This series of books by George Moawad was designed to help dancers learn the English-language translations of famous Arabic songs. Knowing what her songs are about will enable a performer to match the moods of her dance to what the lyrics are saying. Each volume is sold individually and covers 8-10 songs, including many favorites such as Batwanes Beek, Habibi Ya Einy, and Inte Omri. For details, contact Happy Times International, 16531 Caballero Lane, Huntington Beach, CA 92649, USA. Phone: 714-840-7397.

TASSELS: THE FANCIFUL EMBELLISHMENT (Lark Books)
by Nancy Welch

Review by Dina

The author's knowledge of her subject and fondness for it make this colorful book both informative and charming.

Plenty of photographic eye candy, a history of world tassel traditions, well illustrated how-to's, and a gallery of contemporary designers inspire belly dancers to ornament their own costumes and accessories. For more information, contact: Lark Books, 50 College St, Asheville, NC 28801. Email: larkmail@larkbooks.com. Website: http://www.larkbooks.com

A NEAR EASTERN MUSIC PRIMER
by Mimi Spencer

Review by Shira

Mimi Spencer provides sheet music, lyrics, and translations to seven traditional Arabic, Turkish, and Armenian songs that bands frequently play for dancers. Although primarily intended as a resource for musicians who play and sing Middle Eastern songs, it is also useful for dancers who would like to know what the songs are about. For ordering details, contact Vince Delgado, P.O. Box 625, Forest Knolls, CA 94933. Phone: 415-457-8427. Email: vince@vincedelgado.com. Website: http://www.vincedelgado.com

FAT!SO?
by Marilynn Wann

Review by Jenni Morrison

Think you can't belly dance because you're a large woman? Nonsense, Marilynn Wann would say in this revolutionary book that, while not a dance-related book, encourages fat people to reclaim the word "fat" and embrace and celebrate their "flabulousness" by adopting the "fat manifesto." Contact Marilyn on the web at http://www.fatso.com.

Recommendations

ZILS—FATCHANCEBELLYDANCE VIDEO

Review by Jenni Morrison

This video, part of FatChanceBellyDance's *Tribal Basics Video Workshop* series, teaches five different zil patterns. The camera work is well shot so it is easy to see what is being done with the zil. Carolena Nericcio shows that the zils can play anything that drums can play. With a variety of ways to maneuver these seemingly simple instruments, many different sounds can be produced. This video effectively elevates the zil from prop to instrument. For more information, contact: FatChanceBellyDance, PO Box 460594, San Francisco, CA 94146. Phone: 415-647-6035. Email: fcbd@sirius.com. Website: http://www.fcbd.com

HILARY THACKER VIDEOS

Review by Jenni Morrison

Hillary Thacker offers a series of three Egyptian belly dancing videos at beginning, intermediate and advanced levels. These videos provide clear, easy-to-follow instructions and a refreshingly non-Vegas style performer. Thacker obviously enjoys dancing and does not rush through the beginning steps like some other instructional videos. The intermediate video features the music of Hossam Ramsy. For more information, contact: Hilary Thacker's Ghawazee Bazaar, 8 Bellevue Terrace, Edinburgh, EH7 4DT, UK. Phone: 0131 5567976, Fax: 0131 5579606. Email: belly@dial.pipex.com. Website: http://dspace.dial.pipex.com/belly

KAREN ANDES—A WORLD DANCER

Review by Jenni Morrison

Karen Andes teams up with Carolena Nericcio, director of FatChanceBellyDance, for the *Womanpower Workout* video. Geared mainly for advanced students, the video covers strength training, veil work, and American Tribal Style dance workouts. The tape wraps up with a beautiful and thoughtful stretch inspired by temple dances of India. Andes gives brief descriptions of each pose, adding special meaning to the stretches. Overall, this video is an intense workout, but can be modified for beginners.

Andes is also the author of *A Woman's Book of Strength*, *A Woman's Book of Balance* and *A Woman's Book of Power*. These books encompass a variety of topics, including strength training, nutrition, meditation and dance.

Karen Andes' website, www.worlddancer.com, provides information about classes that she teaches, book and music recommendations and a diverse selection of links. For more information, contact: Karen Andes, 1826 5th Ave, San Rafael, CA 94901. Phone: 415-459-5514. Email: kandes@worlddancer.com.

MARY ELLEN DONALD

Review by Toni L. Whyte

Whether you're a dancer or an aspiring musician, Mary Ellen Donald's various series of tapes are worth your time and investment. If you are a dancer, Donald's *Middle Eastern Rhythm* series will give you a **solid** understanding of such rhythms as *ayoub, malfouf, maqsoum,* and *karachi,* as well as the more commonly taught *baladi, chifte-telli, bolero,* and *karsilama.* Donald's *Practice Music* tapes, which feature Donald on percussion and some lovely *oud* and *nay* playing by George Mundy, provide a series of songs grouped by rhythm type, allowing students to practice a particular rhythm for an extended period. If you want to take your musical understanding to yet a deeper level, then I recommend the tape and book combination *Gems of the Middle East,* featuring Donald on doumbec and tambourine and Mimi Spencer on qanun and voice. The book, written by Mary Ellen Donald, gives a detailed breakdown of the rhythm sequences for each song. These rhythmical descriptions are a valuable tool for either an aspiring drummer trying to learn a basic repertoire, or for the dancer learning the structure of the music she is likely to get from live bands. Dancers will also benefit from Donald's instructional finger cymbal products, including *Beginner Cymbal Tape for Bellydancers,* and the *Mastering Finger Cymbals* tape and book. Overall, Mary Ellen Donald offers some of the best educational resources for Middle Eastern musicians and dancers alike. For more information, contact: Mary Ellen Books, PO Box 7589, San Francisco, CA 94120-7589. Phone: 415-826-3786

MIGRATION
by Gypsy Caravan

Review by Toni L. Whyte

If your dancing soul prefers the sound of a small acoustic band over a 40-piece Egyptian orchestra, then the new CD from Gypsy Caravan, *Migration,* is a must-have for your musical library. All of the cuts are good, and the CD is about fifty-fifty fast and slow pieces. The CD has two numbers that would be great with cane: the opening *Stick Dance*—an updated version of one of the pieces recorded on Aisha Ali's *Music of the Ghawazee*—and *Highland,* which also offers a number of drum-solo interludes (would lend itself to a duet or small troupe dance). And oh, the *taqsims!* The song, *Mirage,* is one of the most sensuous *chiftitellis* I've ever heard. In addition, *Migration* has a soulful Spanish-style piece, *The Making,* which features Spanish guitar, flute, and a number of dramatic changes in tempo. This CD has no classic American-style routine or drum solo, but it does have a lot of beautiful, inspirational music that will make you want to dance! For more information, contact: Gypsy Caravan, 4805 NE Campaign, Portland, OR 97218. Phone: 503-288-4355. Email: gypsycaravan@iefx.co. Website: http://www.alveus.com/gypsycaravan/

THE ART OF MIDDLE EASTERN DANCE
by Shira

Review by Toni L. Whyte

Shira has assembled a spectacular collection of information on teachers, dance styles, music, history, and Middle eastern culture (her article, *Styles of Belly Dance in the United States,* should be required reading). Music, video, and book reviews are also available, as well as "how-to" information costuming, teaching, performance, etc. Surfing dancers, start here! Website: http://www.shira.net

ULTRAGYPSY

Review by Tazz

UltraGypsy, a San Francisco Tribal dance troupe, has set a design standard for troupe websites. The solid design represents the spirit of the troupe and Tribal belly dance with a muted modern yellow/green/purple theme. The punky theme serves as a cozy backdrop for pictures of the troupe performing on stage or prepping for a show at Burning Man. Website: http://www.ultragypsy.com

TERPSICHORE MIDDLE EASTERN CLIP-ART CD

Review by Tazz

If you are starting a Middle Eastern website, or just writing a book about belly dance, this is the clip art collection to have. Over 150 images in Mac and PC formats make it easy to give your next project the Middle Eastern look it deserves. For more information, contact: Terpsichore Enterprises, PO Box 90332, Gainesville, FL 32607-0332. Phone: 352-373-4991. Fax: 352-373-4991. Email: kashmir6@ufl.edu. Website: http://members.aol.com/terpsich/clipart/

MELEAH
Photo by Keith Drosin

Source Directory

189

Source Directory

The following list of dancers, teachers, troupes, manufacturers, vendors, artists, musicians and costumers is provided for the convenience of the reader. Backbeat Press is not selling advertising space. These listings are provided free of charge. Backbeat Press is not responsible for claims, descriptions or accuracy of the information. Beginning on page 193, the Sources are listed geographically, with all contact information.

DISTRIBUTORS, MERCHANTS, AND MANUFACTURERS

190

PROFESSIONAL DANCE SOLOISTS, TROUPES, DANCE INSTRUCTORS AND CHOREOGRAPHERS

ATÉA

Photo by Denis Kavemeier

191

ARTISTS, MUSICIANS, PHOTOGRAPHERS AND COSTUMERS

PROMOTERS AND AGENTS

SORAYA

Source Directory

with addresses, by location

■ *Alabama*

BOHEMIAN MARKET
Connie Parrish/ Jamilla Rasa
5883 Hwy 119
Montevallo, AL 35115
Phone: 205-621-0609
email: jparrish@wwisp.com
web: http://www.bohemianmarket.com
Everything from jewelry to custom-made
costumes for Tribal, Gypsy, and Ren Faire.

■ *Arizona*

ANGELIQUE AND FRIENDS
BELLY DANCE
Angelique
PO Box 1813
Gilbert, AZ 85299-1813
Phone: 602-735-3107
email: angelique@angeliqueandfriends.com
web: http://www.angeliqueandfriends.com
Group and private lessons. Performances
for parties, events. Educational lectures,
demonstrations and booking services.

CARMEN—ARABIAN DANCE ARTS
Carmen Evans
5411 E Placita Del Mar
Tucson, AZ 85718
Phone: 520-577-1847
email: carmen@SonoraComm.com
Teaches choreography, costuming, stage
craft. Partner with Shahrezade in Fantasia
Araby Dance Concert Group.

CHIVALRY SPORTS RENAISSANCE
8677 E. Golf Links Road
Tucson, AZ 85710
Phone: 800-730-5464
Phone outside US: 520-546-8223
Fax: 800-410-5464
email: customerservice@renstore.com
web: http://www.renstore.com
Medieval, renaissance and fantasy store
specializing in costumes armor, weapons,
books, gifts and more.

TANYA LIPTAK
PO Box 55051
Phoenix, AZ 85078-5051
Phone: 602-404-8978
email: fantasydancer@webtv.net
web:http://www.angelfire.com/biz/liptak/
    index.html
Performer, lecturer, instructor. Producer of
"International Fantasy" TV show. Instructional
and performance videos available.

THE JOY OF BELLY DANCING
Yasmina
156 W 3rd Place
Mesa, AZ 85201
Phone: 480-962-6303
email: yasmina@syspac.com
web: http://www.syspac.com/~parker
Public Access TV show dedicated to
belly dancing.

■ *California*

ABDUHL & THE NIGHT VISITORS
Sebastian Williams
410 South Church Street
Grass Valley, CA 95945
Phone: 530-273-7705
email: abduhlnv@hotmail.com
Musical group for belly dancers at festivals.
Hand-made instruments and crafts.
Video and music tapes.

ANGELIKA NEMETH
PO Box 4546
Irvine, CA 92616
Phone: 949-786-3111
Fax: 949-654-5745
Performer, instructor, choreographer, producer
of Oriental dance concerts, co-coordinator
of International Conference on Middle
Eastern Dance.

ANSUYA'S SCHOOL OF
BELLYDANCE/YALEIL MIDDLE
EASTERN DANCERS
Ansuya
2323 14th St #5
Santa Monica, CA 90405
Phone: 310-392-7836
email: ansuyas@aol.com
web: http://www.ansuya.com
Classes and seminars locally and abroad.
Solo and troupe performances locally and
abroad. Videos available.

ARABIAN NIGHTS
ENTERTAINMENT
Scottie Schultz
3234 Idlewild Way
San Diego, CA 92117
Phone: 858-581-0135
Promotes Bedouin Bazaar in October.
Instruction in belly dance. Sells music,
videos, costumes, etc.

193

ART / DANCE ACADEMY
Morwenna Assaf
1837 Coast Hwy
Oceanside, CA 92054
Phone: 760-757-4470
Fax: 760-722-3280
email: adacomplex@aol.com
web: http://www.theblendmagazine.com/dance
Studio for dance and drumming instruction.
Home of professional dance company
CEDAR and Oasis Boutique.

ARTEMIS IMPORTS
Artemis
PO Box 68
Pacific Grove, CA 93950
Phone: 831-373-6762
Fax: 831-373-4113
email: artemis@artemisimports.com
web: http://www.artemisimports.com
Complete mail order supplier for US and
world. Clothing , music, zils, veils, everything
the dancer needs.

ATÉA'S MAGICAL MOTION™
ENTERPRISES
Cheryl Simon
12228 Venice Blvd #402
Los Angeles, CA 90066
Phone: 310-301-0045
Toll-free: 800-995-6501
Fax: 310-301-4064
email: atea@magicalmotion.com
web: http://www.magicalmotion.com
Producer of *Bellydance!* video series.
Instruction in classic belly dance and its
holistic health benefits.

AZIZA SA'ID
1040 S Mount Vernon Ave G 360
Colton, CA 92324-4228
Phone: 909-518-5224
email: azizasaid@zilltech.com
web: http://www.zilltech.com
Performs and teaches a wide variety of
styles and skills. Website design for
dance community.

BÁRAKA
1700 Church Street #1265
San Francisco, CA 94131-4037
Phone: 415-435-8727
email: barakasf@lmi.com
web: http://www.barakasf.com
Performer, instructor, author, costumer.
Instructional video: *The Dancer's Toolkit*,
Performance video: *The Best of Báraka*

BELLY DANCE!
Leea Aziz
1235 Boulevard Way
Walnut Creek, CA 94595
Phone: 925-937-7852
email: bellydc@ncal.verio.com
web: http://www.aimnet.com/~bellydc
Retail supply shop & dance studio.
Producer of Belly Dancer of the Year Pageant

BELLY DANCING BY "LA MIRAGE"
34112 Selva Rd #335
Dana Point, CA 92629
Phone: 949-496-8489
email: lamirage@home.com
web: http://www.alienufoart.com/
   bellydancer.htm
Certified Reiki practioner and master teacher.

CONARI PRESS
2550 Ninth St
Suite 101
Berkeley, CA 94710
Phone: 510-649-7178
Toll-free: 800-685-9595
Fax: 510-649-7190
email: bknight@conari.com
Publishes women's books and resources such
as the *Wild Women* series and *Uppity Women
of Ancient Times*

DAWN DEVINE BROWN /
IBEXA PRESS
PO Box 221
Roseville, CA 95678-0221
Phone: 916-772-7570
email: davina@davina.org
web: http://www.davina.org
Author of *Costuming from the Hip* and
From *Turban to Toe Ring*, books on
belly dance costuming.

ELENA
1090 Vista Drive
McKinleyville, CA 95519
Phone: 707-839-7402
Fax: 707-839-7403
email: uzbek.dance@usa.net
Performer, choreographer, instructor of
Uzbek Dance. Uzbekistan native.

FATCHANCEBELLYDANCE
Carolena Nericcio
PO Box 460594
San Francisco, CA 94146
Phone: 415-647-6035
email: fcbd@sirius.com
web: http://www.fcbd.com
FatChanceBellyDance celebrates the female
spirit with a physical display of strength
and beauty.

FLYING SKIRTS OF SAN
FRANCISCO - TRIBAL COSTUME
DESIGNS
Gwen Heckeroth
255 9th Ave. SF CA 94118
Phone: 415-668-9755
email: flyingskirts@earthlink.net
A complete line of Tribal costuming designs
and costumer to FatChanceBellyDance.

GHANIMA GADITANA
315 Crestview Drive
Santa Clara, CA 95050-6505
Phone: 408-246-7646
Fax: 408-246-6746
email: ghanima@anatours.com
Performer, instructor.

HAHBI'RU INC
John Compton
220 Esmeralda Ave
South San Francisco, CA 94110
Phone: 415-641-4510
email: hahbiru@earthlink.net
web: http://www.hahbiru.com
Classes, Instructional Videos, Workshops,
and Performance in "The Hahbi'Ru Tribal
Folkloric style"

HENNA DREAMS
Sally Phillips
Marin County, CA
Phone: 415-721-4226
Fax: 415-389-8218
email: Sally@hennadreams.com
web: http://www.hennadreams.com
Beautiful, all-natural body adornment for
fairs, parties, showers, other events.
Appointments and gift certificates available.

IAMED
Suzy Evans
PO Box 7666
Van Nuys, CA 91409
Phone: 818-343-4410
email: suzy@bellydance.org
web: http://www.bellydance.org
International organization which produces
"The Awards of Bellydance" every August
in Los Angeles. Videos available.

JHERI ST. JAMES
PO Box 492
Laguna Beach, CA 92652
Phone: 949-494-5031
email: jheristjames@webwave.net
Egyptian Cabaret, Tribal, Folkloric,
American, Renaissance, Visionary -
Teacher, Performer, Troup: J.J. & the
Habibis Bellydancers

JORJANA'S GLITTER WORLD
914 W. Marcello Avenue
Thousand Oaks, CA 91320
Phone: 805-498-5274
Fax: 805-498-1384
email: jorjanafiz@aol.com
Coins, costumes, scarves, veils, scimitars,
swords, khaleegy dresses, cymbals, tapes,
jewelry, coin bras and belts

JUDITH'S HEAD
Terri Hendrix and Stephanie Elle
702 Santa Paula
Sunnyvale, CA 94086
Phone: 408-530-0692
email: s_elle@apexmail.com,
terri_hendrix@hotmail.com
web: http://www.judithshead.com
Tribal jewelry and belly dance accoutrements.
Custom clothing and costumes. Waist of
Potential clothing line.

KAJIRA'S BLACK SHEEP
BELLYDANCE, BOOKS, BODYWORK
& BAZAAR
PO Box 14926
Santa Rosa, CA 95402-6926
Phone: 707-546-6366
email: Ghaziya@aol.com
web:
http://members.aol.com/Ghaziya/index.html
Performer. Vendor. Dance writer. Teaches
tribal and classical. Directs troupe United
We Dance. CMT and Reiki Master.

KAREN ANDES
1826 5th Ave
San Rafael, CA 94901
Phone: 415-459-5514
email: kandes@worlddancer.com
web: http://www.worlddancer.com
We explore sacred world dance, express
heart and soul and strengthen the body
with movement.

KATE REED
available c/o Backbeat Press
PMB 253
1647 Willow Pass Road
Concord, CA
Phone: 925-969-7915
email: ocelotsden@yahoo.com,
kate@backbeatpress.com
Freelance web, multimedia, 2D & 3D art,
graphic design. Webmistress for
WWW.BACKBEATPRESS.COM

KEITH DROSIN
953 1/2 Amoroso Place
Venice, CA 90291
Phone: 310-305-8811
Dance Photography

LARK IN THE MORNING
PO Box 1176
Medocino, CA 95460
Phone: 707-964-5569
Fax: 707-964-1979
email: larkinam@mhs.mendocino.k12.ca.us
web: http://www.larkinAM.com
Middle Eastern musical instruments of
all types.

MARGUERITE
Marguerite Kusuhara
1601 N Sepulveda Blvd
PMB 258
Manhattan Beach, CA 90266
Phone: 310-370-5155
Fax: 310-370-7845
email: windhorse@earthlink.com
web: http://www.gypsymagic.com
Upscale entertainment service: belly dance,
magic, fortune telling, children's parties.

MARY ELLEN BOOKS
Mary Ellen Donald
PO Box 7589
San Francisco, CA 94120-7589
Phone: 415-826-3786
Classes in Middle Eastern percussions.
Instructional books and tapes, recordings of
belly dance classics available.

MELEAH
2805 Maple Street
San Diego, CA 92104
Phone: 619-280-8424
Toll-free: 877-378-7945
Fax: 619-255-4575
web: http://www.meleah.com
Performer, instructorm make-up artist for 18
years. 2 videos and make-up line available.

MICHAEL J. MONSON
3275 Shadow Park Place
San Jose, CA 95121
Phone: 408-532-6453
email: mjmonson@earthlink.net
Fine art and dance photography.

NAJMES
Nancy James
134 Berrellesa St
Martinez, CA 94553
Phone: 925-313-8956
email: najmes@hotmail.com
web: http://community.webtv.net/najmes/
najmesdances
Performer, teaches belly dance for fitness.

OASIS DANCE MAGIC
Fahtiem
1840 Nausika Ave
Rowland Heights, CA 91748
Phone: 626-810-9470
Fax: 626-964-9800
email: fahtiem@fahtiem.com
web: http://www.bellydancemagic.com,
www.fahtiem.com
Award winning performer, choreographer,
instructor. Workshops around the country.
Produces annual festival outside Los Angeles.

PE-KO INTERNATIONAL RECORDS
Mher Panossian
5112 Hollywood Blvd
Suite 108
Los Angeles, CA 90027
Phone: 323-664-8880
Fax: 323-664-1614
email: info@pekorecords.com
web: http://www.pekorecords.com
Largest producers of belly dance music.
Top source for music & videos, all styles.
Wholesale/retail.

SAED MUHSSIN
1672 Dolores Street #5
San Francisco, CA 94110
Phone: 415-826-6601
Photographer.

SAROYAN MASTERCRAFTS
Harry Saroyan
PO Box 2056
Riverside, CA 92516
Phone: 909-783-2050
Fax: 909-276-8510
email: ZilsUSA@aol.com
web: http://www.saroyanzils.com
Manufacturers of the largest selection of
finger cymbals, decorative coins and
scimitars

SHAKTI CENTER FOR
TRANSFORMATION
4058 A Tujunga Ave
Studio City, CA 91604
Phone: 818-752-7374
email: shaktistar@aol.com
web: http://www.shaktistar.com
Hypnotherapist, healer, transformer, Priestess

SHIRA
1602 Quail Ave
Sunnyvale, CA 94087
Phone: 408-249-5617, office: 650-926-6551
email: shira@shira.net
web: http://www.shira.net
Instructor, performer, assistant director of
Troupe Wasila and comedy troupe The
Veiled Threats.

SILK SPIRIT
David Ludwig
469 A Magnolia Ave
Larkspur, CA 94939
Phone: 415-456-4989
email: david@silkspirit.com
web: http://www.silkspirit.com
Hand-painted silk theater backdrops and
veils to maximize the impact of your dance
presentation.

196

SIRENS IN SANITY
Yasmine
2333 Old Suisun Road
Benicia, CA 94510
Phone: 707-746-8447
email: fabris@mindspring.com
web: http://www.expage.com/page/belly
Soloists and troupe performers. Instructors,
choreographers, promoters and agents for
belly dancers and events.

SUNARA'S CLOTHING AND ACCESSORIES
Sunara
PMB 52
1710 Broadway
Sacramento, CA 95818
Phone: 916-447-8937
Fax: 916 447-8937
email: Order@Sunara.com
web: http://www.sunara.com
Quality costumes - gypsy pants, belly dance
cholis, jeweled belts, sizes to 4X, and middle
eastern music transcriptions

TATSEENA
Susanne Tatseena
8551 Bandon Drive
Dublin, CA 94568
Phone: 925-828-5714
Teaches group and private lessons, performs
for special events and educational programs.

TOMBO STUDIOS
April Niino
978 Keltner #3
San Jose, CA 95117
Phone: 408-244-7403
email: alkamie@earthlink.net
web: http://www.tombostudios.com
Chainmail and beadmail, beautiful costumes
and accessories, all handmade.

TROUPE WASILA / VEILED THREATS
Kamilla or Shira
PO Box 3653
Santa Clara, CA 95055-3653
Phone: 408-946-9846, 408-249-5617
email: shira@shira.net
web: http://www.shira.net/wasila.htm
Troupe Wasila performs classic belly dancing.
The Veiled Threats specialize in belly danc-
ing comedy.

VICHELLE'S BELLYDANCING
44636 90th Street East
Lancaster, CA 93535
Phone: 661-946-6917
email: vichelle@qnet.com
Performer, troupe director, instruction and
choreography for beginners ages seven-adult.

WALTER RASMUSSEN PHOTOGRAPHY STUDIO
Walter Rasmussen
1247 Solano Ave
Albany, CA 94706
Phone: 510-527-9873
email: wrpphoto@aol.com
Fine art and dance photography.

YEMAYA
3822 Harrison #2
Oakland, CA 94611
Phone: 510-985-1464
email: heathernoel1@earthlink.net
Solo performer.

■ *Colorado*

JEWELS OF THE NILE
Cindy Loader
533 S. Taft Hill Road
Fort Collins, CO 80521
Phone: 970-490-2645
Fax: 970-482-0118
email: nilecindy@aol.com
web: http://www.co-life.com/jewels
Bellygrams, private and group classes.
Instructional videos available.

JOYFUL DANCER DESIGNS
1461 Walnut St
Windsor, CO 80550-5941
Phone: 970-674-1385
email: tomah@verinet.com
Unique and memorable commercial artwork
for promotional materials & websites.

UNICORN BELLY DANCE SUPPLIES
3361 S Corona
Englewood, CO 80110
Phone: 303-762-0124
Toll-free: 800-761-1032
(outside CO, credit cards only)
email: joynan@unicorn-bds.com
web: http://www.unicorn-bds.com
Everything for the Middle Eastern dancer at
affordable prices.

■ *Florida*

INTERNATIONAL PRODUCTIONS BY TAHJA
Tahja
5103 Windward Avenue
Sarasota, FL 34242
Phone: 941-349-3494
Fax: 941-349-4919
email: interproduction@home.com
Theme party entertainment, specializing in
Mid-Eastern, and other parts of the world.
Also Mid-Eastern dance and music of
Yasalaam!

KARINA'S SCHOOL OF HAWAIIAN
& BELLY DANCE
17754 Gulf Blvd
Redington Shores, FL 33708
Phone: 727-319-3949
email: CDErrico@wbtv.net
Professional dance studio for beginners
through advanced, specializing in Polynesian
and belly dance.

MIDEASTERN DANCE EXCHANGE
Tamalyn Dallal
350 Lincoln Road #505
Miami Beach, FL 33139
Phone: 305-538-1608
Fax: 305-538-5320
email: tdallal@aol.com
web: http://www.talion.com
Teachers, performers, workshop instructors,
troupe. Performance and instructional videos
available.

TERPSICHORE ENTERPRISES
PO Box 90332
Gainesville, FL 32607-0332
Phone: 352-373-4991
Fax: 352-373-4991
email: kashmir6@ufl.edu
web: http://members.aol.com/terpsich/
    clipart/
150 copyright-free line & grayscale images
engravings & photos. Available in book and
CD.

■ *Georgia*

BEZENAHS OF NEWMAN
PO Box 332
Newman, GA 30264
Phone: 770-251-8821
email: bizbeeee@aol.com
web: http://hanezbs.com
Egyptian & Turkish costumes and accesories.
Import direct.

■ *Illinois*

JASMIN JAHAL
PO Box 56037
Chicago, IL 60656-0037
Phone: 773-693-6300
Fax: 773-769-6302
email: jjahal@hotmail.com
web: http://www.JasminJahal.com
Teacher, performer, video producer

READ MY HIPS TRIBAL
BELLYDANCE TROUPE
Stephanie Barto
3829 N South Port Ave
Chicago, IL 60613
Phone: 773-975-0242
email: starkana@aol.com
web: http://members.aol.com/starkana/
    tribal/rmh.htm
American Tribal troupe available for club
and special events. Weekly classes in
American Tribal.

■ *Indiana*

INTERNATIONAL DANCE
DISCOVERY
Donna Carlton
108 1/2 E Kirkwood Ave
Suite 5
Bloomington, IN 47408-3330
Phone: 812-336-3632
email: IDD@compuserve.com
web: http://ourworld.compuserve.com/
    homepages/IDD/
Dance instructor. Author/publisher of dance
resource guides since 1987.

■ *Kansas*

SUZANNE SHIELDS
555 S Quentin
Wichita, KS 67218
Phone: 316-687-5033
email: cleopatra@kscable.com
web: http://home.kscable.com/suzanne
Director of Troupe Cleopatra & member of
Big Bad Baghdad Band. Teaches in Wichita
and performs in the Midwest.

■ *Louisiana*

BETTY KARAM AND THE DESERT
DANCERS
Betty Karam
3317 Coliseum Street
New Orleans, LA 70115
Phone: 504-897-0432
email: jdkaram@mailhost.tcs.tulane.edu
Teacher, performer, troupe choreographer,
director. Teaches solo, group, cabaret and
folkloric. Zils a speciality.

■ *Massachusetts*

CHERI BERENS MIDDLE EASTERN
DANCE STUDIO
Cheri Berens
PO Box 374
Yarmouthport, MA 02675
Phone: 508-394-3960
email: cheri@capecod.net
web: http://www.cheri.addr.com
Teacher, performer. Hosts "Cairo Dance
Intensive", an annual tour to Egypt for
dancers.

■ *Maryland*

ELIZABETH ARTEMIS MOURAT
2945 Woodstock Ave
Silver Spring, MD 20910-1249
Phone: 301-565-5029
email: artemisdances@yahoo.com
web: http://www.serpentine.org
Performer, teacher, Oriental dance historian
and writer. Turkish music and videos available.

198

Maine

NICOLAS-HAYS INC
PO Box 612
York Beach, ME 03910
Publisher of *KALI*

Montana

THE CARAVAN OF DREAMS WORLD DANCE TROUPE
Saralyn Sebern & Ginny Watts
890 Hidden Valley Road #33
Bozeman, MT 59718
Phone: 406-587-2006
email: saralyns@montana.edu
Performance in cabaret, folk and world dance styles. Choreography and instruction, all ages and levels.

North Carolina

LARK BOOKS
Nicole Tuggle
Altamont Press
50 College St
Asheville, NC 28801
email: larkmail@larkbooks.com
web: http://www.larkbooks.com
Publisher of *Tassels.*

New Jersey

SORAYA'S MID-EAST DANCE AND MUSIC PRODUCTIONS
Soraya
PO Box 3284
Margate City, NJ 08402
Phone: 609-823-2029
Fax: 609-822-6233
email: SorayaEnt@aol.com
web: http://www.adnetint.com/soraya
www.rickaster.com/pro/soraya
Full-scale entertainment agency. Egyptian dancing, Arabic orchestras, variety/specialty acts. For high-end occasions.

New Mexico

AMAYA PRODUCTIONS
Amaya
PO Box 9157
Albuquerque, NM 87119-9157
Phone: 505-260-1186
Fax: 505-260-1186
email: mariaamaya@web.com
web: http://www.mariaamaya.web.com
Soloist, seminar instructor, video producer. Organizes annual Shake and Bake Festival in New Mexico.

JOAN KAFRI/ MIDDLE EASTERN DANCE CAMP/WORKSHOP TOURS
Joan Kafri
1707 Callejon Veronica
Santa Fe, NM 87501
Phone: 505-983-7725
Fax: 505-983-7725
email: jkafri@peoplepc.com
Hosts dance trips annually, one to Turkey, one to Israel. Includes classes, shows for dancers of all levels.

LINDA REEDER-SANCHEZ
5206 Mescalero Tl
Las Cruces, NM 88012
Phone: 505-373-2936
email: Yallazadeh@aol.com
Teacher, performer of Raks Sharki, Middle Eastern, African, Rhumba, Flamenco & Irish. Costuming, silk dyeing & painting.

MICHELLE MORRISON
7500 Gallinas Ave NE
Albuquerque, NM 87109
Phone: 505-857-0266
email: kenhelm@swcp.com
web: http://www.farfesha.com
Egyptian-style soloist, leader of troupe Farfesha, host of workshops.

New York

ALIA MICHELLE DESIGNS
3801 23rd Ave #409
Astoria, NY 11105
Phone: 718-274-9495
email: aliam@tuna.net
web: http://www.aliamdesigns.com
Fantasy wear for stage, class and your life... Apparel for your adventurous spirit; Oriental, Tribal/Ethnic, Gypsy & Flamenco

DALIA CARELLA
175 E 96th Street #7-0
New York, NY 10128
Phone: 212-987-4281
email: daliac@cloud9.net
Workshops and performances in the styles of Danse Orientale, Dunyavi Gypsy (Rom) Dance and El Mundo Gypsy Dance

MOROCCO
Carolina Varga Dinicu
320 West 15th St
New York, NY 10011
Phone: 212-727-8326
Fax: 212-463-7116
email: morocco@tiac.net
web: http://www.tiac.net/users/morocco
Performer, choreographer, teacher, seminar instructor, researcher, dance historian, writer, lecturer (and general all-around gadfly and trouble-maker.)

199

PUTUMAYO WORLD MUSIC
324 Lafayette Street
7th Floor
New York, NY 10012
Phone: 212-460-0095
email: info@putumayo.com
web: http://www.putumayo.com
World music CDs.

SHIMMYSHIMMY.COM, INC.
Diana Conza
PO Box 402
Greenvale, NY 11548
Phone: 516-759-2609
Fax: 516-609-8493
email: sales@ShimmyShimmy.com
web: http://www.ShimmyShimmy.com
Belly dance boutique selling accesories
including coin belts, jewelry, beaded bras,
shawls and much more!

TARIK ABD EL MALIK
c/o Morocco
320 West 15th St
New York, NY 10011
Phone: 212-727-8326
Fax: 212-463-7116
email: tarikny@hotmail.com
Tarik's explanation of bodily mechanics helps
students master movements in an exciting,
supportive atmosphere.

■ *Ohio*

BONNIE RUPP—CHOREOGRAPHER
400 West Street
Archbold, OH 43502
Phone: 419-445-1246
email: oscar@fulton-net.com
Freelance choreographer.

CASSANDRA AL WARDA &
COMPANY
Cassandra Al Warda
1799 Kenton Circle
Lyndhurst, OH 44124
Phone: 440-646-1061
email: sdassistsu@aol.com
Performer, instructor, sponsor, troupe
director. Specialties: Raks Sharqi, American
Tribal, Westernized Nightclub, Veil, Candles,
Balancing.

■ *Oklahoma*

BELEDI MAGIC DANCE COMPANY
Zenuba
PO Box 720312
Norman, OK 73070-4234
Phone: 405-579-3255
email: beledimagic@yahoo.com
web: http://www.geocities.com/beledimagic
Performance troupe. Classes available.
Creates original belly dance dolls for gift
giving and collecting.

■ *Oregon*

GYPSY CARAVAN/SISTER CARAVAN
Director - Paulette Rees-Denis
4805 NE Campaign
Portland, OR 97218
Phone: 503-288-4355
email: gypsycaravan@iefx.com
web: http://www.alveus.com/gypsycaravan/
Classes, workshops, cds, videos, newsletter
and The Caravan Souk website for Tribal
Style dance.

TRIBAL WHERE?
Sikander Jaad
714 NW 3rd Drive
Pendleton, OR 97801
email: sikander@tribalwhere.com
web: http://www.tribalwhere.com
Publishes books on dance technique,
notation, history, costuming, business;
offers workshops, hand-crafted jewely,
choreography training.

TROUPE AMERICANISTAN
Dunya al Hanna
Eugene, OR
Phone: 541-484-5071
email: dunyah@earthlink.net
web: http://home.earthlink.net/~dunyah/
Musicians & dancers sharing their passion.
Original & traditional music. CD &
cassette, performance videos.

■ *Pennsylvania*

AYSHAH
Shady Hill Farm
PO Box 254
Royersford, PA 19468-0254
email: LadyAyshah@aol.com
web: http://www.ayshah.com
Solo performer.

SHELBY PIZZARRO
40 West Main Street
Mechanicsburg, PA 17055
Phone: 717-791-0323
email: hathor2bastet@yahoo.com
web:
http://community.webtv.net/hathor2bastet/
EgyptianDance
Solo performer available for haflas,
workshops, events. Professional
illustrator/calligrapher.
Work for t-shirts, posters, cards.

■ *Texas*

ODYSSEY THEATRICAL
Nacheska
1604 Mockingbird
Southlake, TX 76092
Phone: 817-238-2180
email: nacheska@nacheska.com
web: http://www.nacheska.com
Teacher, performer, troupe director of
Middle Eastern, Flamenco Moro and
Hula/Tahitian

SCHEHEREZADE'S FANTASIES
Susie Murrell
7101 Park Creek Circle E
Ft Worth, TX 76137
Phone: cell: 817-683-7066
email: suhira@aol.com
25 years as professional dancer, instructor, choreographer. Specializing in group choreographies and performances.

THE BALADY DANCE COMPANY
Thea Smeets
5822 Sabal Drive
Corpus Christi, TX 78414
Phone: 361-980-1586
Fax: 361-980-1586 (call first)
email: baladydc@aol.com
Troupe performances. Raks Sharki, Gypsy, African styles. Costuming and jewelry available.

■ *Virginia*

**INTERGRAL YOGA®
PUBLICATIONS**
Yogaville
Buckingham, VA 23921
Toll-free: 800-262-1008
email: iyd@moonstar.com
web: http://yogaville.org/pubs.htm
Publisher of *Dictionary of Sanskrit Names*, books and videos on health and spirit.

SCHEHEREZADE IMPORTS
2420 Hampden Row
Rockville, VA 23146
Phone: 804-749-3480
Fax: 804-749-3480
email: sherzade@mnsinc.com
web: http://www.dancingturtle.com
Direct importer - Egypt & India. Wholesale and retail since 1985. Seminar producer and teacher.

■ *Vermont*

STOREY BOOKS
105 Schoolhouse Road
Pownal, VT 05261
Phone: 1-800-441-5700
Publisher of *Henna: Head to Toe.*

■ *Washington*

**A'ISHA AZAR/ AL-ZARALAN
DESIGNS**
PO Box 4782
Spokane, WA 99202
Phone: 509-535-7101
email: aazar@ior.com
web: http://kanago.home.netcom.com/aisha/
Egyptian and folkloric dance. Performance, instruction emphasizing cultural integrity. Dance and theatrical costuming.

DINA - THE COSTUME GODDESS
email: dinacg@earthlink.net
web: http://www.costumegoddess.com
Costumer, costume instructor, performer, writer, illustrator, web designer.

DISPLAY AND COSTUME
11201 Roosevelt Way NE
Seattle, WA 98125
Phone: 206-362-4810
Fax: 206-368-6870
web: http://www.displaycostume.com
Fringe, costume coins, jewels, inexpensive coin jewelry, reasonably priced trims, fabrics, too many items to mention.

RHINESTONES GALORE
Lorian Choate
PO Box 404
Maple Valley, WA 90838
Phone: 253-630-7026
Fax: 253-630-7026
email: lorian.choate01@foxinternet.net
Huge variety of sew-on, glue-on and hot-fix stones, costume mirrors, tools.

**SA'IDA FOLKLORIC AND MIDDLE
EASTERN DANCE**
Sa'ida
PO Box 2802
Bremerton, WA 98311
Phone: 360-373-4880
email: saida@ix.netcom.com
web: http://www.homestead.com/
    saidadance/index.html
Performers and instructors for folkloric and cabaret family-oriented entertainment. Costume consultation and historical research available.

**THE SEATTLE SOURCE FOR
MIDDLE EASTERN DANCE**
Zanbaka
email: zanbaka@hotmail.com
web: http://community.webtv.net/
    Iptisam/TheSeattleSourcefor
Website providing up-to-date info on Middle Eastern dance and music in the Puget Sound area.

**VISIONARY DANCE
PRODUCTIONS**
Delilah
PO Box 30797
Seattle, WA 98103
Phone: 206-632-2353
email: info@visionarydance.com
web: http://www.visionarydance.com
Instructional & Performance Tapes. Original music. Elaborate website. Events, retreats, promotions and more.

YASMELA/ BOU-SAADA
Pacific Dance Company
PO Box 2146
Bellingham, WA 98227
Phone: 360-733-4326, 360-733-5409
Fax: 360-733-4326
email: shelleymz@hotmail.com
Old-style (Jamila Salimpour) technique, Tunisian, Moroccan, Ouled Nail, Persian, performance technique/troupe choreography.

201

YASMIN
Caroline Edwards
19220 17th Ave NW
Shoreline, WA 98177-2645
Phone: 206-542-3444
email: skeeter12@juno.com
Performer, instructor, percussionist. Tribal, Folkloric, and Cabaret. Specializing in Moroccan dances and Middle Eastern percussions.

■ *Washington D.C.*

LAUREL VICTORIA GRAY
PO Box 65195
Washington, DC 20035-5195
Phone: 301-585-1105
email: uzbekdance@aol.com, silkroad-dance@aol.com
web: http://www.uzbekdance.org, www.silkroaddance.com, www.egypta.com
Performer, choreographer, instructor, dance ethnologist and costume designer. Specialist in dances of the Silk Road.

■ *Wisconsin*

OASIS BAND & DANCERS
Denis Kavemeier
12448 W Cleveland Ave
New Berlin, WI 53151
Phone: 262-821-0301
email: denisk@execpc.com
web: http://www.oasisband.com
Tapes, CDs. Band available for shows and seminars. Dancer Juli Ana teaches "Belly Aerobics" seminars.

RASHEEDA'S VEILS/THE JOY OF BELLYDANCE/ZENOBIA - PTAH
Glenda-Joy Stace
PO Box 1181
Caloundra, Qld 4551
AUSTRALIA
Phone: (07) 5494 6702
email: rasheedasveils@hotmail.com
Troupe with musicians. Traditional and contemporary Australian instruction. Instructional videos. Hand-crafted swords and daggers.

■ *International*

CARAVANSARY DANCE CENTRE
Linda Hiney
833 Fisgard Street
Victoria, BC V8W 1R9
CANADA
Phone: 205-361-4227
Fax: 250-388-7387
email: caravansary@telus.net
web: http://www.caravansary.bc.ca
Costume, dance & theatrical supply with custom costume service, costume rentals & dance studio space for rent.

GENIES OF THE MIST
Bernadette Dawson
128A Dorthea Drive
Dartmouth, NS B2W 2E8
CANADA
Phone: 902-462-0007
email: montague.onyett@cac.gc.ca
Performance troupe Eygyptian and Ethnic, Cabaret. Instruction through YWCA.

SCHOOL FOR ORIENTAL DANCE
Susanne Potempa
Aarhusgade 108 E, 5
2100 Copenhagen 0,
DENMARK
Phone: 0045-35437383
email: sfod@vip.cybercity.dk
web:http://users.cybercity.dk/~dko5826/ home.htm
Teacher, performer, organizes Oriental dance festivals. Masseuse and Reiki master.

MEDEA MAHDAVI DANCE CO & FOOTWORK PUBLISHING
Philip Walker
7 Stackpool Road
Bristol, UK BS3 1NG
ENGLAND
Phone: +44 117-963-3029
email: medea@footwork.org
web: http://www.footwork.org
Iranian dancer Medea Mahdavi performs dance theatre, incorporating live music, words and design.

AFSANA MAGAZINE
Virpi Virtanen
Raivionkuja 4 B 46
20540 Turku,
FINLAND
email: afsana@nettilinja.fi
Finnish belly dance magazine.

202

AFIFA STUDIO
Afifa / Eeva Rauramo
Nahkurinkatu 8
FIN-20100, Turku
FINLAND
Phone: 358-2-4320869,
cell 358-40-5463127,
358-400-562213
email: afifa@sister.com
web: http://www.afifa.fi
Performances, Instruction. Courses for pregnant, elderly, handicapped, deaf. Dancegroup Nefer. Hosts annual dance festival.

ANDRÉ ELBING - ARTISTICAL ORIENTAL THEATRICAL DANCE PHOTOGRAPHER
St. Lambertusstr. 26
D-47546
Appeldorn,
GERMANY
Phone: +49(0)2824-80 93 95
cell: +49(0) 171-777 67 16
Fax: +49(0) 2824-80 93-94,
+49(0)40-360 307 97 49
email: orientph@aol.com,
AndreElbing@aol.com, Andre-Elbing@big-foot.com
web:http://www.cnphoto.simplenet.com/andre.htm, http://www.Elbing.mysite.de, http://www.Orient.megapage.de
Mobile photo studio archive with 150,000 photos from dancers around the world.

ARC MUSIC INTERNATIONAL
Jesse Wilson-Director of Promotions & Marketing
PO Box 111
East Grinstead
West Sussex,   RH19 4FZ
GREAT BRITAIN
email: info@arcmusic.co.uk
web: http://www.arcmusic.co.uk
Producer of Hossam Ramsy CDs and other world music.

YASSMIN FARRAH
Licia Marcheselli
Via Pirandello 6
Milano,   20144
ITALY
Phone: 02/72023997
Fax: 02/72023997
Professional international dancer, teacher. Studied in Egypt. First performer to make live video in Italy.

MISHAAL
Mishaal Miyamoto
Villa Aoyama 202
4-1-18 Jingumae
Shibuya-ku, Tokyo 150-0001
JAPAN
Phone: 81-3-3402-3564
email: mishaal@hpo.net
web: http://www.hpo.net/users/mishaal
International belly dance performer and instructor.

AISCHA
Dr. Barbara Luescher
Wassergrabenstrasse 3
Binningen,   4102
SWITZERLAND
Phone: 0041-61-421-08-02
Fax: 0041-61-421-63-81
Performer & teacher for Egyptian dance. Egyptologist. Availble for Egyptian dance & culture seminars and lectures.

HILARY THACKER'S GHAWAZEE BAZAAR
Hilary Thacker
8 Bellevue Terrace
Edinburgh,   EH7 4DT
UK
Phone: 0131 5567976
Fax: 0131 5579606
email: belly@dial.pipex.com
web: http://dspace.dial.pipex.com/belly
Professional Egyptian Style dancer. Videos. Bazaar with catalog. Plays cymbals and tambourine in Egyptian group.

204

205

About the Authors

(in order of appearance)

WHY? BECAUSE I STILL LOVE IT AFTER ALL THESE YEARS. —MOROCCO

TAZZ RICHARDS *(California)*

Tazz started his journey as a flute player for belly dancers. Being a fickle person, he has gathered and lost an eclectic collection of hobbies including mime, modern dance, journalism, poetry, and for the last 10 or so years, belly dancing. If all goes well, he'll remain the publisher of Backbeat Press, and make more books on belly dancing and whatever else grabs his hamster-like attention.

SHIRA *(California)*

Based near San Jose, California, Shira has been belly dancing since 1981. She is assistant director for The Veiled Threats, which specializes in comedy, and Troupe Wasila. She is internationally acclaimed for her belly dancing web site at www.shira.net, and is a staff writer for two belly dancing magazines.

KAJIRA DJOUMAHNA *(California)*

Author of *The Tribal Bible,* and a professional belly dancer and instructor, Kajira appreciates all styles and expressions of belly dance, and specializes in the tribal style.

VIRPI VIRTANEN *(Finland)*

Virpi Virtanen is the editor of the Finnish Oriental dance magazine *Afsana.*

DR. BARBARA LÜSCHER/AISCHA *(Switzerland)*

Aischa is an Egyptian-style dancer and instructor, author of books and articles, organizer of dance-tours and workshops, co-producer of "The Stars of Egypt" video series, and holds a Ph.D. in Egyptology.

TARIK ABD EL MALIK *(New York)*

Tarik, Morocco's protégé, began his career in 1986 and performs regularly in the New York area. He has also performed in Morocco and Jerusalem and teaches workshops nationwide in addition to his weekly classes.

ZENUBA *(Oklahoma)*

Zenuba and troupe Beledi Magic are from Oklahoma City. Zenuba is devoted to belly dancing, her two cats and little dog named Spud.

ELIZABETH ARTEMIS MOURAT *(Maryland)*

Artemis has been dancing, teaching and researching dance history worldwide for over 25 years. She has an M.A. in psychology, an M.S.W. in social work and has done postgraduate work in dance movement therapy.

CAROLINA VARGA DINICU, P.K.A. MOROCCO *(New York)*

A veteran of over 40 year as a full-time professional Mideastern dancer, teacher, researcher, et al, Morocco is fond of saying: I came off the Ark with Noah. Been there, done that, seen it all, wrote the book, made the T-shirt & will keep on doing it till 6 weeks after I'm dead. Why? Because I still love it, after all these years.

YEMAYA *(California)*

Yemaya, also known as Heather Crank, has been dancing and performing for eight years, and is continuing to explore and study dance as a priority in her life. She is currently working toward a graphic design degree from California College of Arts and Crafts and resides in Oakland, California.

MARGUERITE KUSUHARA *(California)*

Marguerite Kusuhara is a professional dancer, performer and entertainer, who is also trained as a reptile handler. She has taught classes in movement, Middle Eastern dance and mysticism in Europe, Asia and America.

SUZANNE SHAKTI COPELAND *(California)*

Suzanne Shakti Copeland is a clinical hypnotherapist specializing in the clearing of negative habit patterns and the integration of the spirit and soul purpose. She teaches classes in the meditation movement called Sacred Tantric Dance.

SALLY PHILLIPS *(California)*

Sally Phillips is a henna body artist, belly dancer and writer. She resides in Marin County, California with her husband and two children.

MELEAH *(California)*

Meleah lives in San Diego, where she specializes in personal makeovers. She provides make-up services for film, video, photography and weddings. She has been a professional model, dancer and instructor for over 15 years. Currently, Meleah sells her own line of cosmetics and her make-up video *Face It*.

MICHELLE MORRISON *(New Mexico)*

Michelle Morrison writes articles for *Habibi* and *Zaghareet!* She has studied belly dance for nine years and instructed for five. She is the director of troupe Farfesha.

About the Authors

207

DINA—THE COSTUME GODDESS *(Washington)*

Dina is the writer of the online advice column, "Ask the Costume Goddess", www.shira.net/askcg.htm through the generosity of Shira's website, "The Art of Middle Eastern Dance". She's currently writing a definitive belly dance costume reference, titled *The Costume Goddess Tells All: 1001 Belly dance Costume How-To's*.

AZIZA SA'ID *(California)*

Aziza Sa'id, a performer and teacher from California, is widely recognized for her joyous, fiery and dramatic style and for creating unforgettable feeling in her audiences.

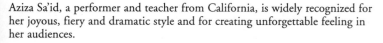

MARY ELLEN DONALD *(California)*

Mary Ellen Donald is a nationally acclaimed author, instructor and performer of Middle Eastern percussion.